Reigning Passions

Reigning Passions

A NOVEL BY

Kathrin Perutz

J. B. LIPPINCOTT COMPANY
Philadelphia and New York

U.S. Library of Congress Cataloging in Publication Data

Perutz, Kathrin, birth date
  Reigning passions.

    1. Sacher-Masoch, Leopold, Ritter von, 1835–
1895, in fiction, drama, poetry, etc. I. Title.
PZ4.P472Re [PS3566.E73]   813'.5'4   77–20701
ISBN–0–397–01247–0

This book is for my parents,
DOLLY HELLMANN PERUTZ
and TINO PERUTZ,
children of the Empire.

Contents

Preface

IF POETRY can be defined as "an imaginary garden with real toads in it," the novelist's license permits him to stock the world of his fashioning with human creatures who were documentably alive. *Reigning Passions* is a work of fiction, drawing on real people and real events, placed in a setting of the imagination. My criterion of accuracy in this historical novel was not that the events actually happened as presented but that they *could have* happened. Leopold von Sacher-Masoch, himself trained as a historian, tells another character, "All history is invented."

Here, then, is an invention.

Acknowledgments

I THANK my family for putting up with my absences and my often preoccupied presence during the past year; Conrad Spohnholtz of the MacDowell Colony, Peterborough, New Hampshire, for finding me room to work when there was none; people in the Ukraine, Hungary and Austria who helped me on my quest for Sacher-Masoch; and Elaine Markson, my agent, who first encouraged me to write this book. Most of all, I thank Edward Burlingame at Lippincott for persistently believing in the novel and convincing me to do the same.

A E I O U

Acronym devised by Frederick III (1415–93) to indicate the Hapsburg sense of mission: Austria rules
the world. The letters were inscribed on public
buildings and in books. In German they were read
as meaning:
    Alles Erdreich Ist Österreich Untertan
and in Latin as:
    Austriae Est Imperare Orbi Universo.

". . . it seems to me that the meaning of man's life
consists in proving to himself every minute that
he's a man and not a piano key."

                Dostoyevsky,
                Notes from Underground (1864)

Principal Characters

COURT:

Franz Joseph, Emperor of Austria, 1848–1916

Elisabeth, Empress of Austria, wife and cousin to Franz Joseph

Gisela
Marie-Valerie } their daughters

Rudolph, their son, heir to the throne

Sophie, mother of Franz Joseph, sister to Ludovica and Ludwig I

Ludovica, mother of Elisabeth

Ludwig II, King of Bavaria, 1864–86, grandson of Ludwig I

TOWN:

Leopold von Sacher-Masoch, Austrian author, 1836–95

Leopold von Sacher-Masoch, the author's father, Chief of Police

Charlotte von Sacher-Masoch (née Masoch), the author's mother

Rosa
Charles } their other children

Karl Eggendorf, dilettante, friend to Sacher-Masoch

Joseph Meyringer
Friedl Zimmermann } friends to Sacher-Masoch
Franz Zimmermann

Wanda, née Aurora Angelika Rümelin, wife to Sacher-Masoch

Frau Rümelin, mother of Wanda

Frau Frischauer, neighbor of the Rümelins

Sasha
Mitschi } children of Sacher-Masoch and Wanda

Anna von Kottowitz, a baroness, mistress to Sacher-Masoch
Fanny Pistor, née Koch, mistress to Sacher-Masoch
Jenny Frauenthal, fiancée of Sacher-Masoch
The Clairmont, née Lichtberg, actress, mother of Lina
Lina, illegitimate daughter of Sacher-Masoch and The Clair-
  mont
Kathrin Strebinger, translator of Sacher-Masoch
Hülde Meister, translator of Sacher-Masoch; later his second
  wife
Nicholas Teitelbaum
Sefer Pasha } "Greeks"

COUNTRY:
Ivan Dmitrovitch Boroduk, peasant
Irina Petrivna, his second wife
Marika
Yarko } children by his first wife

Slavik, idler; later, laborer

Prolog

IN 1815, Count Clemens Metternich, Europe's grandest entrepreneur, staged the Congress of Vienna, where three million doughnuts were consumed—mainly in the Prater—the city's dressmakers took the measure of the world, and Napoleon's defeat added dazzle to Austrian glory, as she held out the scales by which Europe was balanced.

The pattern of nineteenth-century Europe was brilliantly cut, but within twenty years it was to show stains and tears, as cholera, first, then drought, famine and economic collapse wore out the rational fabric and each nation began to look within, for its own measure. By the forties, nationalism was guiding the hearts of many Hapsburg citizens, and the revolutions of 1848 would change the pulse of Europe, after the old beat had become suffocating.

PART I

Vormärz* (CHILDHOOD)

[Man's] will can do everything. Only against sickness and death can it do nothing.
—Leopold von Sacher-Masoch, "The Mercenary"

*Literally, "pre-March," the term designating the period of Hapsburg history from 1815 to the revolutions of 1848.

1

In GALICIA, easternmost province of the Hapsburg Empire, sometimes known as the China of Europe, where the Ruthenian peasants were illiterate even in their own language and Polish landlords could publish edicts as obscure and undecipherable as the cabala, where Metternich's name was unknown and the Kaiser's forgotten in prayers sent up for him—as goodly, God-fearing man; there, in that recess of the Empire, God and man could have their way with the peasants, assured that no one would interfere. When the cholera, which took tens of millions of lives in its deathly pilgrimage from Russia to America, entered Galicia, there were no millions to claim, but it did what work it could, cutting lanes of death between children and the middle-aged, taking strong young men and women, and their grandparents.

The Polish landlords barricaded their mansions and fashioned incredible noses of wax and pigs' bladders, filled with perfumes, to wear against the invading germs, becoming gargoyles in the face of the enemy. During this infected time peasants were buried alive in lime pits on orders of the nobility, that the contagion not spread upward. But the cholera was too strong to be contained by the lower classes (all Ruthenians) and it burst out, so that in the end many a Polish lady had to order the remaining peasants to seize her struggling, retching husband, whose legs, streaming with agony along the muscles, could no longer support him. He, their master, begging for mercy and promising florins, was also thrown into the lime as his widow calculated her chances

21

anew, taking account of the fresh corpse. In Galicia, women were known for their death-dealing.

Only the peasants, some of them, had a way of curing—down by the banks of the Dniester—through submersion and extreme flagellation. Then sometimes their unconscious brothers, faces hollowed and yellowed by approaching death, could be whipped back to life, and the stilled pulse revivified. But cure was rare, since many didn't have a heart strong enough to support it, and most were not reached in time.

When it was over, Boroduk found himself alone with the boy Yarko and the blond little girl Marika. He had watched their mother die first, then his sister, then his own mother. In his family the women had been cut down, though often women were hardier. Each had given birth to children and nurtured them; each died after two or three days of excruciating pain, so tortured she couldn't even recite prayers at the end. No priest offered extreme unction, and the deaths were made more terrible because the lives went unreprieved.

When, sleepy with victims, the cholera slunk away from Galicia, all church bells rang. Ivan Dmitrovitch Boroduk clumsily dressed his little children for church. He carried baby Marika in his arms and led the boy Yarko by hand. The surviving villagers convened to praise the One who, in His infinite wisdom, had meted out His suffering among the poor and the rich with no regard for earthly privilege and now saw fit to bring peace again, after contagion's uprising. All were on their knees and, with hands, mouths, the swaying of torsos, offered their love in prayers and songs of thanksgiving. From the great city of Lemberg and from each Galician village the bells rang out with solemn festivity while people gave thanks in the old manner, even though husbands would now have to cook for themselves and mothers no longer had sons to cook for.

The Galician peasant was accustomed to hardship, familiar with death, and, instead of cursing God for what He had wrought, thanked Him now for ending this plague. The ways of God are inscrutable, they felt, and a poor man who was unable even to name the letters on a piece of paper could never presume to read the Divine Will.

The baby girl whimpered during the long service, but Boroduk held her closer and rocked her gently until she grew calm and fell asleep. Her brother Yarko, four years old, stared at the people around him. Never had he seen such finery. The men wore large capes and belts wide as his whole body, with more straps on them than he could count (but he could count only up to his own age). Others wore fur vests and trousers of heavy wool covered with rich embroidery. And the women were somber queens, in their dark clothes embroidered with strands of every color in the world, their heads covered with scarves elaborate as crowns, the fronts of their dresses hung with corals and chains of coins, interspersed with beads and more coral, red as the sky just before night walked over the Carpathians. And the feet of all the people were clad in boots! Polished boots of black or red, high boots or low, gleaming bright as the wooden cross Papa lovingly oiled every day after breakfast.

On that cross hung a dead man, and Papa said he died for us. For whom did his mother die? Yarko wondered, but the thought confused him and made him feel too hot in his clothes. Later, he would hear many things from his father, not only about the cholera that took his mother and grandmother but about all the evil spirits who inhabit Galicia, its rivers and mountains: spirits of the waters and steppes; ghosts of the dead wandering still over the land by night, seeking revenge; sorceresses in human form whose music is irresistible and leads the enchanted listener to torture, mutilation and death. He would hear, too, about the locusts.

One early morning the sky grew dark as midnight and the people feared a storm greater than any that had ever been. The cloud came over the village, completely blacking out the sun. And then, shuddering with horror, the peasants saw that it was alive, and from this cloud fell the locusts, in millions upon millions, till they were nearly a meter deep. The locusts fell upon the earth and ravaged everything, immolating life like fire, leaving behind bare plains scattered with skeleton trees.

Yarko had been there to see, but he could not remember too well. He remembered nothing well from those times, only modulations in the heavy air of his early childhood. Easter, Christmas and his own name day were feasts that ran together in his mind until their brilliance was muddied and reflection dulled. He could recall, but only with effort, sitting on the roof of their house with the chickens as the floodwaters rose —but had no idea, in thinking back, where the others had been. Another time stood out: one night when his father's voice rose like a lance against a neighbor who was swaying with drink and had dared to curse God.

Like others born in Galicia, Yarko would later regard evil as a palpable force, sometimes revealed in human form, and he would consider brutality and injustice as much a part of nature as trees and rivers. Pain and death were as inevitable as cruelty—and he would come to estimate progress or acts of goodness as astonishing, unexpected boons. His early childhood lay in his memory like a strange sleep of dreams, forgotten until a chance word or sight worries the heart with unaccountable feelings.

Yarko's clear memories really began with his father's wedding. The wedding cakes were decorated with brightly colored paper stalks when Boroduk married Irina Petrivna. Yarko was seven. He watched the women prepare the wedding tree, twining roses and ribbons through the small pine. Irina was beautiful to him (though not known as a beauty) in her bridal tiara with the flowers and shining metal and the many bright ribbons streaming down. How they all laughed and danced at the wedding! The men made fun of him because he drank too much and kept falling over, but little Marika clapped her hands and wanted him to do it again and again. So sometimes he fell over when he didn't really have to, just to please her. All the musicians of the village were at the wedding, of course, with violin, bass, zither, bandura— and the skinny little flutist among them. Everyone was very gay, there was no end of wine, and the singing never stopped. Every kind of song was sung, tunes from the hills and valleys and steppes and then that Cossack song with the lovely melody:

> When I'm on a peak, a high one,
> The other peak seems low—

When I have my second sweetheart,
Then the first must go.

The men carried him about on their shoulders and even threw him into the air, as they did with Marika. She was so red-cheeked with excitement that everyone called her "little apple."

It was a wonderful time, and they soon came to love Irina as though she'd been with them always. She was much younger than her husband, barely nineteen when they married, but was a sensible girl, cheerful in all her work, who wished never to be idle for even a minute. When her chores were finished, she sewed and embroidered clothes for her family or wove shoes for them out of reeds. While she worked, she hummed softly. Or if the children were near, she would tell them stories while the needle flew back and forth in her hand. Sometimes Marika pestered her to tell a story over again, and Irina would look stern and say, "Maria, why is your head like the back of a duck, where nothing will soak in? You must catch hold of the words the first time, not let them roll away."

And Marika, little Maria, would giggle and hug Irina and try to kiss her, but Irina would be unyielding and push her off. Then Marika would lower her eyes and fold her hands and sit very quietly, like a small penitent, with pink skin and pale silvery hair. Finally Irina would look at her and Marika would peer up at the same moment, and their eyes would meet, and both laughed. Then Irina would sigh, put away her embroidery and take the little girl on her knees to begin the story once again. Marika's favorites always contained at least one *roussalka*, that beautiful naiad of Galician rivers and streams who sings as sweetly as the wind, is lovely as a saint, and brings men to their deaths in her watery home.

When Boroduk entered the room and saw the two girls, the little one with hair rippling down her back, two red ribbons carried on the fair waves, and the other, older girl whose hair was dark as strong tea, plaited and folded around her head, then he felt great peace. He was happy with his young wife and many times a day, when his thoughts turned to her in the fields, he gave thanks to the One who had brought him this happiness after the long time of troubles.

His new wife was not beautiful as his first had been, but she was kind and tender, and as clever as any young woman in the village. It was generally acknowledged that her baking was superior even to that of Miroslava Romanovna Kooshnir's, and many of the men teased Boroduk (as he was called by everyone since he'd entered the second half of his lifetime), saying that his young wife was fattening him for the slaughter. He didn't mind their teasing, and when the old bachelors tried to inveigle an invitation to dinner, Boroduk told them cheerfully to come along. Then he smiled with pleasure to see Irochka's happy face as the men swore they had never eaten anything finer, not even in the pastry shops of Lemberg.

Irina was clever in other ways, too, and no one could get the better of her with words. When the men teased her about having such an old husband, she cut them off quickly by saying that old wine was better than new, or that meat before it was hung had no taste and could make you ill. She would tolerate no slights to her husband, whom she considered the best and wisest man in the country. When people mocked her by pointing out that her eyes were neither blue nor brown, she replied that they served their purpose very well, since they permitted her to see the beauty of the world and the qualities of men, whereas the eyes of her questioners allowed them only to see faults.

And so this good woman brought contentment to those around her and was content herself, except that her work was not sufficient to her energies. Irina had taught a proper lesson to a young philanderer of the village, Slavik by name, but she'd taught so well that he now worked with her husband outside, while her own labor was restricted to the house, where she couldn't find enough to keep her always busy. When one day Miroslava Romanovna—mother of the newly reformed Slavik—came by with the news that the wife of the Police Director in Lemberg was expecting, and that therefore the household would be requiring additional help, Irina listened with happiness and conceived a plan.

Next day she put on her sheepskin jacket without sleeves,

her polished boots and a necklace of coins. She dressed little Marika, took her by the hand (Yarko went out with the men that day, as he often did now) and rode into the city. She found the house of the Police Director without much difficulty and, when asked what her business was, announced in a firm voice that she had come about a position. No, she replied to the next question, she was not a wet nurse, but perhaps Their Honors could use a cook, or baker? As she said this, Irina handed her interviewer a doughnut she had baked that morning. He bit into it and looked at her with appreciation.

"Perhaps," he said. "It may very well be. Come, I take you to my wife." Polish did not seem to be his language; his tones were sugared with Germanic sweetness.

"Then you are . . .?" she began, falling to her knees.

He reached out a hand to help her up. "I am Police Director Sacher. Come to my wife. She is of your people."

Within minutes, Irina was assured a position in the kitchen. And so a new way of life was established in the Boroduk household. Irina rose every morning at three thirty, prepared an early breakfast for the family and Slavik, then traveled into the city with the little girl in time to bake fresh rolls for the Police Director's breakfast. Her husband understood Irina's need to be working, and tolerated having his midday meal prepared by Slavik's mother. In the evening, husband and wife supped together, as Irina amused him with lively stories from the city.

The Director's wife, she reported, was a noblewoman, though not Polish. Her family name was Masoch and she was a Ruthenian like themselves, who came from the great city of Kiev, where her father was a professor at the university. She was a lamb, Irina told her husband, gentle as the snow, a lady of simple manners and great dignity, who showed no scorn and treated her peasants almost like friends. She talked to Irina in Ukrainian—about food, naturally, but also about clothes, children, exercise, the ways of men, and even books. Irina had to laugh at that. But Charlotte Alexandrovna, Frau Sacher, simply went on talking, explaining that her father had studied the ways of the Ruthenian people—he was an "expert"—and that in Kiev were many books filled with words about people just like the Boroduks. An angel she was, that Charlotte Alexandrovna, and Irina planned to bake the most delicate pastries she had ever attempted, in honor of the child's birth, expected not long after the new year.

On the twenty-seventh of January, 1836, Charlotte Alexandrovna Sacher-Masoch gave birth to her firstborn, a small, pale boy christened Leopold after his father. Friends of the parents brought christening gifts and ate the sweet delicate cakes baked by Irina in the forms of lambs, bunnies, chickens and kids, their fur or feathers spun with sugar. Visitors commented on the goodness of the child, who rarely cried. But his mother was frightened by the baby's pallor and thinness, and the doctor shook his head slowly above the infant's cradle, in a gesture like the slow sweep of censers preceding a mass for the dead. He was too frail, "too good," as his mother put it, for this world. Prayers and medicine kept the tiny creature alive until the spring, when Irina gave birth to a stillborn son. Then the delicate Leopold was wrapped in blankets and taken, with his mother's blessings, to the house of the Boroduks, where the milk from Irina's sturdy breasts and the pure country air might, please God, in these days following Easter, bring firm, new life to the child.

Irina placed her son in a small coffin of pine made by her husband and buried him under their window. Boroduk forbade mourning: "The good Lord was so pleased with our son that He took him unto Himself." Irina tried to smile at her husband, saying, "I only wish He could have waited a little while." Then she sighed and tidied herself, because there was no point lamenting the dead. They were part of the universe, and not less happy than the living. Some died sooner, some later, and those who died early avoided deep sufferings and troubles. One had to trust in God completely, as one trusted one's husband, and as he trusted in God. Man's only wisdom was in knowing he could never understand the ways of the Lord, but must accept them.

It was difficult, though—the child hadn't even been baptized. She vowed not to let her husband see her grieve. I would have loved him very much, she thought, but then spoke sternly to herself because regret was unfruitful. Sometimes, when she was quite alone, she knelt at the small grave and crooned to her dead baby. Every day she watered the wild-flowers growing above him, who'd been cut down before he could sprout.

But she had the other children—Yarko, Marika and the frail infant Leopold, whom she was keeping alive with the dead boy's milk. And almost every day, Charlotte Alexandrovna arrived in her carriage, her face pale as her baby's, pale as the clothes she wore, her step nervous and apologetic as though she were afraid of offending. Irina's heart went out to her, because carrying hope was more terrible than having no hope at all; and she prayed that God would give her the strength to nurse this child, fragile as a cuckoo's egg, back to health.

Her prayers were heard, and little Leopold Sacher-Masoch, though not as robust as a normal child, was destined to live. His breathing became regular, and when loud, angry screams from him brought the whole family to his crib one night, they all laughed and hugged each other and knew that God was with them. After Irina had fed him, Marika rocked him in her arms, singing:

"Little brother, close your eyes
While the stars are in the skies.
God protects the birds and sheep
And little brother, fast asleep."

She laid him down very gently and held a finger to her lips, so no one would disturb him. Her father kissed her forehead and called her "little mother." Then he gathered her up and carried her to her own bed. He tucked her in, but she defied the covers and raised her small arms to his neck. "God bless you, Papa," she said gravely, "and the Emperor too."

*　　*　　*

The Emperor Ferdinand, known as "the goodly one," had assumed the throne a year earlier when his father, Franz I, died, on his deathbed entrusting epileptic Ferdinand to the care of Metternich, who promised never to forsake him. Ferdinand the Goodly One had no wife and no issue. Despite his long sober face he enjoyed games and toys and would always remain dear to the hearts of Austrians, particularly Viennese, who could overlook simplemindedness if the man was kindly. Ferdinand was that. He made no speeches or proclamations, dutifully signed the papers Metternich presented to him and was known to have uttered only one complete sentence during his reign: "I am the Emperor and I want dumplings!" His nephew Franz, now six years old, was being raised as crown prince, under the stern, ambitious guidance of his mother, Sophie. Little Franz was a charming child, with clear blue eyes, blond hair and the precocious bearing of an officer. He loved soldiering and treated his collection of fine hand-painted soldiers with such care that none was ever lost or even damaged. He knew the uniforms of every Hapsburg regiment down to the buttons. His father, Franz Karl, was a gentle man with no desire to rule. Though not subnormal like his brother, Franz Karl functioned as an accessory to his wife, the beautiful Sophie of Bavaria, making his contribution to history in the form of offspring (three sons already) and leaving her to manipulate the strings of genealogy. Sophie, of the sharp mind, hard ambition and thick ringlets, was the sister of King Ludwig I of Bavaria, a man with a failing for women. Little Franz was, therefore, the nephew of two reigning monarchs both possessed of personal weakness, both to be brought down by the events of 1848. He was learning strength through his mother, and a power of endurance that would later support him during one of the longest reigns in history. He, too, said his prayers every evening like little Marika, but Galicia was as unreal to him, as strange a word as "Emperor" was to her.

*   *   *

The following year, Irina's second baby died a few hours after birth. This time she couldn't be calmed easily. She pulled her hair, screamed, and her husband wasn't able to comfort her with his words or his arms. He, too, seemed weary as he fashioned a second small coffin and dug a hole for it beside the first. His heart was heavy for his wife, who had no children of her own and whose young body passionately longed for a child. Yarko, now nine, tried to kiss Irina, but she shoved him away abruptly. For three days she mourned her second child, doing no work at all except what was essential for Leopold. On the fourth day, she ceased her mourning and resumed her chores. She never went near the graves of her children. She never mentioned them either, and no one else dared talk of them.

As Leopold grew older and stronger, he spent more time with his parents in Lemberg, though basically he still lived with the Boroduks. Two more infants had been born to the Sacher-Masochs: Rosa and Charles, both healthy children who needed no special care. The Police Director was now officially an aristocrat, having received imperial permission to quarter his wife's arms with his own and become Leopold von Sacher-Masoch, Ritter von Kronenthal. The little boy Leopold would inherit the title if he survived his father—though that was unlikely, thought the Police Director, looking at the boy in his miniature sailor suit, the middy blouse and skirt, soft wisps of hair framing a face too thin for a child, too fragile for life.

But his mother and Irina were determined that Leo should live. Charlotte, who adored him, was even willing to sacrifice the natural bond between mother and child during these early years. If Irina's strength could hold the boy up, and if by holding him she earned his devotion, then so it must be. Irina, too, loved the child, who had "dark fires" in his eyes, she said, and who had been brought to this earth from a kingdom of magic.

But when Leo was five, Boroduk died and neighbors saw Irina's face turn black. They took in her stepchildren, fearing that she was possessed by evil, and Leo, or Lev, as they called him in the country, was returned permanently to the house of his parents. The children had been terrified when her face became distorted and her movements turned random and spasmodic. They had crouched behind furniture, whimpering like abandoned kittens until they were taken away. Irina was left alone, though the most hardy villagers crept around the house for a look within. She raged, then became suddenly like the grave. Her screams pierced the night, wounding it, and by day she kept eerie silence. No movement was seen, no smoke rose from the chimney, and the house appeared deserted. Slavik saw her face one day and reported that she was becoming transparent as a ghost. He said she was inhabited by spirits and spoke with the dead.

Her neighbors crossed themselves. They prayed for her soul, for this young, full-bodied woman whose love had run deep as life. Unlike other women, she didn't know how to love through duty, and what she had given her husband was her complete self. She loved him bodily, and now he had no body. She loved him through all her being, and his death removed her from herself. She wanted death too. She wanted to share everything with him because only then would she exist. She was the wife of Ivan Dmitrovitch Boroduk. If he was not on this earth any longer, and if she was not at his side, then she was nothing.

No one could comfort or even approach her. By day the house was a tomb. At night, she could now be seen wandering, in no certain direction, zigzagging the land, aimless as a spirit with no home. The villagers feared she would die of starvation.

Then Marika tied a kerchief around her head and filled a basket with food. Braver than Red Riding Hood, she set forth on a terrain where roaming wolves were nothing compared to the lurking spirits. Pale, holding down her fear, the child walked quickly, breaking into short runs, and stopped at the door of her old home. "Irina Petrivna," she called out, but no answer came. Feeling cold as death, she wanted to run back, but, biting her tongue for courage, she forced herself to step over the threshold. "Irina Petrivna," she called again, "I've come with something for you to eat that you may be well." Still no answer. The child placed the basket on the table and waited. She felt the presence of demons, crossed herself and went to look for Irina; she found her lying in the dark bedroom, the curtains drawn. "Mama!" she called and threw herself on the frail woman. "Please come back. It's so lonely without you." She hid her face between Irina's breasts and sobbed.

Her stepmother held her fiercely for a long time. Then her petrified arms softened into life and she stroked the girl's hair. Marika pulled down the hand from her head and pressed it to her lips. Irina took hold of the girl's chin, pulling it up. They faced each other and Marika saw lines of tears marking Irina's cheeks. The child stood and held out her hand to the woman, who took it. Together they walked slowly to the next room, where they emptied the basket and laid out the food. Together, they ate and smiled at each other.

The following week they moved into the Police Director's household. Leo flung himself so forcefully at Irina that she stumbled back. She laughed. "Easy, my little man. That's no way to go after a woman." She picked him up in her arms and kissed him. "This one," she said to his mother, "is magic. The world will hear of him one day."

"What will they hear?" asked Leo.

She put him down. "That you never wash behind your ears, and that you tell terrible lies."

"I don't!" He pouted. "Those are stories."

Irina nodded. Already he was a wonderful storyteller, whose eyes burned when he spoke and who could make words come alive. He remembered every story, every poem or song he'd ever heard, and he invented new ones of his own. Fantasy's child, he was, earnest and comical, who entertained her while she baked and then crept into her lap and fell asleep from exhaustion. His little body dug a place in hers and she loved him through her grief and strength, fiercely and with dignity, like a tigress her cub.

Compared to this, his mother's love was pale and gentle, the love symbolized by a rose, not a bleeding heart. But her love was wonderful too. It reigned over him whereas Irina's was vented on him. His mother, even in the flesh, seemed something otherworldly, whose voice and perfume enchanted him, whose touch made him feel curiously ashamed, and whose time, when given to him, seemed a gift he was not worthy to receive. Leo was a fearful boy, but "with Mother" —those times rare as Meissen—he was safe as if he had no body, and they played games with the wind, with petals and small stones. When he was older, they often read together, and Mother's voice alone convinced him that queens were real. They read Shakespeare and Schiller in Polish, Adam

33

Mickiewicz and the fairy stories of Perrault in the original. "Why," he asked her once, "am I not afraid when we are together?"

She smiled. "Perhaps because I am not very brave myself."

"Do terrible things thump through your mind?" he asked excitedly, the shame of his fearfulness (which Irina and his father mocked) suddenly disappearing. "Does the wind screech horrible sounds in your ear? Does your skin sometimes not really cover you, does the wind rattle your bones? And do you see she-wolves at night in the shadows? Do you? Do you?" There was so much more—loud sounds and sudden silences, night, thunder, spirits, poison, his own pulse when his heart was trying to leave his body.

She looked at him sadly. All was so peaceful on the grass beside the cypress, and still the terror shook her little boy like autumn winds. Perhaps the peasants' life had been too strong for him, or his physical frailty as a baby had unnerved him forever. She held him tightly but didn't answer, and for the first time he felt fear "with Mother." His tentative hope that she, too, lived with cruel, mocking creatures had made him open up to her, to find himself more alone afterward. Maybe it was better, he thought, to keep the brave front he had with Irina and Marika, who told him that whenever something frightens you, you must go up to it and embrace it. "Hope for the thing you are most afraid of," Irina said, "and then it will never happen." So what he must hope for, the most terrifying thing in the world, was death.

Irina had never hoped for it, and her husband and two sons lay dead. With Yarko apprenticed to an apothecary (on the corner of the main square; the Sacher-Masochs had arranged it), Leo was the only male who remained to her. She was back to her old weight now, her arms stronger and rounder than before, and with these she pulled Leo to her bosom or her lap, carried him about and sometimes spanked him. She told him stories of when she was a young girl like Marika, now growing tall and straight, her silver hair tinseling her shoulders. She told him about her life with Boroduk and repeated stories her husband had told her about his childhood. Usually, they talked in the kitchen, the warm stove loosening smells from the cupboards and pantry. These smells would become fixatives; as a grown man Leopold would hear Irina's tales in a bowl of borscht or a jar of pickles.

Often Marika sat with them, and other times Marika and Leo played on their own. He called her Moon Princess and declared himself her servant, a small star. "My mama is the Queen, is she not?" asked Marika.

"Oh, yes. And my mama is the Goddess."

"My papa is a king at the bottom of the sea on a throne of coral," she told him. "What is your papa?"

He looked at her anxiously and didn't know. If Mama was a goddess, he had to be a god. But he wasn't like that, not beautiful enough, and everyone knew gods were very beautiful. But Papa was extremely important nevertheless; people bowed to him and called him "Your Honor" and "Your Excellency." Some of them wore medals and others had brilliant banners across their chests. "Papa must be the Emperor," he finally decided, though neither of them knew quite what that was. Marika thought of him as a head landlord, the most powerful in all the world, and Leo imagined an emperor as something like a king, who spoke German and lived very far away in another country.

2

No MORE did the Galician peasants know what an emperor was, although they were his subjects. They knew they owed their labor to Polish landlords through the system of *Robot*, a progressive variation on serfdom whereby a peasant was permitted to own his land and work on it, but only after he had completed the required labor for his landlord.* During harvest, for instance, one could see the system in its truest implications. The peasant reaped the crop of his master from dawn to dusk and only then was permitted to attend to his own. He worked through the night with small fires, assisted by his wife and children, and when morning approached, he took a bowl of soup, a piece of bread, a strong drink if he could find it, and returned to the master's field.

So the Polish nobles were absolute lords in their own domains. And, convinced that paternalism, as they referred to the system, was good (it brought furs and jewels), they resented interference (in the form of taxes) from Vienna. We have our land and our peasants, they thought; we all speak Polish here, and we can manage perfectly well without the black eagle of the Empire squawking at us.

But the Galician peasants thought, The eagle is only a small bird, but large enough to protect us. And faith was kept, in the deep snow and rough winds of February, when many

*In other parts of the Empire, this required labor amounted to little and was an easier form of recompense than the taxation that replaced it. Here, however, we are talking of Galicia.

were starving and all knew of the unrest among the nobles. They couldn't tell why it had arisen, or what was to be done, but villages became roosters, spreading news and rumors over the land in minutes. The nobles were concealing weapons, were riding here and there over the countryside in their sleighs. Who could know what they were doing or plotting? In time it would all come out.

And then word carried like a cock's crow from one village to the next, from the first tavern where the Polish landlord appeared and told the peasants to join the nobles, who would give them arms and protect them in the fight against the Kaiser. In the next village, a proclamation was brought and remained unread until the judge was summoned. He began, "To All Poles Who Can Read"—and the tavern burst into laughter. There was not a Pole among them, and in any case no one except the judge could read.

Everywhere the message was the same: "Join us nobles and we will protect you; later we will remove the *Robot* and give you justice."

And from everywhere came the same answer: "Not now and not ever will we side with you, but with our God and the Emperor. You nobles are the ones who have hurt us. It's the black-gold flag, the German officials and the Emperor who will protect us."

The uprising began in the east (near Kolomea) in dignity. At first the peasants allowed themselves to be shot at before capturing and disarming the oppressor. Blood for blood was justice, and all property was meticulously returned to its owners (except firearms). Then the peasants used night's cover, lying in ambush with their scythes, hoes and flails. When a carriage came by, they jumped it and captured the nobles inside, disarming them and keeping the weapons. They carefully removed all personal items, including jewels and money, and handed these over, with the bound prisoners, to Austrian officials.

But the arms bought by the Poles were eventually used against them, and as the fighting became bloodier the peasants showed they could give back in measure what they had taken for so many years. Guns shot into faces, scythes slit noble necks and flails tore the skin off Polish backs. Then all the tumult of war was loosed and dignity overwhelmed through murder.

Yarko, now a young man of eighteen who had learned to read through the teachings of the apothecary (and knew some Latin besides), led a group of men from his old village. He led like a soldier, urging them not to fear death but to welcome it if it came, and meanwhile to fight for their love of God and freedom.

When he was captured by the nobles, they did not kill him outright. "You behave like a soldier, Yaroslav Ivanovitch," they said, "not like a peasant. So we will treat you like a soldier." He was condemned to running the gauntlet three times, a feat almost impossible to achieve, since the first time finishes the boys, the second the men, and the third—well, at best he could hope to crawl through.

True to his own counsel, Yarko did not fear death. He stood with bound hands as the drums rolled, then was abruptly shoved forward to run between two long rows of soldiers, each holding a gun and a scourge and using both on the prisoner's naked skin. At either end, corking the rows, stood a soldier with fixed bayonet.

Yarko ran blindly, and after the first dozen or so blows that seemed to pull away his skin and reach into his inner organs, he no longer felt anything except the difficulty of breathing and remaining erect. In an instant, an eternity, it was over and he was left on the ground, bleeding from wounds that could not be distinguished because his whole back was open.

So he had been brought to them, though his body was covered with a bloody blanket, and Irina howled at the sight of him like a hurt dog. Leo, Rosa and Charles were ordered to go to their rooms, and for the next weeks, while Yarko lay unconscious, they could only guess what was happening by the doctor's stern face shaking from side to side as he left the house and by Irina's taut, angry expression whenever she went in with fresh bandages.

Then one day Yarko woke up and learned he was alive. The peasants had fought bravely and would be rewarded by the Austrians. Sacher-Masoch shook Yarko's hand and congratulated him, while Irina moaned and smiled and continued her prayers. Very soon, Yarko began to mend and it was clear he would regain his health, having lost no more than an ear in all that beating. His mother and sister cared for his wounds and fed him. The Director and his wife ordered medicines and made sure he wanted for nothing. Leo sat on the bed beside him, begging to hear stories that made him weep and then begging for more as his enormous black eyes devoured Yarko's tired face. When Yarko was too exhausted to speak, Leo read to him, from many different books, sometimes in French, which Yarko could not understand (but he liked the sound of it and pressed the boy to read on), and sometimes from his own creations, little adventures and plays he had written. But Leo would only exchange story for story, and kept an exact account of who was owed how many tales.

So Yarko, while he recuperated, heard the wonderful lines of Mickiewicz, Schiller, Gogol, Shakespeare, and Leopold heard the stories that Yarko's father had told him—of the cholera and locusts, the flood, the hungry wolves, evil spirits in the form of women, and evil men. He heard, too, about the fighting that had just passed, when the nobleman dared take arms against the Emperor and the peasant captured him.

Soon Yarko was fully recovered and able to go back to the apothecary's. Leo and the younger children missed him, though he often came by the house with sweets for them and sometimes a book for Leo, who felt very grown up at ten because he understood war. Yarko was the bravest man in the world, and, though even the sight of his bruises made Leo feel faint, the boy resolved that he would become a soldier in the next war. He returned to his toy soldiers and pitched them in furious battle, giving punishment and sermons to the losers when peace was secured and the Kaiser's cause triumphed. Many nobles were imprisoned.

Later the same year the grown-up little Leo had his first taste of the other war on the battleground of a lady's bedchamber. But experience often eludes those it holds, and what happened at that time gains meaning only when one's life has caught up with it. So Leo, playing hide-and-seek, stumbled on

39

a secret in himself but couldn't know what he had uncovered. The wars would catch up with him, though, before he was out of childhood.

Two years later, the revolutions of 1848 began, moving eastward, like fashion, from Paris. Early that year, Sacher-Masoch and his family were to leave Galicia for Prague, where he'd been assigned as Police Director. Before the year was out, the Polish nobles would be exonerated—under a new Kaiser and new regime—and the *Robot* put to an end.

His last Christmas at home was the most beautiful Leo could remember, though it was no different from other Galician Christmases, when snow covers the plain, the sky is pale as a diaphanous sheet, and even the silver birches seem dark against the backdrop. Fragile twigs are encased in sheaths of ice like finest crystal; the sound of a wolf or barking fox reaches you from inside the forest; a large black bird, crow or raven, floats through the air, flops the "fingers" of its wings and glides again; and the long shepherd's horn, the *trembika*, is played across the plain. Long and narrow, three meters in length, the *trembika* looks almost like a spear and mournfully summons the sheep and lambs.

Everywhere, people are rushing in their sleighs to make their Christmas visits, and the tinkling of many bells becomes gay as a circus. Old and young sing Christmas songs, the *kolendi*, first slowly, as in awe, then faster and faster until reverence is no longer distinguished in the merriment. The Holy Family in the manger receives the Three Kings, while in the streets pretty girls wearing crowns of gold paper pelt their admirers with snowballs or accept the arm of a wolf or bear to dance with him around the bonfires. Older people, in furs and boots, walk as quickly as they can through the snowy streets, tempted by the black iron emblems hanging in front of wine cellars. Suckling pigs are roasting on the spit, the vodka flows freely, and at the Sacher-Masochs the smell of Irina's cakes and pastries intoxicates the air to make the children almost mad with excitement. Gifts are exchanged by everyone, and the children proudly present the objects they have been working on for weeks. Night comes, the Holy

Night, and prayers are said, the candles lit. Then the bells ring out the news, and people prepare for Mass.

To Leo, each scene stood out brighter than ever before, each sound was clearer, each sight more moving. He was often in tears as a sense of the future overwhelmed him, and he looked at everything as though it had long passed and was being relived through love and memory.

Then a few weeks later, they were on their way. Irina was not coming with them; she chose to stay in Galicia and return to the old village, remaining close to her husband's grave and caring for Yarko until he married. Marika would accompany them, but Leo felt a part of himself was staying behind in Irina's strong arms. He wept and vowed he would never forget her; she looked at the lean, awkward boy she had nursed and comforted, and shrugged. "Away with you now. Remember to do your lessons, and let us hear some good of you." Then she kissed him and made the sign of the cross over him as he went on his knees before her. Her kiss was always different from his mother's—not delicate like the wings of a butterfly on his cheek, but full on his mouth, imprisoning his lips, making him strange and warm.

As she kissed him now, and felt him trembling like a young fawn in her arms, she feared for his sensitivity. This young boy, who could tell stories that made you laugh till you cried, or others that made you weep with pity on hearing them, who at the age of ten had taken over his father's position in staging theatricals at home and had put on plays so difficult you could only wonder at the music of the words because the sense floated high above your grasp, and who had even taken to writing the plays himself, with high adventure and great moral purpose—this wonder of a boy (though ugly) was like a phosphorescence, strange and brilliant in the dark but unnoticeable in bright daylight. She blessed him and held him tightly until she felt him struggling to be free. Then she gripped him by the shoulders and said earnestly, "Go, young Leopold, and may you always keep the magic you have in you now. Speak only the truth, and the world will believe you. Remember Galicia. Remember us. May God's love keep you for your task."

She turned from him, kissed the hands of her master and mistress, blessed them both, and gave them her daughter. She blessed Rosa and Charles, too, and led her own child aside so she could take proper leave of her. Leo wept miserably in the carriage and thought life could hold no greater pain than this, saying farewell to home and a beloved person. The coachman brought up the horses' heads, and they were on their way.

Irina returned to the house to light candles for their safe journey. Only when they were burning brightly did she permit herself tears. Yarko was the only one left, a grown man with his own life. And hers, at thirty-two, was just about used up.

3

VORMÄRZ ENDED in mid-March, 1848, when
Viennese students and workers invaded the council chamber
and forced Metternich to resign. The demonstrators were
successful despite their lack of organization because the government was inefficient. They cheered the end of absolutism,
centralized bureaucracy and repression. When the Emperor
Ferdinand was told of the demonstrations, he asked, "B-but
how, who gave them? Per-per-mission?"

The catalyst for action had come from Hungary, through
the speech of Lajos Kossuth to the Hungarian Diet. His
words were sped on horseback to Vienna, where they were
read to the waiting crowd by Adolf Fischhof, an assistant
physician in obstetrics at the Vienna General Hospital who
had always loved political philosophy but, as a Jew, was
barred from studying it. Jews, however, were being carried
up by the wave of revolution; two German Jews had just
published a remarkable pamphlet called "The Communist
Manifesto."

Through the stolid mouthpiece of Fischhof, the fierce
plea of the Magyar nationalist roused the Austrians. By the
Ides of March, Hungary had abolished serfdom and remade
itself, using law as the magic wand for instant transformation
from feudalism to modern nation-state. In Vienna, the rejoicing led to action and routed Metternich, the old balancer.
Goodly Ferdinand was bewildered by the young people's lack
of respect.

*   *   *

43

In June, the Princess Windischgrätz was shot dead in Prague while standing recklessly near a window in the governor's palace. Her husband, a true Austrian gentleman for whom no one below the rank of baron existed, had not become Field Marshal for nothing. A soldier to his bones, he observed the corpse of his wife on the parquet, estimated the consequences of ending the revolt immediately, calculated his forces and allowed the rebellion a four-day flourish.

* * *

The new Police Director of Prague, Sacher-Masoch, naturally forbade his family to go into the streets. The people who milled there, mainly students—setting up instant barricades, engaging in hand-to-hand fighting (didn't they see the artillery mounted on the heights of the city?)—were infected with that disease of young people that comes upon them during action and makes them forget why the action ever began, or to what purpose. Sacher-Masoch wasn't quite a cynic, but had worked long and importantly enough as an official of the empire to view the rebel as either irresponsible or juvenile. Young people especially, floating on the vast sea of their identity, scrambled aboard the first vessel they sighted, hoping it would take them in the direction of their lives. Once aboard, they hadn't the courage to jump off again and try on their own. These vessels had different names— "Pan-Slavism," "German Liberalism," "Pole," "Czech," "Magyar," "Slovak," "Croat," and so on: labels to discriminate the cargoes of humanity.

This was "progress": the breaking up of traditionalism, of old values, for the sake of something not yet defined except by the loose tag of "identity." Our Galician peasants aren't like that, he assured himself. He thought of Yarko, that strong, proud man who could tell right from wrong through any disguise and was simple enough—direct enough, was better—to love truth more than his life and to fight for it.

Street fighting in Prague was something different. Who knew who was fighting whom, and to what end? At first sight, it seemed, Bohemians (Czechs) were fighting for independence from Austria. Or was it Slavs against Germans? Then you had to ask, which Slavs and which Germans? The Pan-

44

Slavic Congress just dissolved by Windischgrätz had managed to show the threads but not the fabric. Under Palacký's direction and manifesto, it was intended as a bulwark against the "greater German" feelings of the Frankfurt Assembly. But when Bakunin, the visitor from Moscow, talked about Slavism, his western brothers didn't understand. The Poles hated the Bohemians as much as they hated the Austrians, and were interested only in an independent Poland. So it went, with harassed Palacký pleading for a cultural union, not a political one: a union of peoples, not states. But a cultural union is possible only through a common language, and which was that to be? Raise Czech to an equality with German, of course—Palacký insisted he was Bohemian, not Austrian—but could he ever bring about the acceptance of Bohemia as the Empire's leading Slav nation? Hungary with its Croats and Slovenes, Galicia with Poles and Ruthenians— would they accept Bohemian supremacy? Or would the struggles between the Slavs themselves end in subjugation of all Slavs to the German-speaking federation? The problems of a multinational empire were so complex that, by comparison, a civil war or marital fighting represented only a young child's view of struggle. At the Congress, Palacký announced his startling discovery: "If the Austrian Empire didn't exist, it would have to be invented, in the interest of humanity." For clarification, he explained, "As a means of protecting Slavs from German domination."

The Empire was like a badly cut jigsaw puzzle, thought Police Director Sacher-Masoch. Prague was just one of the pieces. He was basically liberal and even progressive—for he was a cultured man, extremely well-read (and who could read widely without becoming culturally liberal and socially progressive?)—but had absolutist tendencies. He didn't condemn any of the popular assemblies, not even in his thoughts, and did not stand against the impulse toward social equality. However, in this terrible time of famine and drought, poverty and economic disaster, it was wrong to take up arms for a cause when people were blinded by hunger. Despair had found a twin in distrust; the meager soup kitchens provided by the government were as nothing in this famine, so bad, so

45

desperate that one heard of parents eating their children. And yet—what could the government do? This blight of poverty and politics had moved inexorably eastward, from Ireland's potatoes through the prostitutes of Paris into this Empire, sweeping up Slavs and Germans, Italians, Magyars—even the Jews. Businessmen shed their conservatism as easily as dinner jackets in a stifling room, hoping that whatever was forthcoming would restore their fortunes or futures. Students spoke of equality, workers of wages. But the fact was, thought Sacher-Masoch with a sigh, what people really needed was enough food.

He was loyal to the Empire but—like many others in his position or higher—disdained any show of patriotism as being not well-bred. An Austrian was a gentleman first. He was for God and Emperor, of course—the Empire above all, and his truest colors were black and gold—but when he saw the poor wretches who were brought into the police station, his pity outweighed his zeal. He was a good administrator and a kind man. He was reluctant to impose his opinions on others and earnestly attempted to amuse his guests. He was able to drink liters of wine without becoming tipsy—though, if the company he was in were feeling merry, he was amenable enough to forgo sobriety after a single glass. Ladies were fond of him, his employers commended him, his wife adored him, and employees looked up to him. But in the eyes of his elder son, Sacher-Masoch was unimaginative and limited in both emotions and understanding.

Leo thought of Yarko and remembered his resolve to take part in the next war. Though too young, at twelve, for a soldier, he determined to be an observer, at least, and not remain childishly confined while all about him men and women were risking their lives. He was not clear about the issues or the sides—the rebels, according to his father, were wrong—and still felt a stranger in this new land where a new language (German) constricted his tongue. Nevertheless, battles were raging in the streets, and his need for adventure was as sharp in him as his fear.

He told his visitor in the nursery that he had never before

46

defied his father. But he would do it; he would go through hell, he vowed, in his search for life and meaning, because in him trembled the soul of an artist, a seeker of truth. He was too old, he said, for the sugared existence of the nursery or even for the honey of literature, if taken as a soothing agent for the painful rasp of raw truth.

So he explained, in halting German, to the girl who now sat with him upstairs while her mother paid a visit to his mother. The girl was some kind of relation, he'd been told, though he was meeting her now for the first time. She was old as Marika, though smaller, broadly featured (a hint of the Mongol?) and dark. She'd been born in Prague, her name was Miroslava, and she listened to her young relation with the contempt that small males always aroused in her.

"Such theories!" she said, resentful that she was forced to make conversation in a nursery when she was sixteen years old, of an age to bear children herself. "You sit in the house and expound theories. Why don't you just go out?"

"What, now?" He was shocked.

"Why not now? Or after dinner, or tomorrow morning? Or are you waiting for the rebels to come and fetch you?" she mocked. "I've been on the streets myself and intend to go again."

He stared a moment, as familiar strings of terror jerked him. "Take me with you," he begged, going on his knees before her. "Please. I'll be your slave, I'll do anything you say."

Miroslava looked down at him, and though he was a ridiculous boy, the thought of having a slave didn't displease her. "All right," she said. "Order our dinner to be served here. We'll see what can be done."

An hour later, Leopold huddled behind the barricade, his skin the color of fresh milk, his teeth chattering and a film of sweat cooling his face.

Miroslava looked over at him scornfully. "Why did you come?"

"To—to see," he answered feebly, feeling that the depths and connotations of the word "see" contained meanings too profound for explication. Often this young magician with words felt them disappear, vanish suddenly, leaving him alone on life's stage with a stick and handkerchief. Besides, this newly learned German could not yet be trusted to convey actual meanings.

"Coward!" she said, almost spitting. Her eyes flashed, her broad face showed the cruel lusts of Genghis Khan or Attila the Hun. "You're just a baby who belongs in the nursery. And now here you are, I've got you hanging onto me, and I can't let you get killed. Damn." She looked as though she'd like to, her eyes narrowing into slits, her face savage in its anger, her nostrils and mouth quivering with the smell of prey.

He was thrilled by the wildness of that face and wanted to immolate himself before her. And, as the strange thrill invaded him, he perceived this was not the first time. Something similar had happened to him before; this sensation had already been felt. Maybe, he thought confusedly, his mind lifting him a moment from his body, feelings were acquired like knowledge; you start with almost nothing at all and then are taught, learning in small steps until the knowledge (feeling) becomes part of you. In early childhood you grasp only the dim outer edges of thought or emotion, then slowly begin to penetrate them. He had a sense that whatever he'd known or felt until now was only the shadow cast before the body of truth.

Or perhaps it was the other way around: you knew (felt) everything at one early time, perhaps at birth, and as you moved through life, events hinted at what was forgotten and reminded you more and more of what was once known.

"Brat!" She hissed at him. "Do you always gather wool on fields of battle?"

That was witty, he acknowledged. She was a dark girl, barely taller than himself, with flashing teeth. He pictured a cutlass between them. Her skirt was above her ankles; she wore high boots and a bright red Polish vest trimmed with fur over a simple puckered blouse. A bullet whizzed by; a horse reared. He would be killed, he knew; he was as if dead already. A demon had entered him, to make him disobey his father and join this evil sorceress. He would be shot, stabbed or trampled

48

if he remained here. The screams sounded like gushing blood. Better to go home and die through Father's punishment, be whipped and imprisoned and starve to death. A thick club hit the side of a face, and the face disappeared. No, this wasn't happening. This was not actually going on, he wasn't here; he was dreaming in bed and his mother would come soon with chocolate. An explosion somewhere—and people ran out in all directions like ants from a trampled hill, but they were running, blood was on them, some wore bandages. More screams and angry voices. A hot, terrible smell, and then a horse tripped on the cobblestones, fell to its knees, tried to rise, couldn't, thrashed, kicked, struggled and wounded itself more, death coming into its eyes.

This eternity of war had been less than fifteen minutes, and now he just ran, not knowing how he had become erect or what new demon drove him, hearing only his heart in his ears and feeling the ground move under him but knowing this was wrong; the ground was still, and his legs were carrying him over it. Miroslava's scream echoed—"Stupid infant!"— and then came the shot and he knew he was dead. He fell forward on his face on the stones. Hands gripped him. He would die an inglorious death, delivered to the enemy. The hands pulled him up, shook him, and a voice called his name. He was being shaken like a young tree in storm. He kept his eyes tightly shut, his teeth locked. The voice repeated his name, angrily, then pleadingly, a voice he'd heard before. He opened his eyes and Marika was standing there, shaking him as if he were a doll. He was so astonished that he fell and grabbed her legs. She gave him a hard kick, and he lay on the ground, his face beside her foot, pain rising with shame, and dared not look up at her. She was speaking, in a low growl like a she-wolf guarding her den. "You naughty child! You wicked boy! What if you were killed? What then? Or wounded so that you could never walk again? You are mad, mad. What will your father say?"

He burst into tears. "Marika, Marika." Her power over him was so great that she seemed a god or Nature herself, who could protect and nurture or maim and kill. He kissed the foot beside his lips, and again she kicked him with it. Then she raised him up—what strength in this girl slim as a reed with hair like tassels of corn!—hit him smartly all over to dust him off and told him to get behind her. So she led him, retching with self-disgust, through the battling streets, winding between humans and animals. From her belt she drew a pistol, flourished it over her head and shot in the air. He recovered himself through amazement and followed the stern, extraordinary girl as she ran past a man with one eye missing, a young woman whose forearm was dangling, almost completely severed from the elbow, a dog's corpse, a man lying on wet red stones with only one leg. Sometimes she pulled him down and they crouched a moment; then she jerked his arm and they raced further. He had no breath, no thoughts, but his body moved, his feet flew behind hers and they were home. She dragged him to his room, boxed his ears and locked the door behind her when she went out.

He lay in stupor first, until he became conscious of pain, of soreness and a buzzing in his head, and sharp shocks as the muscles of his legs jerked to ease. What had happened was both real and not real. Scenes returned with captions, and cries wove into dialog, as a play slowly spun out in his mind. The heroine was tall and dark with a pistol in her belt, the hero a strong peasant and the backdrop included examples of the city's most magnificent Baroque. "The Last Days of Prague" or, perhaps, "A Woman Soldier."

But as he coughed, gagged and retched with his coughing, he remembered that he was in a locked room, that Marika had saved him, her beauty pale as long grasses in moonlight, and that the events, the moments, had all taken place. She had actually flourished a pistol. She'd been a soldier; he a coward. The other girl, who had taken him along, was ready to kill him, and her ferocious look had brought him a sensation both strange and remembered.

His thoughts moved back from the play. His body was hot and cold at the same time. Something in the past, as yet unreconstructed, was troubling him.

Galicia, at home. But not really home, not in their own house. During a game, with children. He was second oldest. Not too long ago, maybe during the time of the uprising? Yes, that was right; the strange feeling located itself close to the fear he felt when they'd brought in Yarko.

A woman—someone like this Miroslava but older. Much older, not a girl at all, but a relation too. Her silks rustled; she wore brocade. In her closet, the clothes imprisoned him. Closet? Yes, definitely: closet. He was hiding there, must have been part of the game; the furs made him sneeze. She was very angry when she found him, and dragged him out by his hair, or maybe ears. A man was with her—two men? Or had they gone? He fell to the floor to ask forgiveness. She kicked him with her small boot—red, polished, trimmed with ermine— then raised him up and smiled. Yes, so it was. That was when the sensation came. Heat showered down on him and made him shiver. She saw he was trembling and drew her fur around him. She was the most beautiful woman he'd ever seen, skin pale as the moon, soft as an eider. Auburn hair caught loosely at the crown, the rest of it falling free. When she kicked him, when she caressed him, the feeling was so strange he first thought he was dead. Then the intensity became less; he moved down from a peak and was brought slowly back to his corporeal self. When he'd regained his body, his first wish was to die in her arms, killed by her hands in some magnificent, silky way.

Yes, that was it, he remembered now. Today too . . . his agitation was growing, he would soon have a fever. If his mother saw him, she'd make him lie down with a cool compress on his head. The agitation continued, tears came to his eyes and spilled over, and he fell asleep as abruptly as falling down a deep hole.

Marika woke and released him at teatime. Seeing his pallor, she massaged his feet and sang softly to him a mournful tune from their childhood:

> "Down to the river
> my sweetheart goes.
> Who will find him
> When the water flows?"

Then she pinched his cheeks for color and warned him to act as though nothing unusual had happened. He understood, but could hardly believe, that his parents hadn't discovered him and would not be told.

At tea, no one noticed his wild thoughts. He was silent, but then he often said little while "scribbling in his head," as his father put it. In any case, his parents were too concerned with developments in Prague to pay close attention to their children. His mother told her husband she'd had a tedious visit from Miroslava's mother, and one of many stones rolled from Leo's heart.

* * *

Two days later, Field Marshal Windischgrätz bombarded the city and took it. He dissolved the government and the national guard, establishing martial law. His victory was stunning (no need to remember that the rebels had expressed willingness to discuss terms hours before he ordered the bombardment). This was the first victory of conservatives over revolutionaries (government over people) in all these battles. Windischgrätz could travel to Vienna with Prague in his pocket and a bitter though pleasurable foreknowledge that his wife's death would be avenged all over Europe. He could feel in his soldier's bones that the tide of revolution had been stemmed and now would turn. In the fields of summer, the great Hapsburg confederation would weed out patches of nationalism, he predicted.

And so it happened. On the last day of August the March laws of Hungary were declared invalid and the Austrian army invaded the land. All Hungarians, even the great poet Petőfi, fought with valor, remembering the months when they lived in freedom and everything was possible. Women fought with the men, leaving motherhood and cooking to the old as they cropped their hair, put on soldiers' uniforms and manned the barricades. The fight would be long—into the next year—but hopeless.

In Italy, Field Marshal Radetzky, with the Archduke Franz at his side, took Verona.

In early October, Austrian grenadiers on their way to Hungary found the railroad station occupied by revolutionaries. Having no desire to kill or be killed by Hungarian brothers as hungry and underpaid as themselves, the soldiers mutinied and joined the crowd of students and workers. From the station, they marched to the war ministry, gathering more to their ranks at each step. They demanded Count Latour, the hated Minister of War. "Latour," they called. "Give us Latour, or we will come in and get him." But the Count didn't show himself, so the crowd had to force its way inside and find him. When they did, it was butchery. Kitchen knives and carving knives, the ends of muskets, bare hands were all used on him, and when they dragged his body to the street, with its hundreds of wounds, they stripped it and strung it up on a lamppost. Blood streamed to the street while the crowd sang. Women dipped their handkerchiefs in his blood and laughed. Men cut off pieces of his skin.

Civilized, charming Vienna couldn't believe it. Dropping their newspapers in the coffeehouses, 100,000 Viennese fled, *schlag* still clinging to their mustaches. Ferdinand and his court were removed to Olmütz in Moravia, the feeble Emperor believing he was taken there for reasons of health.

*　　*　　*

At the castle in Olmütz, Archduchess Sophie, most formidable member of the Imperial Family, showed the stresses of Europe on her face. At forty-three, she retained the beauty of seven years ago, in red velvet with pearls around her neck and delicate drop earrings, captured by the portraitist for her brother Ludwig's Gallery of Beauties. Now Ludwig had just been forced to abdicate the Bavarian throne because of his affair with a common woman, supposedly a Spanish dancer, for whose pale skin and dark hair he'd emptied the coffers of the country. All Europe appeared to be going mad, and those rulers not out of their senses already (like Ferdinand) seemed determined to take leave of them. Her brother had actually paraded this Lola Montez, had been stupid enough to give her a position in his government, and so became the laughing stock of Bavaria through his "Lolaministerium"—a ministry that would no longer dance to the tune of Lola's golden castanets.

Sophie hated stupidity and for that reason had few friends. When she found someone whose intellect she could admire (like Metternich), she didn't trust him; and in the immediate circle of Hapsburgs—her husband, brother- and sister-in-law—she found it impossible to take seriously anything that was said, except a request for food. Her hope lay in her sons, particularly her eldest, her Franzi, who would take up the reins while she stood behind to guide him.

The massacre of Latour unhinged her to violent anger, a rage that carried her, white and shaking, through the next sleepless days, immolating the last shred of liberalism in her, wiping out every memory of the one sweet time in her life when she was young and beautiful and tenderly in love with her husband's nephew, the delicate son of Napoleon.

She became a fury. Seeing her pace the night with her ringlets in disarray, courtiers thought they understood the deadly danger of the lioness. Then Vienna was proclaimed in a state of siege and Windischgrätz named supreme commander. Sophie returned to herself, to the clear-mindedness that had earned her the sobriquet of "the only man at court." Franzi would become emperor; she could count on Windischgrätz and Metternich to help her. She and the old statesman had always understood each other, though they maintained distance. He had helped rear the crown prince, advising Sophie on tutors and subjects. Through Metternich, Franz had learned to take command.

Now serving under Field Marshal Radetzky, the future Kaiser was an unusually good-looking young officer whose elegance of bearing and figure were in no way diminished by the open sensuality of his features. His tight white cutaway jacket with gold buttons emphasized his leanness, falling from broad shoulders in a V to the waist. He was accustomed to uniforms, loved them now and would always love them, having first worn a jacket like this (though much smaller in size) five years earlier, when he was appointed colonel of a regiment. Now, at eighteen, with clear blue eyes and dark blond hair, Archduke Franz made a splendid picture.

He'd always loved soldiering; when he began to receive serious military training in his teens, he welcomed the clean order, the precision of maneuvers, the efficiency of discipline. But he was no dedicated militarist. He admired the army for its formality and decorum, its reassurance that good breeding would always rule.

He had a passion for horseback riding. Though unresponsive to what was known as "the finer things," he was enthusiastic about the fairer sex. On the dance floor, he was most graceful of all the dancers and court ladies flushed with pleasure to be in his arms. At table he showed equal grace, his lack of pompousness and the naturalness of manner combining in what women called virility and men, authority.

He appeared older than his years. Trained for command at the inevitable price of spontaneity, the Archduke had seen his adolescent dualities channeled into streams of Man and Official. The man was sentimental, kind and erotic. When Sophie and his tutors undertook the task of his sexual initiation along with other necessary lessons, Franzi showed himself remarkably adept. Women delighted in his energy, attentiveness and the surprise of finding him imaginative in bed.

In the official, these traits were expressed as conscientiousness and public zeal. He worked hard and diligently, read every memo, memorized every necessary fact. The public figure of Franz was not sentimental or even particularly just; he was disciplined, and control was a far more salient trait than sympathy.

He remained in Italy as fighting continued in the streets of Vienna, in the barricaded inner city. The revolutionaries had thrown back Windischgrätz's call for unconditional surrender, believing rumors that the Hungarians were near with reinforcements. Though the rumors were true, the Hungarian army was defeated just outside the city walls. In protest rose the last brilliant surge of resistance and blood, the worst fighting of all, beside the Hofburg, the Imperial Palace, in the spot where the Turkish siege of 1683 had reached its climax. Windischgrätz cut down the bloody flower of resistance and proclaimed a military dictatorship.

This time he traveled to Olmütz, to receive congratulations and confer with Sophie on the establishment of a new government. He called for his brother-in-law Prince Schwarzenberg, whom Sophie trusted no more than Metternich, but no less either, and in a cool appraisal found him to be a suitable mentor for her son. Calm, cynical and shrewd, he would be an excellent prime minister who could prune the deadwood of feudalism, placating Metternich's enemies and bringing new growth to the political organism.

Schwarzenberg was Sophie's match, the more so because she was an attractive woman and the prince had made an exhaustive study of this species. His affair with Lady Jane Ellenborough had given him his doctorate. She was a honey-blond beauty whose portrait hung in the Gallery of Ludwig, having been painted pre-Lola when Lady Ellen was sleeping with the king. She scorned values and considered morals to be childish. She was the kind of spirited Englishwoman produced regularly in every century, varying in degrees of wit (Lady Ellen was no Lady Montagu) and beauty, but always ruthless adventuresses of the heart, always finding whatever they sought and ridiculing it in the same moment.

They had a daughter together, whom Schwarzenberg loved. She and the moral he could extract from the affair were more than enough recompense for loss of love. The time spent with Lady Ellen had cured Schwarzenberg of his own adventurousness. At forty-eight, he was ready to settle down and take up the government. Though he was to die in four years, he would manage before then to get Austria on the road she would continue to travel until the end of the Empire.

It was settled. Franz Karl relinquished his claim. Franz returned from Italy. On the second of December, 1848, the Emperor Ferdinand I abdicated the Hapsburg crown in favor of his nephew, to be known henceforth as Franz Joseph I. (Schwarzenberg and Sophie had chosen Joseph, the name of Maria Theresia's eldest son, who reigned from 1780 to 1790. He'd been Austria's most progressive Emperor, and Franz Joseph would in time reverse part of his legacy.)

As his uncle passed over the crown, the boy Emperor said under his breath, "This is the end of my youth."

Goodly Ferdinand whispered, "God b-bless you. You'll have n-need, n-need of that."

PART II

Anna (<u>YOUTH</u>)

"We want only to flow into each other. We dip our soul into the strange soul; we climb up into the strange, inimical nature and receive her baptism. . . . We give ourselves over—like a thing, like cloth: Make from me what you are! . . .

"Then comes the terror of losing oneself completely.

"We feel almost a hatred against the power of the other. We think ourselves dead. We want to revolt against this alien life, to find again our selves in ourselves.

"This is the resurrection of Nature."

—Leopold von Sacher-Masoch, *Don Juan of Kolomea*

4

IN SPRING, the river Mur tumbles down from the eastern Alps, pale green as new grass, its froth white as baby lambs, accompanied on its course by swallows and martins, wagtails and hawks. Sometimes a golden eagle will glide across it, and where the Mur is held still as a lake, ducks and coots settle in for their mating and later hatching. The river is cold, then, but its glacial green means spring is here. The peasants smile and encourage its gurgling, for to them this is the sound of birth and the long labor is over. The season will grow and gain strength until it no longer needs human care.

After the planting and sowing, summer comes and brings forth of itself, offering life and crops, food for animals and humans, tapestries of color in the fields and on the slopes. Then the girls put on their prettiest dirndl blouses, their best necklaces, fresh aprons and finest silk shawls and waltz the night away in the arms of young men in lederhosen. When they fall to the floor from dizziness, a large bell is rung and a tray of beer or young wine is brought out. Everyone drinks and sings:

> *Ein prosit, ein pro-o-sit—der Gemütlichkeit.*
> (Let's drink to it, let's drink to it—this together-
>   ness.)

And then there is laughter; the musicians set down their glasses and pick up the instruments again. Late at night, on the way home, some boys will take their sweethearts into the bushes, vowing they love them in the cool darkness.

The season becomes still riper until the grass calls for the scythe, golden tassels signal that the maize is ready to be picked, birds crowd the air on their passage south, grapes are in the press and bacon in the smokehouse. The days will become capricious, hot or cold, as the hay is spread out to dry and then gathered into stacks or ricks, sprouting on the slopes like stunted forests. Sunflowers strain for the sun's last warmth as women in the arms of lovers turn and smile, lingering at the end before they must rise and dress and return to their husbands' coldness.

The Mur is quieter now, more contemplative, as it slides down its narrow bed from Bruck to Graz. In the city, women are rushing to appointments at the dressmaker, carriage wheels are being oiled, the cook seals the jam and packs the butter, and bachelors notice, too late as always, that the fur collars of their overcoats should be replaced. Coachmen bring out blankets for the horses and rub their hands together, anticipating and recalling numbness despite gloves when reins are held too long or too tightly. The opera has just opened and soon the theater season will begin. The jail is emptied of summer miscreants and awaits new clients. Students and professors will be returning to the university; schoolchildren already animate the streets each morning on their way to school, the bags on their backs filled with books and food. In the Styrian countryside, peasants prepare for short days and long sleeps on the bench by the stove as the year moves toward its death—but in Graz, townspeople feel just the opposite and await the new season of balls and festivities.

Police Director Sacher-Masoch observed that people walk with a faster gait in the fall—at least the young ones. Here, as in Prague, in Lemberg, fall meant beginnings for young people, who prepared their books, their minds, and set their lips wryly for the reopening of the university. His son would be one of them, starting out at the University of Graz in his second year of studies, after a successful first year at Prague. Young Leo was an excellent student. He had finished *gymnasium* (high school) in Prague covered with praise from his teachers, who found that Leo's school-leaving composition, "The Influence of Music on Human Character," showed clearness of mind and literary proficiency astonishing in so young a person. And Leo had only begun to learn German when they moved to Prague! It was an achievement, a source of pride for a father, and Sacher-Masoch had presented his son with an impressive gold-plated watch engraved with his initials and the motto, "Excelsior!"

But Leo was changed, he thought, wearing his grief like a bearskin since Rosa had died a few months ago. She'd been a lovely, fresh, bouncing girl, and the typhoid had driven her through pain, then madness, in a few short weeks before releasing her to calm and early death. Charlotte behaved well, only shrinking and becoming more pale during the illness and after the death. Her smile now could pierce the coldest heart, with its gentleness and deep, unreproaching sorrow. Leo, though, was unhinged, partly mad himself during his sister's delirium. Now that morbid, thin face was waxed with death and brought the freshness of Rosa's suffering back each time he had to look at it. Rosa had been his favorite: an enchanting girl, who ran to her father with open arms, sometimes stumbling in eagerness. She played with his mustache and teased him for growing too fat. At only fifteen! The Director felt the horror of her death like a sickness in his own body. It was fortunate that he was offered this post at that time. Better to forget, to bury the dead in the Prague cemetery and move to a new place, gather fresh impressions, take up the task again.

But Leo had never relinquished his mourning. He hardly spoke to any of them, as though they'd been responsible, as though the suffering were his alone. He was not a man but a mother's boy, who would always indulge himself in excess of feeling, incapable of restraint, with eyes fixed inward to observe his own emotions as though they were of utmost importance. He'd always been the frail one, Rosa a blooming, healthy child. Nature should pluck the weakest first. . . . No, he must not think further along these lines. He was a responsible husband and father, a citizen and official who could take honest satisfaction in his self-discipline. Leo should have learned by now to take himself in hand.

61

"Your Excellency!" The assistant bowed. "A lady is below. She says she is the wife of a Count Attems, who has abandoned her and three children, and that—"

"Yes, yes." The Director waved his hand. "All right, but tell her I am on my way to an important meeting and can give her only a few minutes." Young Attems' "wives" had spread like creepers since the old count died and the inheritance passed to his son. Women could be vultures. With every corpse of a rich man came droves of women hoping to nourish themselves on the cadaver. Hateful hordes, small-minded creatures. Sacher-Masoch thought of his own wife. Women should all be aristocrats; then they would have the dignity of their sex.

The "lady" was brought in, her rouged cheeks showing her at once to be a charlatan. Sacher-Masoch assured her briskly that he would look into the matter, and, before the tears could spill from the reddening rim of her lower eyelids, he saw her to the door, saying he was already late for an important conference. Then he combed his hair and mustache, refolded his handkerchief and went out for a pleasant, well-earned dinner.

Leo unburdened himself only to Marika. Her simple heart, he felt, could understand depths of grief. And Marika was well acquainted with death. Her mother died before she could remember, her father died when she was very young, and at sixteen she had parted from her brother and second mother. She understood.

"It's a weight pulling you to the center of the earth," he said.

"No," she replied calmly. "You must not allow it. Rosa is in heaven. She would be sad to see you as you are. Make songs for her; dance to her memory."

"How did you feel when your father died?"

"Nothing."

"Nothing? How's that?"

"I felt nothing. The world was flat. I couldn't raise my eyes. I was nothing."

"But it was he who was nothing! *He* had become nothing and you were trying to fuse your nature into his."

She shrugged, patted his hand and stood up. Slim as a young tree, with her rain of silver hair, Marika was Leo's Moon Princess from a lost childhood, not now the stirring heroine of Prague. He rose and embraced her, kissing her with brotherly tenderness, his own Marika, "little mother" of his babyhood, his Irina, Rosa, his girl, sister, his bright star.

For weeks after the event in '48 he hadn't touched her, frightened by the new light she stood in, her assumption of power that made her both wonderful and a stranger. But life continued its usual round and her glory faded as he thought less often of her brilliant role and the tumble of feeling she had thrown him into. In little less than a month, she was his old Marika, that solid, loving girl who was strong as a boy and gentle as a pussycat. She, too, reverted to her old manner and shed the haughtiness she had shown toward him, loving him again as a brilliant but weak boy, half son, half brother, whose frailty must be protected and whose mind was a rare ransom. Now they were seventeen and twenty-one, their love for each other still nourished by the streams of Galicia, of home, still held by the arms of Irina and the smells of the kitchen. They hardly observed changes in each other, the strange developments of growth and grafting that make separate branches, even from the same tree, amazingly varied. Leo was aware that he loved Marika, that she belonged to him, but he regarded her as a constant part of the landscape of existence, neglecting to remember times when she astonished him or forced him to see her as exceptional.

"Lev," she said, still holding him in her arms, "you will do very well here. I can feel it. You must hold the past deep in yourself and let your mind go out fearlessly in this new university."

He ran his hand over the soft sleek hair. "I will try, Marika. You give me strength as your mother used to. Bake me your pastries and I will become the best student in Graz for you."

"For me? No, you must do it for your mama and papa first. And then," she said with a little laugh, "you will be doing it for your sweetheart."

"But that's you!" He forced himself into the game, hopelessness still struggling to claim him. But her laughing eyes won, as she twirled easily from his hold, caught his hand and twirled again. He joined her in a quick dance, then stopped abruptly, feeling ashamed. She saw that he wanted to be alone and left him, pleased by her small accomplishment of faint color rising in his gaunt face.

Alone, he went to the next room, sat down at the old Biedermeier secretary, took out pen and paper, and wrote his resolves to:

Devote myself entirely to studies, with the exception of conversations with mentors or otherwise well-informed persons who may offer enlightenment.

Sleep no more than six hours, and rise early.

Play no more games of cards or otherwise.

Avoid female company except members of the household and their guests. Gentlemanly behavior, however, will be shown in the presence of all females, whatever their rank or station.

Smoke less or not at all.

Forswear daydreaming.

Take one meal a week (at least) away from the family.

Spend only a moderate amount of time (no more than two hours daily) in coffeehouses.

Read serious books mainly; no more than two works of Pure Literature a week.

Be cordial with Papa; make Mama laugh at least three times a week; guide Marika in her reading; be patient with Charles.

He read it over, signed at the bottom, and stood up to meet his father.

"Why are you using my desk?" asked the older man coldly.

Be cordial with Papa. "I'm sorry," said Leo. "I just had to jot something down."

"What is it that was so important?" He held out his hand for the transcription.

"No! I mean—nothing important. I'm sorry, forgive me." Paper in hand, Leo ran out, up the stairs to his own room and there wept.

Later that night he found himself again in his father's study, in nightgown and cap, with bare feet. Though it had happened a few times during his childhood, this sleepwalking

64

then disappeared—until a few months ago. Now it had recurred a few times, but since he always returned to his own bed and never harmed himself or any objects in the house, the good doctor with whom his mother conferred advised only that Leo take a medicinal tea each night before going to sleep. The stress of his sister's death and the move to a new place was upsetting Leo's delicate nature, said the doctor, but this was merely a phase and would pass in time.

Moonlight lay in sheaves on the small polished rosewood table with lion's feet. Caught in silver-bluish light, the marble figurine seemed something otherworldly, beyond life but not contained in art. Paleness animated her, more an embodied spirit than human, and this tiny goddess grew before his eyes, her lips parted, her nakedness amazing. He knelt before the Venus, his lips moving in prayer. Her blind eyes looked on him with contempt. He shivered and stretched his hand to her, but she disdained it. Edging forward, he kissed the goddess' feet, as peasants in Galicia kissed the feet of the crucifix.

His eyes blurred; her lips trembled. He caught the statue, kissed the cold lips, and a blaze of heat passed from the goddess to himself. In horror, he tried to rise, but instead bowed his head, hitting it on the table's edge, and felt her foot hold him down. Faint high laughter circled around him. A voice he had never heard before said clearly, "You will be mine!" and the high laughter rose again as all his senses came together and he lost consciousness.

He woke in his bed, shivering under the down, in a dark stillness he could recognize as between two and three in the morning. His heart pounded; he was sweating coldly. He diagnosed terror and remembered the statue. Again he heard laughter, high as the wind, and lit his lamp. Nothing out of the ordinary in his room, but he sensed, like small animals long before the hawk's shadow is on the field, that something dangerous was near. He extinguished the lamp, murmured a Hail Mary, and was immediately gathered into the arms of sleep.

When he woke again in daylight, Marika was entering his room with the breakfast tray, which held tea, rolls and his nightcap. "A fine thing!" she said laughing. "It was on the floor in your father's study. I found it before he was awake. Now up with you, lazybones! It's after seven."

"I'm not well," he said, closing his eyes. "No breakfast today."

Marika had seen the black flash in his eyes, the light she recognized as meaning he was in another place, here only in body, and she decided to say nothing to his mother. He would return from there, as he always had, with fresh stories, and as he told them the strange light would be rekindled but would shine with less blackness. His eyes were like no one else's, sometimes inhuman, black diamonds in a pale setting, brilliant and fixed, unable to cut even the thinnest glass. Or they were small creatures held in the fur of lashes, absorbed in their own life, unconnected to the large frame that was their host. Others, she knew, were frightened by those deep eyes and their fires, but Marika understood the flashes as signals, and she left him in peace, or torment. He was the gentlest soul alive, and the most generous, who would protect small animals from the cruelty of boys and give everything he had to whoever wanted it. Patiently, he'd given her his time with the slow letters that refused, for long weeks, to become words. And then, when she finally learned, he carefully guided her reading, bringing her new books, helping her with anything she didn't understand. No one else had given her so much. He presented her with words and, through them, gave her journeys over time and across seas, to lands her parents had never been able to imagine or dream about. She sometimes thought that life had been only a wide plain before she began reading, and though she didn't read too often or too quickly, she knew that books elevated her and words conferred on her something special, like the mark of a princess.

* * *

In Possenhofen, a small town in Bavaria on the banks of Lake Starnberg, the young Emperor Franz Joseph had fallen instantly and completely in love with his cousin. Her bright eyes and flushed cheeks turned him into Romeo, as he defied his mother by refusing the princess prepared for him, insisting on her fifteen-year-old sister, the wild tomboy Elisabeth. Though niece of King Ludwig I and of his own mother

Sophie, Elisabeth (called Sissi) had grown up as the child of her father, madcap Max, Duke in (not *of*) Bavaria, resisting the refinements her mother Ludovica hoped to polish her daughters with, to make them shine as the brightest prizes in the most exalted marriage market of Europe, servicing ruling monarchs and their heirs.

Sissi had been eleven when her cousin became Austrian emperor, but she cared for politics no more than for French lessons or any of the other graceful arts her mother took pains to have her tutored in. Sissi was happiest when out of doors, racing through dewy grass, climbing trees, jumping on a horse bareback and urging the animal to greater and greater speed, leaping over stiles, until her face turned red from whippings of the wind and her own long hair. Her mother was a lady, but her father was her darling. Like her, he loved everything fast, colorful and unconventional. Over the years they were twin, free souls, escaping their fetters early on a Sunday, silently letting themselves out of the house while others prepared for church and riding to a village to see the circus performers. There Sissi danced, holding out her apron for copper coins from bystanders, laughing and singing with her father and the jugglers, tumblers, acrobats. Then all went for beer, Sissi ceremoniously paying her own way and inviting gypsy children to a pitcher with the money she'd earned.

When Franz Joseph met this fairy's child, stumbling out of the woods behind the house with laughter streaming in tears down her bright cheeks, her breath struggling to keep up with her explosions of happiness, his own breath caught and he stumbled back into a golden dream he had forgotten. She would be his Empress, beautiful and clear as the glittering Starnberg, who would irradiate the dullness of rule while he laid his empire at her charming feet.

Both mothers were against the match—the girl was untutored and unsuitable for Europe's highest throne. Her older sister Helene (Nené) was the proper choice. But, for the first time in his five-year rule, Franz Joseph was deaf to Sophie's advice. Last year he had proposed to a princess chosen by his mother (and happily—he thought now—had been refused). Since the attempt on his life earlier in this year, when the

67

nationalist Libenyi, shouting "Long live Hungary!", struck with a knife from behind, stabbing the neck but missing the artery, Franz Joseph had grown more independent, as though confirmed by the foiled assassination that he was Emperor through God's will.

He proposed and she accepted. He was wonderfully handsome, he swept her through air when they danced, he attended to her constantly at table and, when he caught her eyes across a room, she felt the world was exploding into brilliants and stars around her. She was a young girl, in love with the great Emperor, but she could think of him only as her Franz, who knew her completely because his eyes held her as no others had. She loved him through all the enthusiasm she felt for life, joy, speed and her own lovely being.

But when they went together to the small church in Ischl, where the Hapsburgs had a summer castle, Sissi was afraid. Crowds welcomed them, crooning her name. The little town was gauded in bright ribbons, the blue and white of her Bavaria mingling with his black and gold. At the church, after Mass, Franz Joseph drew her by the hand and went to the priest to ask his blessing on both of them, for Elisabeth, he said, "is my future wife."

The priest, the town, all Austria blessed them and sang the praises of the beautiful young couple. The commotion unnerved Sissi. She loved her Franz, she would certainly marry him, but, alone with her mirror, she wailed to the pretty image, "If only he weren't the Emperor!"

*　　*　　*

"Here comes Sacher," said Karl Eggendorf, a fair young man with a broad forehead. He nudged his friend's paunch with his elbow.

Joseph Meyringer, handsome as a tenor, smiled. "You can recognize him a hundred meters off by his shuffle."

"Strange," said Karl. "When you sit with him, or even when you're standing, he's all straight lines. Did you notice? Lines, vertical and horizontal. But when he walks—should we call it that?"

"Locomotes?" suggested Joseph.

"All right. Then he curls up and moves along like an old man with bad feet."

Leo approached them. His childhood fragility hadn't left him: a thin, flat body with a delicate head placed on a long neck, a long nose dividing his face into two flat planes, and below the nose, at right angles, a long seam of mouth. He hailed them. *"Servus,* my hearties. Are you grinning here at my expense?"

Karl embraced him, Joseph made a small bow. *"Servus,* old man," said Karl. "Not entirely at your expense. It was my treat."

"How you Germans torment us poor Slavs. Go on, laugh. Tomorrow you will be our servitors."

"Master," said Karl, "would you permit your servants the honor of inviting you to a beer?"

"Thanks, no. I'm off to the library."

"A glass of white wine?" offered Joseph, remembering that Sacher preferred it.

"Ah, you're a better servant than this other one. Come along, then. We need something to moisten the dry pages of learning." More than that, Leo usually found himself in need of refreshment after the walk from home, through the inner city, out by Paul's Gate or Palace Gate, across a patch of the City Park eastward to the university. Thirty or forty minutes, sometimes longer if he stopped to watch the henna squirrels with their bushy tails, or the great tits squawking at the newly arrived snow finches. He tried to vary his walk by at least one street every day, never returning the way he came. In the mornings, he passed tradespeople, servants and ladies hurrying through the gate into the inner city and its shops, while he shuffled out to lectures and learning with usually nothing more than a cup of coffee or glass of wine on his mind.

It was good to have friends. A man needed companionship, and here in Graz was the first time Leo felt comfortable in the comradery of men. Though he hadn't known them long, Eggendorf and Meyringer afforded good company. He could relax with them, forget the cares that flew at him like homing pigeons when he entered his house, and be himself, or at least a self he took pleasure in and otherwise rarely encountered.

Both were very handsome, in Leo's estimation. Karl was taller than himself, with hair the color of sand, deep blue eyes, a narrow waist and long, elegant fingers. The son of a baron, Karl showed aristocratic amusement and tolerance toward almost everything, regarding the phenomenology of creation as a performance presented especially for him. He was cultured and intelligent, curious about anything he had not encountered before, agnostic but not cynical (because nothing, not even God, was serious), and his natural aptitude for the game of life was daily refined through new skills.

Joseph was a bourgeois with smooth cheeks and emerald eyes, a kind young man with the innocence of a groom on a wedding cake, his handsomeness nearly pretty and as unspoiled as his heart. He was a student of life who took great care to learn his lessons and whose smile was perennial as lilac.

Sometimes Leo wondered what he had to offer them, why they had so readily accepted him into their friendship. He knew he was ugly and pale; on the other hand, he had a good heart and good mind. Karl had occasionally observed that Sacher was "hugely amusing," and Joseph listened open-mouthed to his stories.

"Prosit." They clinked glasses and drank. Karl turned and surveyed his new friend from top to bottom, like an inspector of meat. He sighed and asked merrily, "When, my dear Brussels sprout, will you ever learn to dress yourself?"

"I have been dressing myself since the age of five."

"And no improvement in all those years! We must take you in hand, Sacher—or better, take you to a tailor."

"What's wrong with my clothes?"

"It's not the clothes so much as what's behind them. You wear them like saddlebags."

"Are you calling me an ass, sir?"

All three laughed. "Good," said Karl. "But really, my dear, you look quite the Bohemian. You should have your trousers pressed and wear your scarf as though the center of gravity were beneath your feet and not off in the direction of your left shoulder."

"I do not believe in gravity," Leo pronounced.

"Nor I!" said Karl, patting him on the back. "Well"—he sighed—"I've done what I could. You will not take advice from a man of the world. Let fall what may—you have been warned."

"Thanks, old one," said Leo. Joseph was cocking his head at the waiter for another round, but Leo stopped him because the lecture would begin in ten minutes, hardly time to get out and up the crowded staircase to the large hall. All of them had to attend the lecture on "Transition from Babenberg to Hapsburg Law." Within the Law Faculty, Karl was studying philosophy, Leo history, and Joseph law itself. "This evening? Five o'clock?" No need to say where; they habitually met in the coffeehouse off the main square, closer to home for all three.

By five fifteen, Joseph hadn't joined them. "He's been abducted," said Karl. "Carried off by a nymph of the outskirts with black hair and danger in her eyes. You are not a virgin, I take it?"

"You cannot take it, it's gone."

"Well, then, what do you think of the fair sex, our beautiful adversaries?"

"I don't think, I feel."

"How very German of you. And what do you feel, my dear Werther?"

"Strange, hot, confused—to tell the truth. I'm no Werther, the Romantic Dream is counterweighted by another view entirely: the evil woman, who tempts men and destroys them and to whom we must pay homage."

"Which only goes to show you frequent the wrong whorehouse. A few florins is all you need to pay."

"Not that. In Galicia the peasants know there's evil in woman. We have many legends of sorceresses and death-givers. And then we have the true stories, from a generation ago, when Polish mistresses treated the male peasants like pigs or worse."

"Tell me one."

"A story?"

"A true one. Tell me about a peasant who actually lived."

Leo opened and closed his mouth to imitate a dying fish.

Karl grinned and understood. The fee must be paid in advance, in liquid currency.

When it arrived, Leo began: "You've met Marika, who lives with us and whom I regard almost as my sister." He paused a moment, in sadness. Karl mistook the pause and grinned lasciviously. Leo shook his head, annoyed. "No. Now I will tell you a true story about her father, a good and fearless man whom I can hardly remember. I knew him when I was very small. I lived in his house for reasons of health. He had strong hands and a deep, comforting voice.

"His name was Ivan Dmitrovitch Boroduk, and his first wife, Marika's mother, was Lyubov Orestivna, a beautiful woman with hair of wheat and gentian eyes. She was beautiful, but not kind. I will tell you how it came about that Ivan Dmitrovitch married her." When Leo narrated, he unconsciously affected a different style of speaking, moving into the Galician past with cadences conforming to the language of folk tales. He had the ability to weave truth and elaboration together so finely that not even he could tell which threads were which. His memory provided him many details he had heard, and his native talent gave him whatever transitions or specifics he lacked. When he told stories, his voice was soft and hypnotic, holding his listeners in the same trance he was held by. His whole face seemed to soften, though his eyes became brighter, emitting small flashes whenever inspiration guided his tale in a direction he hadn't expected.

"Marika is her mother's child, with gentian eyes and the moon in her hair. Ivan Dmitrovitch could never know if she was his own child as well—but even the wisest man in the world can never know, and he was very far from being the wisest.

"His troubles began when he was twenty-two, though some say they began much earlier, and go back to the day he was born, in the cold winter of 1793, the eighth living child of his parents. At the age of twelve, he joined his brothers and father to fight the Poles, each of them carrying around their necks a little metal cross and a small bag filled with earth that the mother had dug from under the threshold of their house. So did all our soldiers venture forth.

"The war ended in summer with the Peace of

Schönbrunn, which ceded Poland the whole of West Galicia and Cracow, retaining most of East Galicia for Austria. Of the five Boroduks who marched out, only two returned: Ivan and his fifteen-year-old brother, Timofy. Their father and two brothers had kissed the cross and the piece of earth from home, and died.

"At the time of the new troubles, those that would lead to his marrying the beautiful and cruel Lyubov, Ivan Dmitrovitch was a peasant of the Count Dolubovsky and his wife. The count was still young, barely thirty. His wife, a magnificent woman of twenty-two, had small feet and slim ankles, hair rich as velvet and skin so translucent that every narrow vein showed through. She was known by all for her beauty and cruelty. Ivan had heard of both characteristics, but felt no curiosity about her whatever."

Joseph, who had not been carried off by a fair nymph, but whose watch had stopped, now joined them. Karl put a finger to his lips, Leo paused for Joseph to give his order, then resumed:

"One day Ivan Dmitrovitch was sitting at table, finishing his prayers before dinner, when he heard carriage wheels coming to his door. With a hasty 'amen' and a quick crossing of himself, Ivan went out to see. There was his mistress, beautiful as Salome, descending her gilded wagon with tiny feet shod in fur-trimmed boots. He fell to his knees and kissed the hem of her skirt, in the old manner of our peasants. She whispered to her companion in uniform, who told Ivan that the mistress deigned to visit his hut; she was interested in seeing how her peasants lived.

"Ivan rose, bowed low and escorted her in. At the sight of his dinner she laughed softly and asked if this was what peasants ate. 'It is, so please Your Excellency,' Ivan said, and she would not be denied the tasting of it. He poured her a glass of wine and stood respectfully to the side while she tasted the cabbage soup, sausage, bread, and his cucumber, a treat he had looked forward to since the evening before. She appeared satisfied and left the hut without looking at Ivan. Her escort returned to tell the peasant that the countess would visit from time to time and sample his food."

Like a good actor, Leo could be absorbed and still highly

sensitive to his audience. This was the moment to have a sip of wine. He wouldn't lose them; they were both completely his.

"Ivan was confused and premonitions took hold of him. She was the most beautiful woman he had ever seen, delicate as a baby bird, strange as a bittern's cry in the night—a creature too complicated for his simple understanding. It was as though an angel had descended to his hut, and he prayed she would not come again.

"But scarcely a week passed, and she returned. Ivan Dmitrovitch did not comprehend that the capricious little Polish lady had taken a fancy to him, to his large solid body, lean from work and not puffy in places, like her husband's. His thick dark hair and intense black eyes interested her more than anything she'd seen in months. Her days were dull, on the whole, her companions predictable and their conversation stale. In the peasant's hut, with his eyes burning her skin, she was aroused. She wanted to overpower this strong, independent man.

"After she had visited a few times, she motioned him to sit with her while she ate. He felt this was wrong; his crudeness and the roughness of his hut offended her delicacy. But he did as he was bidden, keeping his eyes on the floor and his hands crossed.

" 'Look at me,' she demanded. 'Do you think I am beautiful?'

"His answer was a bleat but she insisted. 'Am I beautiful?'

" 'Very,' he mumbled.

" 'Would you like to touch me?'

"He couldn't speak, neither could he draw his eyes from her, and he felt he was burning in hell.

"She laughed and told him to come lace her boots more tightly. He knelt, and when her foot was in his hands he lost his reason, bent and kissed it. Then he sprang up as though his lips had touched fire. She smiled calmly and said, 'That was naughty. Your punishment is to come dine with me tomorrow. Yes. That is an order. I'll expect you no later than midday.'

"In his wretchedness, Ivan could not sleep throughout the night. He prayed, kissed the crucifix and vowed that, for all the whippings he might receive, he would disobey and not attend upon his mistress.

"But on the morrow a courtier entered his hut and took Ivan to the manor. There, the poor peasant was led into a small room furnished with red velvet set in gilt frames, the walls almost as rich as the chairs. Two strong maidservants bathed and scented him despite his outcries, and then dressed him in clothes so delicate he dared not move for fear of tearing them. In a white silk blouse with wide sash over soft white trousers ending at the knee, white silk stockings and boots of white kid, he was presented to the lady. In contrast to the white, his dark hair and black flashing eyes looked wilder than ever; his mistress flushed with pleasure and murmured, 'My Cossack prince.'"

Leo's throat was dry. He paused and drank, noticing that Joseph was as flushed as the countess. "Am I talking too long?" asked Leo disingenuously.

"Go on!" Karl commanded. "The night is young. Ivan's troubles have just begun."

Leo thought of his resolves and momentarily reproved himself. He must not while away the evening in the coffee-house; at home they'd be expecting him, and he'd drunk enough wine already. But he was in good form, his friends were hanging on his words, and it was impossible to resist one's own performance, particularly if it was going splendidly.

"From that time on, Ivan's life was not his own, and always tortured. The frivolous countess used all her charms to have him make love to her, but he resisted, because adultery was a mortal sin. Then she beat him with her pearl-handled whip and, when he still remained adamant, gave orders that he be stripped and flogged until blood streamed down his back. Day after day, one week after another, Ivan took his punishment in silence, praying inwardly.

"When she saw she could do nothing to make him bend, she became bored and sent him away. He returned to his hut, cleaned out the dust and dirt that had settled in his absence,

75

and gave thanks for deliverance, ignoring his bruises. Perhaps beauty was cruelty, he thought, but he felt no anger now it was over.

"He was not to remain in peace for long. A few days after his return, he was summoned to the count, who whipped him and raged at him. 'You dog! You dared try to make love to my wife. No, dog is too good for you, you worm, you piece of filth, you vomit from a she-dog. You don't deserve the grace of death, but in kindness I shall give it to you.'

"How could a peasant dispute the words of a countess when in the presence of her husband? Ivan was beaten with whips and chains until no part of his body remained un-lacerated. When he fell unconscious, he was taken away. Then his great strength brought him back to health and his wounds mended. But the count was not satisfied. 'You snake, you viper, you lowest of all creeping things, you will learn your lesson!' he vowed.

"At that time in Galicia it was easy to teach peasants their lessons: they were whipped and beaten until they either died—in which case the lesson may have been learned, but could not be practiced—or survived, with bodies and wills so broken they were less than work animals. The Polish gentry in the early part of this century, my friends, thought nothing of subjecting their peasants to treatment they would not toler-ate for their horses or pets, on grounds that it was inhumane.

"However, Ivan survived and was given, at her request, to the pretty countess as a toy. She used his back as a seat during picnics (flesh is softer than the ground or wood), as a mount when she went riding, and she amused herself by ordering him to bring her a bottle of wine when she lay in bed with a lover or was doing her toilette in negligée. She even summoned him when she was completely undressed, then ignored him, as though he were invisible.

"Her husband used Ivan for anything unpleasant. When one day two of the horses became ill and could not do the plowing, the count borrowed his wife's plaything and yoked Ivan to the plow."

"No," Karl interrupted. "You're inventing now. That was absolutely not permitted in the Austrian Empire."

Leo smiled. "Of course not. But remember, Galicia was considered the China of the Empire, very backward, and its links to the west at the time were delicate as the countess' silver chain. You wanted a true tale," Leo reproached him, "and I'm telling you one."

"Go on," Karl said brusquely.

"For years, Ivan led a life no better than that of a dumb animal—much worse, in fact, since he was still a man and could remember the sweetness of human love and the mercy of Mary. For a man to live contentedly like a beast is only possible when he has no philosophy, and Ivan did not lose his philosophy when he became a slave. Though he could neither read nor write, he had memorized many passages from the Bible, and he persisted in believing that God was good, man was capable of goodness, and our life on earth was the passing of a dream.

"He was strong and did his work well. After a few years the count came to Ivan one day and spoke to him in a direct manner, without the scorn of earlier times. He told Ivan of an embarrassment he had with a certain woman of the countryside, extremely beautiful but without scruples. She had not understood the droit de seigneur, and was now making demands on him, threatening disclosure. If his wife learned of the sordid affair, she would surely kill the other woman and make his own life a hell besides. Would Ivan Dmitrovitch, certainly of an age to be a husband, consider marrying this very beautiful creature?

"Ivan replied that he would not, whereupon the count ordered him to do it. Then he softened, appealing to Ivan in the name of Christian love to take unto himself this woman —otherwise she would die, or at best live abandoned and alone. Also, the count promised Ivan and his bride a pretty house, money and two very fine horses.

"Ivan reflected a moment. 'Make me your foreman,' he told the count, who began to shout, suddenly stopped in mid-rage, laughed and said, 'Why not?'

"So the agreement was made and both parties remained true to their word. Ivan Dmitrovitch married Lyubov Orestivna, the most beautiful woman of the village. The countess left him alone, the count treated him in a friendly manner, and he was respected by all. So it ended."

"Bravo!" exclaimed Joseph, but Karl shook his head. "This Lyubov must have made his life miserable," he said. "What happened to her?"

"She died in the cholera, as did the countess. Ivan and his master let the evil of the past bury itself and they became friends. Ivan soon married a kind and lovely girl, my beloved Irina Petrivna, and the count sent them a very valuable silver samovar as wedding present."

"So the good man had a few years of happiness before he died?" asked Joseph.

"Great happiness," Leo told him. "His new wife was a wonderful woman, who brought him such love that he could forget the past. He was always smiling—like you."

Joseph smiled broadly. Even though he was nearly nineteen, he liked stories to end happily. "You have a great gift," he said.

Karl agreed. "You're younger than either of us, and you tell tales like a master. What will become of you, Sacher? Will your name fall as reverentially from lips as Goethe's?"

Leo felt exhausted. It was an effort to speak. "I am a scholar," he said.

"Nonsense. You are an artist. All that you're studying now will probably serve you later only as material. No, don't bother to answer. I can see you're tired. Strong coffee is what's prescribed." He ordered. "When you've drunk it, you can answer me, if you want to. But I predict you'll have difficulties with the professors and mentors of the university. They'll declare that you are too colorful, and they'll eat their hearts out while choking on the dry bones of history. If they can have no gravy, neither can you. Dust to dust—from the old pages of texts to parched prose. You'll see. I know them."

"That may be," said Leo, revived at the sight of coffee, "though I doubt it. Telling stories is just amusement. History is something else, and I intend to be a historian."

"And I a philosopher, and Meyringer a judge. Do you really think, you loons, that we'll be sitting here in ten years as 'Doctor Professors' and whatnot? No, I predict Meyringer will be singing in the opera, Sacher will be writing novels, and Eggendorf will be living very comfortably with a full-bottomed wife, writing essays of wisdom and contributing fitfully to civilization's dance."

"Won't I have a wife?" Joseph pleaded.

Karl looked him over. "A harem."

"And I?" Leo asked, amused.

"A strange mistress, or perhaps a large dog."

"I'd prefer a cat."

"Cat, then—you shall have it. And now, my esteemed colleagues, I must take leave of you. Important matters." He winked at Leo.

It was much too late. Leo also stood up and returned home, each step carrying him further from the legerity of the coffeehouse, bringing him back to his accustomed pain.

5

In VIENNA, the fiacre drivers decorated their horses with blue and white rosettes. Blue and white were the colors of the milliners in their ribbons and bonnets and of the flower women selling posies of white narcissi and forget-me-nots, or blue and white hyacinths. A portrait of the Bavarian princess hung in every shop, and the entire city was being cleaned, polished, adorned in anticipation of the wedding.

On a bright day, in a pink dress, Sissi set out from home to become the Empress. With her parents, she rode to Munich, from there by steamboat along the Isar to the Danube. Madcap Max was gloomy at the beginning of the journey, brooding over restrictions imposed on him by his daughter's betrothal. Only yesterday the Bavarian King had "suggested" he mend his ways, after a particularly ribald evening in a Munich tavern. A lovely party, he thought ruefully, where he'd been in top form at rhyming puns and erotic limericks, and the girls were plump and tasty as dumplings.

But Sissi could always lift him from gloom, and by the time they reached the Danube, father and daughter were "up to their old tricks," as Ludovica disapprovingly put it, sharing their old delight in each other's company. At Linz, the first Austrian town they came to, Franz Joseph greeted them on the quay with flowers, having traveled from Vienna to surprise his bride, escort her to the mayor's house, where she was to spend the night, and then return by himself to the capital. She embraced him enthusiastically, reassured that he was the handsomest and kindest of men.

Next day the Bavarian family rode toward Vienna on a

yacht covered with roses, past banks of the Danube crowded with people in finery, who had left their work and brought their children to see the beautiful bride of the Emperor. Sissi spent the night in the 1400-room palace of Schönbrunn, in apartments prepared by Aunt Sophie.

On the following day she was dressed in a gown of pink and silver embroidered with roses. A diamond crown sparkled on her chestnut hair. She mounted a glass coach with panels painted by Rubens, drawn by eight white Lippizaner horses, escorted by outriders in gold and black. The crowd called her a fairy princess and broke through police cordons to gape at her. "Like a freak in a sideshow," the princess whispered to her mother, who shook her head in despair.

So she was displayed to her future subjects on the day before her wedding. On the morrow, in white and silver, stepping on rose petals in her path, Sissi took the hand of her Franz, and a cry went up, echoing through the streets of Vienna, through every wine cellar and coffeehouse: "Long live our Empress!"

In the wedding party was Sissi's small cousin, heir to the Bavarian throne, eight-year-old Ludwig with sapphire eyes and thick dark curls, an enchanting child. Some guests were reminded of paintings in Schönbrunn, showing the wedding of Maria Theresia's eldest son, Joseph II, with five-year-old Mozart in attendance. Ludwig stared at his cousin and decided she was the most beautiful woman in the world.

Next morning at breakfast, Sissi's aunt, now mother-in-law, asked, "Did my son do his duty well? Did he perform satisfactorily?" The sixteen-year old Empress let out a shriek and ran from the room, leaving Sophie to her opinion that the girl was still green, and potentially hysterical.

*   *   *

"Pretty, isn't she?" remarked Karl, stopping in front of a portrait of Empress Elisabeth displayed by a jeweler on the Herrengasse.

"Beautiful." Though dark, she reminded Leo of Marika —the same fineness of features, the small resolute mouth.

"I wouldn't mind marrying her myself. To be served by such a woman—"

"Never!" Leo broke in. "Such a woman must be served.

Such a one places her foot on our necks and we become her slaves."

"Not I," said Karl. "Women like to be treated roughly. Furthermore, I could never be the slave of anyone. I am possessed of my own free will."

"Which is determined," Leo pointed out.

"In part, from the perspective of infinity. In finitude, however, I am free. My personality is its own imperative."

"Hegel?"

Karl grinned. "In part, from the perspective of the university. In philosophy, however, I am my own goulash."

They turned and walked slowly up the cobblestones of the Sporgasse, looking in shopwindows as they talked, nodding to acquaintances. Sundays were lazy, though the ritual must be kept. Others, in lederhosen and with alpenstocks, made excursions to the surrounding mountains. Students, however, had to tend to their studies even on the day of rest and took their Sunday exercise in mild form, going up the Schlossberg, listening to the music awhile, then descending to serious labors at home or in the coffeehouse.

Leo could feel a palpable love for Graz—this eclectic, cacophonous little city that somehow attained harmony, like an intricate, self-contradictory woman who captivates admirers through undefinable, though irresistible, charm. As capital of Styria for three hundred years (1400–1700) when the region was large and powerful, Graz had been a Mecca for architects. Classical and Baroque, Renaissance, Gothic, and Roman, even modern styles, all blended in the colors of Graz, the deep egg yolk of the Hapsburg buildings, the blue dome of Fischer von Erlach, the pastels of the main square with the bright stucco patterning, the house painted over with heroic scenes from history, the columns and statues. The old tower and giant clock on the Schlossberg looked down at the town, spreading on both sides of the Mur, blooming with flowers, trees—the colorful houses tempered everywhere with living green. Now the city was known as "Pensionopolis" because of all the retired civil servants who lived there, but the old people kept to themselves at home, in coffeehouses, on benches in the sun, at chess tables in the park, and the city was enlivened by its thousands of students who chattered, sang and animated the streets.

Though at the beginning had Leo been indifferent to Graz' charm, now he felt he would like to live here always, where small courtyards opened onto other courtyards, magic boxes that continued their delight in familiarity, where alleys ran like rivulets between larger streams, and ripe fruit from the south gleamed fat in the marketplace among the bright sprays of flowers. Prague had the magnificence; she reigned in the world's most splendid Baroque. But Graz was quixotic, and enchanted him.

At the top of the Sporgasse they turned left through the gate for the more leisurely of the ascents. Traversing back and forth, they smiled at the descending promenaders returning for an early dinner or late Mass. The women, even the old ones, looked charming with their Sunday dirndls and rosy cheeks. Leo and Karl walked in silence, Karl striding, Leo shuffling, trying to match their disparate steps and letting go their thoughts to savor the warmth of the day and the companionship. But when they passed the large crucifixion, at an early bend, Karl remembered Leo's remark about being a slave. "Do you know about the miracle? Ah, you must."

Leo shook his head.

"Really? Amazing. I suppose it's such an old story that everyone assumes all others know it, even the newcomers. I'm no storyteller, as you know, but the legend is this:

"On top of the Schlossberg was an old prison—that's a fact—where prisoners were kept in chains. Only one prisoner ever escaped from there. Despite iron chains around his arms and legs, he somehow managed to get all the way down the mountain to this cross. When he reached the foot of the cross, his chains sprang open. He was a free man. He disappeared and was never seen again."

Leo nodded appreciatively. He had a vivid impression of the deep wounds made by the chains and could feel through his own lungs the man's gasping for breath as he pulled himself down the mountain. "Freedom through Christ," he said aloud, testing the theme.

"What did you say?" asked Karl.

83

"I said, 'Man is born free and everywhere puts himself in chains.' "

"That's good. First class. Did you just make it up?"

"I read it somewhere."

"Yes, it does have a familiar ring to it. Could you be misquoting slightly? Is it possible that you were referring to the words of the great Social Contracter, that precocious prerevolutionary child of Nature, who said (if one may believe the translation), 'Man is born free and everywhere he *is* in chains'?"

Leo felt himself blushing, a terrible, shameful trait, and he merely nodded, keeping his head down. Karl continued, "Is it to be believed that you, Dr. Sacher, misquoted from the heart, as it were? Is it possible that freedom weighs too heavily on your slender neck and that you seek the chains of love to release you?"

"Perhaps," he mumbled, in a confusion of secrecy and embarrassment. He had honestly thought he was quoting correctly. Karl was damnably clever and could see like a hawk. The misquote, Leo recognized, changed the context. Rousseau was referring to man in society, while his own version pointed to individual psyche. The prisoner of the Schlossberg had actually been in chains and broke free through love.

Mercifully, Karl resumed silence until they reached the top, leaving his friend to solemn thoughts while he congratulated himself on his perspicacity. Strains of music accompanied them on the last leg, and then they joined a crowd of Sunday listeners, the early arrivals seated in chairs around the podium, the later ones—like themselves—leaning on trees or standing with legs apart.

"The Austrian army," Karl whispered, "may not be the most effective in Europe, but it's certainly the best-dressed."

"And the most musical," Leo added. Uniforms gleamed and gold buttons dazzled in the sunlight. And how they played! Though not especially musical himself, Leo knew that such musicians would be hard to match. From marches to waltzes, polkas to mazurkas, effortlessly they flowed from one melody to the next with impassive faces and combed mustaches, leaving the audience breathless at intermission as though they had been dancing to all of it.

While they applauded, Leo observed the crowd. Children were laughing, pretty ladies fanning themselves, and men bowing on all sides to acquaintances. He saw his father, standing near the podium, and quickly moved his eyes to the right. There she sat, her face in three-quarters turned in his direction, the most beautiful woman present. He kept his eyes on her after the applause ended. She stood up to stroll, a tall woman of about thirty who walked like a queen. Her deep auburn hair was parted in the center, falling loosely in waves to frame her majestic face and caught up in a chignon at the back, covered with only a small piece of black lace. She wore deep green, edged in white lace, and carried a white parasol. Her skin was pale, but with no suggestion of illness, and as she moved through the throng eyes turned to her. Older men blinked, remembering the dreams of their boyhood, and young girls stared to see the ripeness of their hopes. A small dark-haired child reached out as the woman passed and touched her skirt, then looked up at the face with such reverence on her own small one that she might be regarding the Virgin Mary herself. The woman looked down and smiled, then moved on.

Karl had noticed her too, and both boys stood gazing at this woman whose magnificence was unapproachable. She stopped beside Leo's father and gave him her hand to kiss. Leo and Karl looked at each other with amazement and, in unspoken agreement, set off simultaneously in Sacher-Masoch's direction.

"Studying seriously, my boy?" said his father by way of greeting, acknowledging the baron's son with a slight ironical bow.

"Good day, Father. I'm glad to see you here."

"You are? How so?"

"It's such a beautiful day."

"Hmm."

The audience was returning for the second half. All three men caught sight of the woman in green and followed her with their eyes to her seat. "Beautiful woman," Leo ventured.

His father frowned. "The most beautiful in Graz. She is the wife of Baron von Kottowitz, has three children, and her virtue is as powerful as her beauty." He scowled at the young men to impress them with that fact.

"A pleasure to see you again, Director," said Karl, bowing. "We must take our positions; they are about to begin."

They moved off quickly, to the outer edge of the crowd and then away.

"Quite something," said Karl.

"That's the kind of woman I want," confided Leo. "Proud, beautiful, self-contained. She makes me think of a tigress."

"When you get her, let me know, will you?"

"You'll be our first guest," Leo promised and, laughing, they ran down the steep side, taking the hundreds of steps at the base two at a time.

"*Servus*, till tomorrow," they called at the bottom, and each ran off in the direction of his dinner. His mother kissed Leo when he entered, warned him not to exhaust himself and suggested he lie down before the meal, which would be late, she said, because his father had gone to a concert.

He embraced her. "Little Mama, don't worry. I'm big now, it's for me to take care of you." She looked pale; she'd become smaller and more anxious since Rosa's death. "You should lie down. I'll collect you, if you'll give me the honor of coming to dinner on my arm."

"Let me see"—she looked through an imaginary *carnet de bal* at her wrist—"it seems to be free. With pleasure, my cavalier." She gave him a low curtsey and went, smiling, in the direction of her bedroom.

Leo was driven to the kitchen by hunger, calling plaintively to Marika that he was starving, dying—she must throw him a crumb, a pastry, anything. When he arrived in the room, she was standing with hands on hips grinning at him. Behind her sat a plump-cheeked, pleasant man who was also grinning. Leo recognized him: Friedl Zimmermann, the cabinetmaker, who twice before had lingered after his work to enjoy Marika's company.

"Bolt the windows, the beggars are coming!" Marika told Friedl.

"Oh, the poor lad. Take pity on him, he's so thin."

"Yes," Leo agreed, "and will surely die of starvation if he is not fed this instant." Dramatically, he fell to the floor. Marika bent down and placed a strawberry between his lips. His eyes opened. "Ah," he said, chewing, "the kiss of life."

"I'd prefer a kiss from her lips to any berry," said Friedl audaciously.

"Away with you, Zimmermann. You see?" she said to prostrate Leo. "See how he taunts my honor?"

"Nay, that is too much," said Leo, leaping to his feet. He grabbed a spoon, cried, "Choose your weapon, villain," and charged.

Friedl caught him in an embrace. Laughing, he begged Leo's pardon, claiming he'd been carried away by the young woman's loveliness. "Well you might be," Leo agreed. "She's pretty as the empress and can bake a lot better."

"I know." Friedl's tone changed so suddenly that Leo now looked at him and frowned. Was it possible that the man had serious intentions? Unthinkable. And yet, she was twenty-three. But Zimmermann? Who else? Marika was cloistered in the household. Leo grasped his arm. "You will stay and dine with us?"

"I don't know." He looked tentatively at Marika, who was smiling broadly.

"Do. For my sake," Leo urged him. He knew his parents wouldn't mind. An extra plate was nothing, and a guest was always welcome.

"Well—perhaps."

"Good. It's settled, then. Now I leave you to your own modesty, Marika—and you to your honor. We'll meet anon."

He left them and thought of the possibility of Marika marrying. He couldn't bear it! He'd marry her himself. Why not? The image of her on that day in Prague flourishing a pistol came to him, in a current of heat shivering up his legs. Her small mouth; the long, soft hair. He trembled. She was like a sister. But when she walked, the wind blowing her skirts against her body, he could see the outline of her thighs, firm and long, ending where he would like to die, in the warm nest, the soft, moist heart of Marika.

She was strong and good, a daughter of Galicia with

round arms and a laughing voice, who cast the same unastonished gaze on everything in the universe, whether grief or cabbages, and who knew that all was according to God's will. He loved her. . . . The Baroness Kottowitz strode into his mind, fierce as a tigress, shimmering in green. It was not to be Marika, his beautiful girl, but some woman who could put him in danger.

Marika had had suitors before, of course, but Leo had never thought seriously about them. He'd been too young, too busy with his studies, too preoccupied with death; mainly, he was unable to believe in emotions of living people that differed from his own. When he invented stories, he could imaginatively produce the feelings of his characters, and even when he heard about someone in a different time and place, his empathy was such that he could experience in himself the pains, griefs, and elations of the unknown person. But in these inventions and creations he was free to carve from his own imagination the feelings—as well as thoughts and actions—of characters, and from his own heart he gave them loves and fears.

With a living person, one he knew well and loved, he was constricted by the Other. Though he could understand why Marika would be wooed, with her open, laughing ways and her beauty, he had never thought that she could return affection to anyone except himself and the immediate family. But now he was eighteen, and his own experience had showed him it was possible to feel warmth, closeness, even deep love for someone you hardly knew. Furthermore, he understood the practical aspects: at twenty-three, Marika was nearing the age when matrimony would no longer be offered to her, except possibly by old widowers. Though bachelorhood was respectable, and even admired in men of intellect, talent or charm, spinsterhood aroused pity at best.

He was too big for her to look after, and Charles, at fifteen, was no longer a child, despite his seeming resolution to remain one. In a few more years he, too, would be grown, and Marika would find herself unwed and childless in this exiled land. Better that she marry and remain in Graz, where he could visit her daily and be godfather to her children.

And so, in the manner of brothers and fathers, Leo suppressed the wish that his girl belong to him exclusively and instead joined forces with the enemy, as it were, determined to find a friend in his darling's suitor, in case she accepted him.

With Friedl, the task was easy. A round man with red cheeks, Friedl resembled a cherubic Bacchus. He was always in good humor, had a chubby, cheerful joy of the grape, and saluted each new day in the morning with a large glass of fruity white wine. His hair was thin and retreated from the high color of his forehead, his lips were full and his nose small. Even the sight of him raised one's spirits; he was a simple, good man and so skillful in his work that he would soon become a master.

Now twenty-three, a few months younger than Marika, Friedl had been apprenticed to Graz' most esteemed cabinetmaker for seven years. Last year his master had died, and Friedl took his place. Some said that the young man's inlays and intaglios were even finer than his master's, and all agreed that young Zimmermann's artistry was as great as his craftsmanship. He seemed destined from birth to be a cabinetmaker; his name (meaning "carpenter") was another example of the little jokes played by Fate for her own amusement. Leo and his friends collected these: Josef Bachofner was a baker, Otto Mahler a painter, Frau Schneider a dressmaker, and Professor Hegel naturally taught philosophy. Such discoveries particularly delighted Karl, who saw in them the natural casting for life's role. When he first met Friedl, having heard about him from Leo, he called him "Zimmermeister," and the name stuck.

Despite his natural modesty, Friedl quickly warmed to Karl and Joseph, who both thanked Leo for bringing him along. In him, the students enjoyed escape from university, their theories of history and justice meeting the solid material of daily life. Karl took snobbish pleasure in having a cabinetmaker as friend, Leo felt an almost brotherly fondness for Friedl, and Joseph was delighted in a companion who could match glass for glass, unto the liters.

Friedl had proposed formally in the first week of May, on his knees in the kitchen. He offered himself, his abilities and his love in a small, uncertain voice. Marika accepted all three, and he couldn't rise to embrace her, but remained on his knees, weeping softly with happiness. Then she knelt beside him, put her arms around his neck and kissed his round, hairless forehead. Even then he could do nothing, as his sobbing grew stronger and happiness uprooted all his control.

The marriage was to take place in fall. "She is the best of women," Leo assured him, "just like her mother." They were sitting in the coffeehouse, where Friedl could only join them one time in five, and a full liter stood on the marble table. "I'll tell you about Irina Petrivna," Leo said. "Look to the mother and you see what will become of the daughter. Irina Petrivna was only the stepmother of Maria Ivanovna, of course, but she was like a natural mother to Marika, who knew no other."

Joseph poured. "Good," he said, smacking his lips. "Another story."

Leo noticed ashes on his coat sleeve and flicked at them. He rubbed the remainder, making a circle of dull gray. He cleared his throat. "Irina Petrivna was the second wife of Ivan Dmitrovitch. She was nineteen when she married him, three years after his first wife had died in the cholera. His first wife had been beautiful and cruel; Irina was more plain, though with a pleasant face, and she was kind and clever as well. I loved her—I still do.

"Her clever remarks were repeated by the villagers, but mostly they spoke of a lesson she taught to one of the young men. A clever woman can always change a man.

"Though she was only attractive, and not a rare beauty, many admired her. The most persistent of admirers was Yatoslav Dmitrovitch Kooshnir, son of Miroslava Romanovna, whose baking was almost the equal of Irina's. Yatoslav Dmitrovitch was a broad-faced, husky man of twenty-five who loved to laugh, especially at the expense of others. He was one of those Galicians—perhaps I should say one of those peasants—possessed of the queer notion that his life should be different from what it actually was. He spoke with scorn of those who were content with their lot, calling them 'no better than cows or sheep,' and if he entered a house that was neat

as a pin, the first thing Yatoslav would notice was a crack in
the table leg. If a woman wore a sheepskin with magnificent
flowers embroidered on it, he opined that the stench of the
jacket was overpowering; and when he was served steaming
vareniki—our cottage cheese dumplings, with sour milk or
cream poured over them—he announced that a man needed
meat for his dinner. He was the first to know if someone had
gambled away his money, or if a wife committed an indiscretion. He usually predicted rain, and if the sky was completely
clear and blue, Yatoslav complained that the sun hurt his eyes.
Women were either too thin or too fat, too young or too blond
for him. He worked as little as he could get away with and
spent much time in taverns talking about the difficulty of his
labors. He was, in short, a lout and troublemaker."

"Amusing chap," said Karl. "I can think of a few students
at the university just like him. When is all this taking place?"

"Before I was born: 1835, I'd say."

"Continue, please," urged Friedl, who loved hearing
about anything that concerned his beloved Marika.

"Well then, this Yatoslav—or Slavik, as he was called—
was irresistibly drawn to Irina Petrivna, Boroduk's wife.
Many mornings she had literally to sweep him out of the
kitchen, using her broom to drive him from the chair and out
the door. Because Irina was tenderhearted and kind, she had
warm feelings even for Slavik and would often listen sympathetically to his laments. But she couldn't tolerate idleness,
and the big oaf interfered with her work.

"However, he was a good-looking fellow, with hands so
large they could cup Marika's bottom like a ball—remember,"
he said, placing a hand on Friedl's arm, "she was only three
—and his eyes were gray as the Carpathians on a fall morning.
His hair was thick and sand-colored—like yours, Karl. His
expression was quizzical, for, though his lids were heavy, they
drew out his eyes to an amused look, not a sleepy one. He
often teased Irina. 'Ira, Irina, you're so plain.' 'Like the
steppes,' she'd answer. 'Ira, Irochka, your husband is old.'
'Like the earth,' she'd say.

"But she usually laughed when he teased her, and Slavik
laughed too, because his words were meant in fun and he

liked seeing her draw out her neck like a turtle before giving him a sharp retort.

"Sometimes she served him tea, and they sat chatting while she did her handiwork. It was not long before those neighbors whose tongues grow more active when their teeth fall out were calling Boroduk's attention to his wife's 'unsuitable conduct.' He paid them no heed, of course, but the ugly rumors continued, and they troubled him. Because he trusted his wife he knew she would speak only the truth, and he resolved to ask her.

"He chose a cozy evening, when the children were in bed, the fire burned cheerfully and the samovar was lit. Irina was knitting, as it was too dark for needlework. Boroduk took out his pipe and prepared it in the old manner. He clicked open the lid and scraped the bowl with his knife to loosen the ashes. He pushed in fresh tobacco and carried out the next steps in the way he'd learned as a boy, fighting his first battles. He took out the flint he carried on his belt, placed a small piece of sponge on it and struck fire with his knife. Sparks glittered. The glimmering sponge gave off an herbal smell, and he threw it into the bowl of his pipe. He inhaled a few times, took strength and asked Irina if it was true that young Kooshnir was paying court to her.

"She dropped her needles in amazement. 'What a terrible thing to ask, Ivan Dmitrovitch!' she said in sorrowful earnestness, her usual spark of gaiety extinguished.

" 'I ask forgiveness, Irina Petrivna,' said her husband humbly.

" 'As I love God,' she told him, her eyes holding his squarely, 'I am true to you in mind and body.'

"He went on his knees before her and kissed her hands. 'My flower,' he said, 'my star. Forgive this stupid old man.'

"She looked down at him, whose lips were pressed to the hands he held together as in prayer, and suddenly she laughed, in her high, gay tones."

"Like Marika," said Friedl.

Leo nodded. "Ivan looked up in astonishment. 'Stupid old man indeed!' she said through her laughter. 'And what does that make me, then, who has chosen to marry such a creature? No, my husband, you are old only in knowledge, and your body is young and strong. As for that Slavik, don't think about him again. I'll teach him his lesson.' "

Hans, the young waiter, was standing with empty tray poised at the side of their table, listening intently. Leo smiled and included him in his audience.

"On the next day Slavik appeared for breakfast. Irina brought out a lavish meal of sausage and cheese, bread and butter, wine and fruit. He was delighted (though commenting that butter was inappropriate at breakfast and should be saved for tea) and embraced Irina around the waist, trying to kiss her. She broke from his grasp, and ran around the table with him chasing her; then he caught her again, tried to kiss her lips, and again she broke free. The third time he had her so firmly she could not escape. She smiled lovingly in his arms. As he bent to kiss her, she placed a finger on his lips and said gaily that he must wait a moment. The door was un-bolted, the curtains not drawn—anyone might see them.

"He released her and waited, full of pompous self-con-gratulation. He could see the truth behind any woman, he told himself; Irina's apparent fidelity had never fooled him.

"He waited a long time and became suspicious. He called her and received no answer. He went to the door and found it bolted from outside. So, too, were the windows when he tried them. He called out, 'Irina, Ira, don't keep me here. My mother is waiting for me, let me go.' But his pleas grew softer and in time stopped entirely, for he knew they were useless.

"When the whole family returned in the afternoon, Boroduk looked at Slavik with wonder. 'What have we here?' he asked.

"Irina grinned. 'Here is a man who feels he deserves what belongs to others. He would like to eat your food, drink your wine and make love to your wife.'

" 'Is that so?' asked Ivan Dmitrovitch. 'It appears, then, that Slavik would like to be me. Very well, he shall be.'

"Now both Irina and Slavik looked at him in surprise. The young man had expected to be beaten within an inch of his life. 'Yes,' continued Boroduk, smiling faintly, 'you shall learn to be as I am. You shall assist me in my work and do as

I say. In time, if you work well and diligently, I will invite you to share my food and wine and take your place in my family.'

"Slavik could not refuse, as he had been disgraced. Next day he went to work for Boroduk, and every day after that he worked hard in the fields and forest, caring for livestock and crops, chopping trees and preparing lumber. Every morning he brought in the eggs and milk and made himself useful in all ways. He was no longer proud and caustic, and he kept his eyes lowered after grace when Irina brought in the midday soup.

"Now the people in the village repeated to each other how it came about that Slavik the cynic was turned into an honest workingman through the lesson given him by a good woman. Slavik's mother was grateful, and Slavik himself, to his own surprise, felt content with his lot.

"That is the story of Irina, and because of the lesson she taught, she came to us. You see, she had taught it so well that Slavik now took over many of the chores she had formerly done, and she felt a lack of work at home. So she came to my mother, who was carrying me at the time, and entered our household. After I was born, she took me to her own house and nursed me."

"A wonderful woman," said Friedl joyfully, "and her daughter is worthy of her. I hope to have the honor of meeting Irina Petrivna one day."

"I say bravo to the storyteller," said Joseph. "Hans, another liter here."

" 'A wonderful woman,' " repeated Karl slowly, converting Friedl's enthusiasm to irony. "But you said that women in Galicia are evil and fascinating."

"Not Irina!" Leo burst out, and blushed.

"Do you think about her? Do you miss her?" asked Friedl kindly.

"Often. What you don't understand, my friend," he said to Karl, "is that Woman in our stories and legends personifies Nature herself, who kills babies while they are in their mothers' wombs, takes off the strongest men of the village, brings fire and drought and still comes up with sweet spring. That

Nature is pure force, unthinking, selfish, magnificent, before whom man is nothing. And women, who are closer to Nature than men, are sometimes like her. But not Irina, not Rosa, not the laughing young girls of the villages."

"And yet, the happy girls are not for you," Karl said.

Leo remained silent. After they left the coffeehouse together, Karl said to Leo, "I have the sense that in you women and art are closely bound. Your talent is your mistress, who drives you beyond your control and brings you images both terrible and beautiful."

"Perhaps," he said, not daring to refute him.

"That's not a bad thing. It gives you depth. Or at least," he said, smiling, "the contradictions that usually pass for depth. In any event, I believe that Woman, in reality or in your concepts of her, will always be driving you, in your life and work, and that the woman who already exists in your mind will be stronger than any you will ever meet." Karl, with his arm through Leo's, could feel him tremble. He added, for assurance, "You may be an important writer one day. You must gather your energies. Women will come and go, but you must take care of your temple."

"Temple?"

"Up here." Karl showed him with a finger. "The temple of your talent. Don't let anyone in who might make a mess."

"Ah," Leo said, grateful for Karl's warm interest, "don't worry about that. I will set them in little niches and describe their beautiful plumage while I listen to them sing."

Karl extricated his arm to pat his friend's back. "Good work, Sacher."

"Don't you have a Woman who lives in your mind?" Leo asked.

"Only bits and pieces—parts of the body, you know." He winked comically. "When I find one who's managed to put all the pieces together in the right proportions, I'll snatch her up."

"They are a bother, you know," said Leo.

"Quite right, my dear. And men are fools, because they like nothing more than being bothered."

Their spirits lifted, the two young men continued on

their way in a peculiar little dance—Karl's version of Leo's shuffle—and sang,

> "Good-bye, Mother,
> I'm off to the war.
> Good-bye, sweetheart,
> I'll see you no more.
>
> Soon you'll be crying
> To think I am dying;
> But I'll be kept warm
> In another girl's arms."

"Should I come in with you?" asked Karl at Leo's door, "and embrace your pretty Marika?"

"If you like." He shrugged, and was shocked.

Neither Irina Petrivna nor Yarko could come to the wedding. Yarko had written a long letter, also on behalf of his mother, explaining that this season of year was harvesttime and they could not leave the land. Irina was frightened at the prospect of undertaking such a long journey to distant lands by herself (she had never traveled farther than Lemberg), and Yarko could on no account accompany her.

Shortly after the Sacher-Masochs left for Prague, Yarko had asked the apothecary to release him, that he might return to the village and help Irina. The apothecary was a kind man and sent his assistant off with books and chemicals. Yarko made a study of agriculture, of the new agrarian principles set down by men in Kiev and Petersburg; he ordered new fertilizers and experimented on his own soil. Soon he had the richest crop in the village, and the other peasants came to him for advice, which he gave freely. He had not yet married; he and Irina worked side by side along with others they were able to employ. Irina sent her blessings and love to Marika and assured them that she had said a special prayer for Marika's husband-to-be. She knew he must be a fine man and a good one; she wished them both many healthy children and a long and prosperous life. To this, Yarko added his own wishes, and both sent their blessings for the Sacher-Masoch family. Irina was proud to learn that Leo had become such a fine scholar.

Irina sent Marika her own wedding dress, saying (through words set down by Yarko) that, though old, it held memories of the greatest happiness Irina had ever known, for it had given her the best man in all the world and his two loving children. She advised Marika to take it in, if necessary, because (and they could hear her laughter as she dictated), she had been well-larded when she married, and Marika was surely still slim as a larch tree. She sent along the ribbons also, though they were slightly faded, and suggested Marika add to them fresh flowers from her new home. Yarko sent her a necklace of silver and coral, and for Friedl a precious book from Lemberg, filled with engravings of the city and countryside, so he could see the beautiful land where his bride was born.

Marika wept when she read the long letter, and wept again over the gifts from home. Then she dried her tears, fitted the dress to herself so tightly that she could not get into it without assistance, and baked a special cake for her future mother-in-law.

The wedding took place on a clear Saturday in a small church north of the city, not yet in the mountains, close to where the Zimmermann family lived. Frau Zimmermann, in a beautiful old brocade dirndl, dabbed her eyes and leaned for support on her elder son, Franz; but she assured everyone that the tears came from happiness, and Marika was the loveliest daughter she could dream of having. Leo felt a moment of pain when Friedl took his new wife in his arms. He walked off by himself, then returned to join the wedding feast. He drank and sang, ate from the heaping trays, accepted more wine, whirled to the music with Marika, his mother, Frau Zimmermann, and then with others, until the excitement made him ill and he ran to vomit in the bushes.

The feast lasted through the day and even after the stars came out, long after the abducted bride had been found and returned. According to tradition, Marika was "stolen" during the festivities and then bridegroom and father-in-law, Leo, and others went in search of her. Karl, the abductor, showed great skill at elusiveness, moving her quickly from place to place, leaving behind the required clue but always snatching her up a moment before the party arrived in search.

Wherever they stopped, they ordered something to drink, and the men who sought them were also compelled by custom to order wine or *schnaps*, inviting everyone in the tavern or inn, spending a decent amount of time there before moving along the trail of the bride, leaving behind a few silver coins for luck. So it had been for generations, the bride and abductor fleeing husband and father (usually hers) with decorum and drinking, the search itself tipsy and joyful until the groom showed his nervousness and the posse, amid teasing, agreed she'd been missing for an abnormally long time. Friedl became nearly sober in his anxiety, and his father placed an arm around him, saying, "I worried in the same way, but I found her in the end and never afterward let her out of my sight."

The missing pair were sighted walking demurely down a lane after Marika had forced them to go more slowly. She loved the excitement of the game, but when Karl tried stealing a kiss from her, she decided it had to stop. The men saw them and the cry went up: "The bride is here!" Friedl ran to her and kissed her full on the mouth, throwing Karl such a ferocious look that everyone laughed. Then they returned to the wedding party, where Karl was teased by the men and Friedl was warned that his wife was too pretty for one man alone. He must make a leash for her, they said, or surely she would be abducted in earnest.

Marika had never been so happy, except for moments of sorrow that rose and ebbed as she thought of Irina and Yarko and wished they could be here.

When the moon was already bright in the sky, she entered the carriage with her husband, and among the cries wishing them health and happiness, they rode off. A group of men chased them, wailing for Marika, who waved her handkerchief out the back while Friedl made motions to shoo them away. Finally the men dropped behind, and the happy couple rode on in moonlight to the inn where they would drop to sleep, exhausted but still laughing, in each other's arms.

6

TWO WEEKS after his marriage to Sissi, Franz Joseph mobilized his troops in Galicia as protection against the Russians. The Crimean War lasted two years, during which time the Emperor conferred with his mother, not wishing to upset his beautiful and overly sensitive young wife. He felt she needed all her forces to accustom herself to the demands of her position. At the beginning, the delightful child had made numerous mistakes, some charming, others that brought Sophie to his room in white anger.

First, she had removed her gloves during dinner. Sophie, the diplomat, understood her guests' consternation, and relieved them by following the girl's maladroit example, though immediately after the meal she told Sissi that, while such behavior might do in a Bavarian farmhouse, it must never again be exhibited in the palace. Another time, when the serving men behind each chair leaned forward to inquire whether it should be Burgundy or Bordeaux, the Empress was heard to ask for beer, which, though it could not be refused her at the moment (indeed, she was insistent and told her valet she *always* drank beer at home), was subsequently removed entirely from the cellars. While being dressed, she asked for a pair of shoes she had worn a few days earlier and then burst into tears to learn that the empress wears a pair of shoes only once. But worst of all was the time when Sissi put on the clothes of one of her ladies-in-waiting and escaped from the palace, to be found hours later emerging from a public bath in the city!

Like a madwoman, she insisted on going riding every day even though she was bearing a child—possibly the heir!—and, to Sophie's disgust, the Emperor permitted these romps on horseback simply because she pleaded and begged. She stared in the faces of parrots, despite the risk that her unborn child would then look like one, and would have continued her irresponsible, girlish ways up to the time of birth had not the doctor and Sophie together been able to convince the Emperor that his bride was placing her own life, as well as the infant's, in jeopardy.

Then the girl was nothing but long faces and melancholy sighs. Sophie complained in letters to her sister Ludovica about the negligent upbringing she'd given her daughter. When the child was born—christened Sophie—the Empress Mother obligingly removed her from Sissi's side. A year later little Gisela was born and again, naturally, placed in the care of her grandmother. Sissi was not capable; still unformed herself, the only influences she exerted were unpleasant. A few months after Gisela's birth, she persuaded her husband to grant amnesty to Hungarian revolutionaries, against Sophie's protests.

Despite her mother-in-law's antipathy for that nation, the young Empress flaunted her affection for Hungary. In the months before her marriage, when she was being tutored for her future role, Sissi had been unwittingly taught by a Hungarian, who told the girl stories of his country, explained its position in the empire, sang its songs and spoke of its people. Sissi was fascinated, and with her usual intensity, the quick brilliance that allowed her to comprehend in a flash (though she then moved on like a skipping stone, indifferent to the depths below), she mastered the language and acquired fluency within that short space.

She learned of the revolution in Hungary, when even the poets and the women fought. In 1849 Czar Nicholas I sent in his troops, and shortly thereafter Russia could announce its good deed to Austria: "Hungary lies humbled at the feet of Your Majesty." Sissi had been too young at the time, but in preparation for her imperial marriage she learned that the leaders had been killed or gone into exile, Kossuth fleeing with the sacred crown of Saint Stephen. Thousands were arrested or shot or hanged, and the Austrian general left to supervise the "peace" was so proficient at torture that England protested and even Russia expressed shock as Haynau butchered his way through, earning his nickname of General Hyena, saving his most bloodthirsty acts for women.

This her teacher had told her; though he couldn't know that at the time of Russia's gift, the new prime minister, Schwarzenberg, had smiled politely and murmured, "Our ingratitude shall know no bounds"; nor did he know that the letters arriving from Hungarian mothers, begging for their sons' lives, were dealt out by the Empress Mother in a game of Patience.

But what Sissi did learn inspired her to her only political audacity, and though she was not recognized as fit to be a mother, her husband listened to her on the subject of Hungary. The year after amnesty, a dream was realized as she traveled with her husband and two small daughters to the beloved land she'd never seen. Incredibly, despite bloody memories, Hungarians fell in love with the Empress, and she returned it. Franz Joseph noticed her powers and understood how important she could be to him in regard to this land.

The dream ended abruptly in the death of little Sophie, and the mourning parents returned to Vienna with year-old Gisela. Sissi avoided the eyes of her mother-in-law and tended to her own grief. She mourned through her next pregnancy, till the birth in 1858 of her first son, heir to his father, the Crown Prince Rudolph.

Franz Joseph kissed the boy and prayed for God's guidance over him as the guns roared out their salute. But the guns reminded him of Italy, and he gave orders to strengthen his troops against the Italian threat. Then his old field marshal, Radetzky, died; then Cavour rejected Austria's ultimatum to Sardinia, and the Austrian declaration of war brought on a declaration against her by France, through the schemes of Louis Napoleon.

In the summer of '59, the Austrian army was defeated at Solférino. Franz Joseph wept for the bravery of his men and the lives lost, but his sorrow impressed neither his subjects nor his neighbors. Austria was slipping, and the gold buttons of her uniforms were being dulled by blood and dirt. Napoleon III could smile, especially when the Czar, unwilling to forget the betrayal in Crimea, shook his head against Franz Joseph's pleas and grinned.

The Emperor was left alone by many, including his darling wife, who, dressed in black, had made a secret visit to a doctor and there learned with horror the nature of her shameful disease, contracted through her husband, who had received it along with the attentions of a vivacious countess. Sissi fled in disgust to Madeira, then to Corfu, while Sophie raised the imperial children and Franz Joseph remained alone in his study from the dawn of every day until he prepared for sleep in his narrow iron bed. The sixties had begun, and he slept badly.

*　　*　　*

In 1855, at the age of nineteen, Leo received his doctorate from the University of Graz. This astonishing achievement of the Police Director's son was remarked in many homes of the city, as fathers urged their sons to take example, and mothers of pretty girls calculated how soon he would be thinking of marriage. Two years later, despite strong opposition within the faculty, young Sacher-Masoch became Graz' first *Privatdozent* in the subject of History. The *Dozentur*, a postdoctoral position permitting its recipient the honor (and duty) of teaching at the university while attending to his own research, is a high point of academic accomplishment. A Dozent carries the authority of the chosen few who have demonstrated intellectual excellence, valuable scholarship, pedagogical ability and seriousness. The subject of History was not considered of enough weight to stand with Philosophy or Medicine or Law as a citadel of scholarly discipline, and Sacher-Masoch's Ph.D. had been in the combined field of History and Law.

His dissertation for the *Dozentur*, "The Uprising in Ghent under Emperor Charles V," was acknowledged by the reviewing board to be well-written and lively. That was reason enough for the more august professors to distrust it. A lively style belonged to the world of feuilletons and did not

102

convey the rigors of academia. "It has come to our attention," wrote one professor in his report, "that Sacher-Masoch is publishing stories and novellas. While the candidate might find personal amusement and private profit in the little adventures he writes, the publication of these literary attempts must raise serious doubts as to his qualifications for the highest university degree. Critics have found his writings 'colorful,' 'imaginative' and so forth. . . . We suggest that Sacher-Masoch pursue his career of letters. . . . We find him unqualified for the *Dozentur* and recommend that he be rejected."

His oral examinations revealed shocking lapses in his chosen field, in particular medieval Austrian history. Though his mathematical and philosophical knowledge proved adequate, he was, said the majority of his interlocutors, highly deficient within his own specialty and undeserving of the proposed honor. But his mentor, Doctor Professor Weiss, a highly esteemed colleague, pleaded that this man be awarded the degree. His unusual perceptions, his originality of mind, his exceptional and proven ability for writing placed Sacher-Masoch in a position different from other candidates. He would bring honor to the university, Professor Weiss assured them. He personally would guarantee the young man.

After days of debate, the good professor won, and Sacher-Masoch, the writer of stories, was awarded the first *Dozentur* in History ever given in Graz, or indeed in any Austrian university. His detractors insisted that no one had been so unqualified as he, and that no degree had been so misplaced as this one. Nevertheless, the honor was bestowed on him, and at the coffeehouse Hans brought out several bottles of champagne, compliments of the management, for the new Herr Dozent and his friends. From then on, his favorite table would always be reserved for him, and his favorite paper brought immediately in its wooden holder. In Austria, the measurement of a man's success is seen more clearly in the coffeehouse than in his place of work, though the means of measurement may differ. A regular customer rises in rank over the years: five years makes him an Engineer, ten a Doctor, and after twenty he may be awarded the aristocratic "von." Bad customers, on the other hand—those who are unpleasant in manners—may be demoted from whatever position they hold in the world outside, and even a count may be referred to in the coffeehouse by his last name alone.

But Sacher-Masoch earned his degree doubly, though with more enthusiasm in the coffeehouse than at the university. His friends shared in his decoration: Karl became "Herr Baron," Joseph was "Herr Professor," Friedl "Herr Doctor"; and Friedl's brother Franz, a wine merchant, became "Herr Director."

Police Director Sacher-Masoch showed his pride by ordering his son the best suit available in Styria, made of the finest materials—English wool and Italian silk for the lining, with old silver buttons and a thick pile of velvet at the collar. Leo looked quite the dandy for a few weeks, and then this magnificent suit took on the characteristics of its wearer: the buttons became dull, the trousers wrinkled, their cuffs sagged, and the jacket, bearing ashes and stains, gave up its shape.

"You will never be a gentleman," said his father. "You look like a tramp."

Leo shrugged, his gesture parting the jacket further to reveal the spot where a dumpling had landed, to the fury of the older man. If precocity and brilliance led to the appearance of walking garbage, it was better to have no mind at all. Charles was not a dozent, but at least he looked civilized. This one wasn't fit to be seen in decent society.

Leo thought sadly that he would never be able to please his father. The bureaucrat required correctness, and even though he possessed intelligence, personal bravery and benevolence, he was the Director above all else. Handsome, Leo admitted, but insensitive. How could this person unfurl the delicate petals of his wife's character? She loved the man, adored him even. She loved her children, naturally, but it was different—with her husband, something overtook her. Once —Leo was tiny then—he and his mother were playing "the flower game." Each petal they gathered was a word. When they had collected enough, he threw them all in the air. They fluttered down and lay scattered on the ground making a poem, a secret message only the two of them could read. Then Father entered the garden in his uniform, and she looked up at him in a strange and beautiful way, her face emptied and altered, as though the soul-snatcher had come. When he left, the petals were no longer beautiful phrases, just torn parts of a living plant.

. . . She knelt at his father's feet, helping him on with his boots. . . .

"A gentleman shows himself by his actions," said Leo haughtily, conscious of the usual discomfort he felt in his father's study.

Sacher-Masoch smiled. "In that case, sir, be so good as to sit up straight."

Leo stood and bowed. "I am taking you from your work," he said with purposeful irony.

His father was unaffected by it. With a cheerful wave and "Till dinner," he dismissed his son and turned to his desk.

The girl on Merangasse watched the gentleman go by in the morning and was struck by the sadness in his face. "That's the son of the Police Director," her mother told her. "He's a famous writer. At his age!"

Aurora didn't understand what that meant; he was a grown man. Though maybe her mother meant he didn't have a long beard yet, or a mustache. In any case, he was famous, and the young girl made him part of her collection. For several years, she'd "collected" people in Graz, making up names for them when actual ones weren't furnished and inventing stories about their lives. She amused herself with these, which became the stories she told herself at night before falling asleep. Her greatest heroine was Baroness von Kottowitz, the most beautiful woman in the world, whose skirts she had touched on the Schlossberg.

Leo walked past the house many mornings and never noticed the girl in the second-story window. He couldn't know that he figured in her make-believe, or that through the child's invention he was courting the beautiful baroness, whom he actually thought of very often, whose magnificent form he followed with his eyes, and who entered his own imagination when he sat at his desk trying to mold queens and goddesses out of the limp stuff of words.

Since his first sight of her a few years ago, she'd remained with him. He'd seen her often since then, though the most intimate meeting between them had been no more than a slight bow and a faint smile. He noticed that her lips were small and her eyes blue-gray. Her bearing was queenly, and the strength of her body suggested a hidden power, a wildness behind the elegance, like a tigress or panther, containing danger. He learned that her Christian name was Anna, and she became for him the manifestation of Nature expressed through Woman, in her beauty and force.

His friends teased him whenever he mentioned her, but Karl, who had a knack for cutting a straight path through the jungle of Leo's imagination, said, "You know her in the sense that you invent her. She's become the object of your love because you see her emblematically, through your own needs."

"How else do people love?" he asked innocently.

"I don't know about others," said Karl, "but I, for one, require more active participation in the game." Karl's conquests were so numerous he was required to make notes opposite each name in his address book. Joseph once remarked that "Karl plucks the hearts of women as easily as they pluck daisies"; his charm, his looks, his nonchalance made him, seemingly, irresistible. His "girls" were as assorted as boxes of chocolate, for he had sampled every variety of Graz' womanhood, married and single, widows and mothers, from blue eyes to black. Though some lasted longer than others, none, so far, had captured his heart. He never permitted himself much time in a lady's company, explaining to his friends that "even the most delicious comedy becomes tiresome if carried on too long." Though he willingly shared the company of men from afternoon till early morning, he gave his time sparingly to women as though he were a rich dessert, to be taken in small samples and enjoyed most in the aftertaste of lingering sweetness.

Joseph was in love with an actress a few years older than himself, whose miserly favors prompted Karl to pronounce her "coldhearted" and Friedl to find her "virtuous." Friedl was happily married; his brother Franz was hoping to find a good cook with a warm belly. Leo was like none of them, though his flirtations with a number of pretty women brought him close to Karl's honorable vocation as Don Juan.

Yet Leo remained shy with women, and with them his natural awkwardness intensified. He felt himself to be extremely unattractive, and if a woman showed him kindness, he was sure she was pitying him. He was repelled by his own looks because he thought women were, and that conviction circled on itself, so that if a woman was attracted by him, liked the way he spoke, listened to his words with fascination while her eyes moved over his soft hair, his sensitive expression, his large, hungry mouth, then Leo decided she lacked taste, and he couldn't take her seriously unless she herself was ugly. His twenties didn't release him from that horror of adolescence, when a person projects his self-disgust onto others and trusts no one who will not confirm his own miserable estimation of himself. Not all his triumphs had freed Leo from the shame he felt for his personal appearance.

He desired women, however, and all the women he desired were beautiful or at least pretty. Despite himself, he was beginning to learn that his mind, or character, was a reasonable barter for feminine loveliness, and from time to time he was able to accept the affections of a charming woman. In their arms, however, he was often disappointed, and each year he felt it more. Though he always managed to "perform," in the terminology of the pretty actresses, he often experienced overwhelming sadness when he lay in soft arms, hearing sweet words, and feeling that this act was banal; he'd missed the sensation that brought him here. Ordinary "polite" lovemaking was a set of exercises done by the body independently of mind. He longed for something else: a tension of man and woman powerful as a drama of creation, wherein the two came together through ritual. As in a morality play, She and He must represent far more than their simple selves, and if She was Nature, then He was humanity, owing his fealty, his very life, to Her. Without the dance and without the danger, sex could not go back to the savage begin-

ning, to Creation, and therefore it neither informed nor inspired. With a woman like the Baroness Anna, he would be
held in thrall, and in the homage she would surely demand
he could expiate himself, lose himself willingly through abjec-
tion. He understood, though darkly, that his sexuality took
uncommon paths. He might be afraid of ridicule if he revealed himself, except that what he had to reveal was as in-
stinctive, powerful and unanalyzed as his creative forces.

But one thing remained sure through all the years: the
woman he longed for had to be majestic, independent and
strong. Whoever she was, he would have to look up to her; she
would have to inspire in him the awe he had never been able
to feel in churches, a reverence he had felt in Nature and, a
few times in his life, at a woman's feet. Anna was such a one,
and Leo "knew" her, as Karl suggested, through the discoveries he was making about himself.

He'd never talked to her, but he knew her voice. He'd
never touched her, but his fingers understood her skin was
smooth as marble, though soft and fragrant. When she entered the room that day where he stood exchanging banalities
with a retired colonel, her roan hair braided in pearls with
one lock dangling free, her breasts and shoulders gleaming
palely against wine-colored velvet, his breath caught, his ears
were stopped, and a coldness like death came over him. So he
stood, transfixed, until a cool social voice was pronouncing
his name, then hers, and his back loosened enough for him to
bow and kiss the hand she extended. He feared he would
freeze, but society is a great restorer, and he released the hand,
straightened and smiled into the exquisite face.

"At last," she said, her voice harsher than he'd imagined,
and at the same time richer, "we meet properly. By now all
Graz is talking of you!"

"Madame," he murmured.

"You haven't changed much," she said, cocking her head
as though to see better. "I remember you many years ago on
the Schlossberg with your father."

"You remember?"

"Naturally. You had an unusual face, striking, and I
thought how unlike your father you were. It seems I was

right." She smiled kindly, in the manner of older people who feel flattered when younger ones develop in the way they predicted. "Your career is very different from his." Her tone changed and she said brusquely, as though blurting out a secret, "You have enormous talent. I've read some of your work."

He bowed, feeling his insignificance, his unworthiness even to address her, while his limbs stretched to unmanageable lengths and words skittered from him before he could harness any. The terrible silence went unnoticed, though, by Anna, whose hostess had come to guide her to an elderly visiting countess.

He followed her with his eyes all evening, and whenever she caught his gaze she nodded, smiling faintly, as though his homage were both predictable and proper. He spoke to others, not hearing words, while circles formed around her and her laughter rose, rumbling and sparkling. Sometimes her husband joined her, a man with blond mustache and sideburns styled like the Emperor's, his embonpoint buttoned in snugly, his cheeks ruddy and his eyes clear. He was the obvious possessor of a comfortable and comprehensible life.

When she was leaving on the baron's arm, she gave Leo her hand. "The evening has gone by so quickly," she said, "and I had hoped to be able to talk with you. Your ideas interest me very much. Will you come visit me?"

He felt soft challenge in the way she flung her invitation, drawing back her head. He murmured affirmatively.

"Tomorrow then," she said, "for tea."

Through the night he cursed himself, remembering his awkwardness, his dumbness in her presence. He thought of the morrow, planned brilliant phrases, imagined her eyes widening with pleasure as he brought new ideas for her delectation—then remembered his mute performance of the evening, and despair overtook him. His second suit was not pressed, and the one he'd worn tonight was in even worse condition, rumpled and stained. It was too formal for tea in any case. But his gray Styrian suit with horn buttons needed ironing, and he would have to take it out first thing in the morning. He had planned to spend the morning in work, and he always worked in his dressing gown. He could not do both. If he left aside his writing, or even interrupted his usual routine (he would have to dress completely in order to take out that cursed suit), then he would become nervous, he knew, and would be at his worst with the baroness. His day depended on a balance, the weight of work holding down mornings, permitting him to draw into himself, use himself, so that later in the day the confidence held. And to work meant keeping a strict order of activities: rising at seven to a cup of coffee with milk but little sugar, taken in bed; then a quick toilette, ending with the brushing of his hair; elimination of yesterday's wastes; donning of the robe; preparing five cigarettes (so he would not be interrupted later by the need to roll one); inspection of pens and their sharpening, if necessary; then work. At ten thirty precisely, breakfast was brought in, and after the short intermission (though his mind was free to continue), he resumed writing until shortly after noon, when he dressed for dinner.

That cursed suit with its wrinkles would destroy the day and make him unfit to entertain Anna. Better not to go at all, to put it off. But what could he say in the note? That he was suddenly ill? that he had a previous engagement he'd neglected to remember? No, no—it had to be done, Fate decreed.

In such minute problems and complexities that seem always to overtake the mind when emotions are engaged, Leo spent many exhausting hours, until the first paleness of day calmed him and he could sleep. He woke at midmorning, to the breakfast tray, his decision made for him since it was too late to accomplish anything before dinner. At teatime, in his freshly pressed suit, he pulled the bell at the door of the Kottowitz villa and was let in by a servant who merely glanced at the card and seemed to be expecting him.

The baron was not at home. As though it were all perfectly natural, as though her virtue would cover them like light, she motioned him to take a seat beside her. Some of her hair was held in a clasp, the rest falling loosely down her back. Around her neck hung a small silver cross set with garnets. Her deep green déshabillé was etched with beige lace and her feet were shod in green silk slippers fashioned like boots.

Goddess of the forest, a Diana misplaced among the Bieder-meier of her apartments; he stared, could feel himself staring, and blushed. He sat down abruptly, jerkily, shame for his actions carrying him further and further into inarticulate-ness. He was unable to make the choice between tea and coffee, but her smile smoothed out his confusion as she lifted the coffeepot and poured for both of them. She selected a few small cakes from the platter and gave them to him on a white plate with gold rim. He was overwhelmed by her goodness and couldn't speak.

An hour later, as they both sipped apricot brandy and smoked cigars, he was considerably more at ease and they were talking almost like friends.

"Your *Galician Story* was the first I read. Fascinating. I hadn't known what went on there in '46. Quite horrible, though the bravery of your characters reaffirms one's faith in man."

That novella, a combination of history and fiction con-cerning Isaac Mendel, a Jew and Galician revolutionary, owed its being to Karl. He'd insisted that Leo's stories of Galicia be set down, so that other Austrians, not only his immediate circle, learn of the land and the time. Karl urged him and badgered him until he wrote it, and then Leo em-braced his friend, who'd served as midwife until the issue.

"I then read *Count Donski*"—it, too, concerned the Gali-cian uprising, seen through a heroine named Wanda—"and I am most impressed by your lively sense of history. One al-most lives through it."

Her hands were large, but narrow. Her voice seemed less harsh today, though it contained no girlishness. He was en-thralled by that voice, for which he tried to find an image. Rich and heady, but with sharpness to it: a red plush seat sprinkled with iron filings? a sable hiding small pins? No, because the sharpness brought humor to the voice, as a scat-tering of freckles mocks the perfection of smooth skin and makes it more endearing. But she was conversing and he must reply. "*Too* lively," he said and smiled. "My academic col-leagues refuse to take me seriously. History, they feel, must be dead—or it isn't worthy of the name."

She returned the smile. "And yet you lead readers into the past as easily as into a sitting room, so they may observe their surroundings at leisure." She blew out dark smoke from her cigar. He was bewitched by the understanding of this lovely woman.

"I write fiction and plays now, though I always imagined I would write books of history."

"Is that a great loss to you?"

"Not really. History was my first love, and my major study at university. But when I wrote about it, even in my dissertation, the events and characters took on such life that I could see actual scenes which had never taken place in any textbook, and could hear the dialog between historical personages, and even among their servants. The buried past became unearthed in my mind and reanimated. Horses cantered and their breath hung in the air. Gowns rustled, and sometimes the bodices were laced so tight they pinched their wearers. Forks and spoons had to be polished, cold winds blew through the castle in winter, and kings had nightmares. In whatever period, whatever historical moment, I find the woman who actually ruled, behind the throne or the man. She's always there: the strong woman at the eye of all events, remaining immovable herself while soldiers fight and die and the country is reshaped."

"You mean," she said, looking at him keenly, "that your history is invented."

"All history is invented," he told her authoritatively, and she gave him a sharp look, full of interest.

"You can't be saying that what we read about from the past didn't happen," she protested, puffing vigorously to revive her dying cigar.

Leo's lay cold in the ashtray. "I mean that between what did happen and what could have happened lie many generations of dead men. The historian is someone who makes guesses within a context. His personality, biases and predilections will all influence what he finds. For instance: I'm now working on a book about Maria of Austria at the time of Hungary's defeat by the Turks. Though we can accept that Suleiman the Magnificent sent out his army, which completely annihilated the Hungarians at Mohács, we know nothing at all about the individual soldiers of either side. They were men, with real mothers and sweethearts, who felt actual fear and ate their breakfasts. The writer of fiction can often bring out a truer sense of history than the historian—"

"As you do," she interrupted. "You bring me to the actual place and let me see with my own eyes."

"You could be Maria," he said eagerly. "She was beautiful and powerful, a queen. . . ."

She placed a finger to her lips as though in warning. He wanted to throw himself at her feet, become her Turk, be used by her for whatever she desired. Instead, he noticed that the hour was late, the glasses drained, and he had probably overstayed his welcome.

"Forgive me," he said, rising, "I talked too much and didn't realize the time."

She held out her hand. "Neither did I, I was much too engrossed by your words. This has been a wonderful afternoon for me—one so rarely talks with someone who has anything to say. You will come to see me again, won't you? Very soon."

In answer, he pressed his lips fervently to her hand. He would live for those visits; her inspiration was already commanding him.

When they became lovers, the imperious Anna sometimes met him secretly away from home, or in his own apartment, where she would come disguised as a laundress. He had rented three small rooms near the university, the presence of Anna in his life strengthening him to forgo the uneasy comfort of home and live in humble accommodations paid for by his small teaching stipend. In his rooms, they ate simple meals of cheese and bread and fruit and drank Styrian wine. In her villa, they sometimes dined together when the baron was away, on fillet of veal or venison, a roast of hare or beef, following the champagne that preceded the main course with a rich Burgundy. He rarely saw her children, though during one of his early visits, Anna's eleven-year-old daughter, a charming girl with her mother's small mouth and a precocious presence of mind, asked suddenly, "Who is this person?"

Unlike other mothers, Anna didn't reprimand the girl's abruptness. She smiled, answering, "He's a friend—to both of us."

"Which both?" insisted the girl. "You and me, or you and Papa?"

Anna laughed brilliantly and looked to Leo to join her merriment. "Well, he's definitely a friend of mine. The rest of you may decide if you want him as friend—and then must try to win him."

"Will you be my friend?" asked the girl straightforwardly.

He kissed her small hand. "With the greatest pleasure, my dear." Later, he would remember this transaction guiltily. He preferred not to become an "uncle" to the children, and Anna, too, seemed to feel it best to maintain privacy. However, she would not tolerate secrecy and always answered her husband with the truth when he asked where she had gone or what visitors she had entertained in his absence. When she disguised herself, it was to keep from prying eyes of those who neither knew her, nor wished her, well. She explained to Leo, "I am obliged only to those I live with, and those who love me. I don't tell my husband all that you and I do, but I don't hide our friendship from him, either. He trusts me, and sometimes that makes me sad. He is a forgiving man, and he's never felt there was anything to forgive you."

Leo told no one, not even Karl, the extent of his liaison with Anna—her honor stood above everything. Also, Leo couldn't have explained. Anna had brought him a voluptuousness he'd sensed but never experienced before, which now became the truth of his existence. She transformed him, he felt, as though for the first time in his life he was capable of confronting reality—a thing as life-giving and mysterious as the Resurrection.

She wore a long silk cloak of aqua lined with sable. Pearls lay around her throat and in her earlobes, gleamed from her hair, and the blue-green silk fell from naked shoulders like a sheet of water, parting below the knees to disclose the rich soil of her opulent fur. The first time she appeared like this, sweat varnished Leo's face and color drained from it. She was the most majestic and beautiful creature in all the world, the incarnation of terrible beauty, and when he thought that she might spread the cloak to reveal her own warm, naked flesh pale against the dark hairs, he began to tremble violently.

She didn't speak, but strode like a goddess to the couch, her head high, a distant smile softening her lips. She placed herself carefully on it, arching her arm back and over the side, and waited. He fell to his knees and gazed at her, this work of art, this manifestation of the eternal female that he dared not approach. His head touched the ground, as if he lay before a saint or sheikh, and then he felt her small, naked foot on the nape of his neck.

"Would you do anything for me?" she asked in a low voice, peaked by faint mockery.

"Of course," he murmured.

"Would you die for me?" The peaks rose.

"Yes. Yes. However you desire." Her foot burned against the skin of his neck and his feelings became thick cords that were strangling him.

"Get up," she said softly. She removed her foot and his neck felt the absence. He couldn't rise. She repeated her command and, like a sleepwalker, he moved outside of will, obeying her. When he stood above her, she slowly parted the cloak, her lips still held in distant humor. The aqua flowed to either side; on the dark fur lay a body perfect as marble and luminous, but the flesh was ripe. . . . He couldn't bear to see it; closing his eyes, he fell on her and was overcome.

Later, he heard her soft chuckles, laps at the edge of a small lake, and knew she was pleased. "My Anna," he said, "you have caught the soul of me."

"My trout," she said lovingly, her eyes wetly caressing his face, "how will I remove the hook?"

"Never remove it. Leave it to go deeper and deeper until I no longer struggle and am done."

"No," she said, "you must remain with me."

"Always."

"Always," she agreed, her tongue tasting the strange word shyly.

And, though neither had known such love before, or

believed that it could exist, still the love seemed to grow more brilliant every day. He cared for nothing but her; not his writing, his studies, his friends, or his old haunts. She felt the same. Leo delivered her from the drab bourgeois life she led with her husband and carried her into a world of passion, words, ideas. She had never felt such excitement in her life as now came upon her each morning when she woke and realized that a day spread before her, varied and amazing, filled with color and joy. The world was transformed from a dull sitting room into a golden hall of mirrors, reflecting objects and the reflection of objects, as both her body and mind glistened in their rebirth and her new pleasure animated the streets sprinkling diamonds into the Mur.

They told their love to each other again and again, describing how they felt, how everything appeared to them, how food tasted to their new appetite. Soon they possessed their own language of love and couldn't bear speaking to others, strangers to the tongue. They detailed their feelings, their joy, and then—because nothing pertaining to humans can remain static—they needed more. They cursed the long separations from each other in the name of family and decorum. His apartment turned into a stark prison whenever she left it, and her villa had become her tomb. For the first time in her existence, she had encountered Life, and now she hungered for it, was addicted to it, could not tolerate what had sufficed before. She was a person of exceptional honesty, and this trait had kept her virtuous. She had always told men what she thought of them, and, since this was usually very little, her would-be admirers had slunk away with hurt pride, sometimes to return as her husband's dinner guests making nervous patter about affairs of state, and commenting later on their hostess' chaste virtue.

Her honesty had made her realize long ago that she wasn't happy, but she told herself it was foolish to expect happiness when she had everything else that humans wish for —position, wealth, handsome children, an attentive husband (when he was there), furs, jewels and, as she'd learned to acknowledge, powerful beauty. Since with all these she was still not happy, she came to the conclusion that happiness was not a true condition at all. It was, as she saw it, the afterlife offered on earth by church and society to imbue human existence with a seeming direction. Happiness was simply a regulatory policy to maintain people in their work and duty through the constant hope that they would be rewarded.

She recognized that others, lacking her honesty, usually accepted baubles or heightened moments as happiness. The woman who wished for a fur coat all her life and then finally received one said she was happy and probably believed it. But once she owned the fur, she could no longer wish for it or dream about it. The actual possession destroyed hope. Humans swaddled their lives in dreams created for them by history and art, to protect themselves from the sobriety of actual existence. So Anna saw it. The term happiness was a motto to commemorate the achieving of something that had formerly been desired. Others looked at her life and said she was happy. She herself had thought she was happy when a bride, and then again at the birth of her first child. But what she had then designated happiness, she understood later, had been only the attaining of another rung on life's ladder, which was said to lead to heaven but actually ended in nothingness.

"You are the only one who understands," she told Leo. Many considered her proud; others called her hard, because she refused to take expectations as actualities. Everyone, but most particularly a woman, was expected to enter the conspiracy of lies, flatteries and illusions known as society. When she used her God-given eyes instead of rosy glasses, people said she was hard. "You've thawed me like a frozen river, and now I rush to you."

"And you," he said, kissing her naked arm, "have burst my dam." They laughed and caressed each other.

"I am the little Mur and you the great Danube."

"You are the rivers and mountains, the wide steppes, the owl's cry at midnight, wind rustling the birch leaves, soaring eagles and the hungry tigress."

"Surely that is too much," she protested.

"No, my Anna. You are whatever is wild and uncontainable. You are Nature herself, free and magnificent."

"I never knew that," she said laughing, but believed him

because in the freedom she now felt, she was indeed a child of nature, spontaneous, unbelievably alive, with powers in herself she'd never known. Through Leo, she escaped the conventions of her marriage and society and entered into her own nature.

She had done the same for him, though he was not fleeing convention so much as opening locks within himself, permitting desire and imagination to pass freely on the heretofore closed waterway of his sexuality. He assumed that she was teaching him, through her own passions. When she appeared naked against the furs, he was overcome by her beauty, overwhelmed by the most powerful, most essential feeling he'd ever known toward a woman. She'd never told him that this had been her first time in such a costume, that she had ordered it when the two became so intimate she understood his unspoken—unspeakable?—desires through patterns of his stories. He often mentioned a *kazabaika*, an eighteenth-century cloak worn by noblewomen in Galicia, of silk, velvet or Turkish woven cloth, lined and trimmed with fur. The garment itself, in Leo's stories, seemed to bestow desirability and power. He told her of an older relation, a countess, who had worn *kazabaikas* and inflamed his childish fantasy.

In Austria, such a cloak was not known, but Anna had taken an old fur to the dressmaker and, pledging the woman to secrecy (with the explanation that this was to be her costume at a masked ball and she was hoping to go undiscovered even by her husband), ordered the fur to be sewn into blue-green silk. She gave herself to Leo dressed only in this as a gift to him, and he assumed she wore the fur to incite her own lusts. He begged her to wear it often, and in time the cloak became an instrument of desire for both of them, each believing it increased the appetites of the other.

Then he presented her with a pearl-handled whip, and she stood holding it in her fur-clad nakedness, as a tableau of the cruel mistress. He was ravished by the sight, and she was aroused by the theatricality of costuming herself, as most women become more desiring when they feel they are most desirable. Though no coquette, Anna had lived since girlhood with the fact and power of her own beauty, which she regarded at times as a thing apart from herself, a jewel placed in her custody, and she took pleasure in changing its setting, to show it off more brilliantly.

Gazing at this proud, erect woman with eyes the color of morning lakes and rich hair cascading down her back, Leo felt the mystery, composed of adoration and terror, that cruel beauty inspires. He forgot the Anna who braided her daughter's hair, smoked black cigars or spoke kindly to tedious officials and saw only the quality he desired, the strange womanhood that had always, he felt now, called to him, though he'd never before heard and understood.

In their happiness, each found meaning. "So," she said wonderingly, "it is possible to be happy."

"Yes."

"For a moment." Happiness does exist, she thought, but how could it last? It was a freak of nature, like the rainbow, its brightness fading the longer one gazed on it, indescribable, touched with gold, will-o'-the-wisp.

"For as long as you desire, my darling Anna, my heart and pain."

"It doesn't last through separations." In sadness, her voice became smooth and deep, the barbs leveled.

"I will always be here."

"And I in my villa squandering my life in tea gowns talking to people of no consequence about nothing at all? No, that's intolerable."

"Then come. Leave him, come to me, live with me."

"And the children, what of them?" But they had rehearsed this often before. She knew the lines by heart.

"They're old enough," he said. In fact, it was she who had told him that.

The little one was only eleven. Quite a young lady, self-assured and clear-minded, but whose body was still flat as an ironing board—could she fill out with no mother? A girl needed a woman, but so did a boy. The eldest, Anna's favorite, was fifteen. Her firstborn, he had convinced her of happiness by his coming—she remembered now—three years into her marriage. His hair in ringlets, color of old gold. His first sailor's suit (on her dressing table in daguerreotype), and his baby name for her: Manna. He was already taller than she, though not yet Leo's height, and they had always confided in each other, sweet private moments questioning God and the ways of men.

Her babies, who were no longer hers but already belonged to the world that framed them. If she stayed, they would either emulate or despise her life. Either was intolerable. If she stayed, they would know her as an unhappy woman and soon they would grow up, leave home, and she would be left with heavy furniture and a dull husband. What then—Sundays on the Schlossberg forever and books in the evening? She had been granted this rebirth so late in life; the boon would never come again; how could she deny it?

"It is for you to decide," he told her. "Your drawing room or your own kingdom; subject or queen."

They had gone over this terrain many times, and both knew that these words were like aimless scribbling, as distraction and protection against thought. They rarely mentioned the difference in their ages. Though Anna had tried to bring it up in the early days of their love, Leo had rejected it so thoroughly, seeming almost offended by the topic, that she let it rest. And certainly, she couldn't feel those years. She had been thirteen when he was born, but her growth was sapped by marriage, eighteen years of sleep from which she was now waking, kissed by intimacy; her inner self, the being that was Anna, rising fresh and young to meet her prince.

But always, even in the "sleep" of matrimony, she had met the challenge of honesty, her ruling trait, through which she reigned. And now, despite shame, scandal and complete discreditation by her family and society, the beautiful Baroness Anna von Kottowitz, formerly known for her virtue, left husband and children, wealth and privilege, in order to live with a young author—young enough to be her son, said the gossips of Graz—in his apartment near the university.

"Amazing," said her lover, holding her in his arms. "Formidable. You are an Amazon, a truly noble soul, brave and fearless, empress by nature. My lioness, my eagle." She listened and, though pleased by his praise, she wondered why he crammed so much adulation in one embrace. His ornate-

ness was like a late-Baroque chapel, where profusion of ornament suggests a collage of afterthoughts.

He told himself she was undaunted, open, fearless as a
warrior queen—and more besides. In truth, he was shocked.
Like other creative or highly imaginative people, Leo had
somehow taken for granted that all acts of originality would
be committed by himself. Despite his age, inventiveness of
mind and seeming disdain of society, he was still tied to the
conventions he ridiculed. Son of a police director whose values he found trivial, Leo nevertheless took his duty and honor
as citizen quite seriously. Though he reviled social oppres-
sion, spoke out against Austrian censorship, imperialism and
falsity, he was, despite his convictions, as loyal as his neighbors and equally dependent on the structure of the community he lived in. Perhaps more; in a false setting, even
semiprecious stones can be mistaken for emeralds, and, as a
young writer not yet embarked on the magnum opus of his
life, Sacher-Masoch depended on a blank society to make his
mark. He was not sure how he would be regarded—would he
be noticed?—in Vienna. Here in Graz, he was famous.

In short, young Leopold was nervous. His old cowardice
reappeared, and this extraordinary, original, sexually adven-
turous artist didn't admit, even to himself, his shock that a
wife could leave her husband. Yet he felt some shame for all
of them and would have sent his apologies to the baron if he
could.

The doors of the villa were naturally closed to him. Even
on the streets, mothers put a restraining hand on their daughters' shoulders and whispered in their ears when he walked
by. He thought of the baron's disgrace and felt sympathy.
Alone with servants and children, forsaken by a wife of eighteen years on whom he had lavished his gifts and affection, the
man—who had done no wrong—was to be pitied. Leo didn't
know him well, and had actually felt scorn for his pomposity
and self-congratulation when dining there, but now he was
alone, his daughters too young to play hostess, his servants
laughing behind his back.

"Dull, yes, but a kind man," Leo said.

Her hands covered her ears. "Stop it! You must never

mention him to me again, or my children. No one can bear a cross for me. You asked me to come to you. Here I am."

He threw himself at her feet and tears came to his eyes from a source he didn't understand.

During the first weeks they kept to themselves, inviting no guests and refusing even the staunch friends who begged to visit. Leo went out to give his lectures, and Anna did the marketing, but otherwise they remained in the rooms, talking of love and planning their empires. Leo didn't dare confront his family, and avoided Karl through a sense of his own betrayal, since he had not taken his friend into his confidence. He had even lied the day Karl came to see him at the university, by claiming that his writing occupied him fully. (Karl's smile, suggesting he knew the actual reasons for Leo's seclusion, seemed to exonerate him, but he was still ashamed.)

When he ran into Friedl on the street, Leo was unable to turn away from his warmth or refuse his invitation for supper. He longed to see Marika again; she was part of his family and yet independent of it, his lovely sister, the wife of his friend.

He apologized to Anna, who smiled. "I'm glad," she told him. "You will enjoy the evening, and I will be left in peace for a while." He felt jealousy for her independence, jealous of the self that was sufficient unto his beloved, and would have preferred to stay. Next time Anna must come along, he insisted. "We'll see," she said, as though it were a matter of indifference. "Perhaps you should brush your jacket before you go."

He brushed it carefully under her watchful eye, kissed her with a hunger for the time they would be apart and left only when she physically pushed him out the door. He walked to the Zimmermanns', where he was greeted by Marika with "Lev, darling! But wait, first let me brush you off." He laughed and resigned himself to her vigorous sweeping of him.

The children, she said, were in bed already. For a moment Leo suspected that their parents were shielding them from exposure to his wickedness. Then he forgave them, embraced them both and inquired after little Johann (named after her father) and Hannerl (after his mother). The children were healthy, he was told, and very amusing. He must come one afternoon and play with them. Johann had been born after five years of marriage. He was now nearly three. After his parents' long wait for their firstborn, they were doubly rewarded by the birth of his sister twelve months later. "I wish Irina could see them," said Marika sadly. "Johann is already like his grandfather." She would have preferred to call him Ivan, not its German equivalent, but Friedl's parents had protested, and since the father of Friedl's mother had been named Johannes, the baby was christened in compromise.

Against the image of his magnificent Anna, Marika still maintained her loveliness. Fair and slim, even slimmer than at her wedding, Marika looked like a girl. But her face was not as calm as it had been, and her slimness no longer had the natural grace of a sapling but seemed harder, more like a stick, as though a hunger gnawed at her. "I'm bored here," she said at supper. "Friedl works all day and the babies are not enough occupation." She played with her fork while she spoke, a sign of nervousness Leo didn't recognize in her, though Friedl had already become used to it.

Her husband smiled apologetically. "She is in the house too much. She should be out amusing herself in gay company."

"And where am I to find that? And who will care for the children while I am away? Or prepare the meals?"

Friedl shrugged, embarrassed by her displeasure and his own inability to satisfy her. He longed to talk of something else, yet dared not ask Leo about his life. That would be an indiscretion; Leo's sensitive situation demanded tactful silence. Marika suddenly smiled and said, "You are like a bird, Leo. You fly on your wings above us all. No one can put you in a cage." Softly, she added, "You taught me to fly, you know? When I couldn't read or write, and you showed me words."

"Do they bring you happiness?"

"Yes," she said eagerly. "I read a lot now—I have so

much time." Aware of the complaint in her voice, she turned to her husband and smiled warmly at him. "Forgive me, Friedl. You are a good husband and an artist. You give me everything I want and are a loving father." To Leo she said, "I thank God for bringing him to me. And yet, my soul weakens in this city. I grow restless."

"She walks for hours," Friedl affirmed.

"When the children are older," Leo said soothingly, "you will be able to find work outside the house."

"Why should she?" asked Friedl. "I am able to care for her. She is my wife and must not work for others."

Marika smiled sadly. "That is true, my treasure. I am full of nonsense." Her eyes flashed at Leo for an instant, and he saw the young girl drawing a pistol from her belt, her hair like tassels of corn, her arm pulling the recalcitrant child. "Marika . . ." But he could say nothing; a brush fire started up in an instant and then died. Other fires smoldered under ashes long after they seemed extinguished. "Marika," he began again. She looked at him questioningly. He was thinking of Anna, the fierce-spirited woman who placed herself in danger, and he held his palms open, with nothing to say.

"We miss you in the coffeehouse," Friedl ventured.

"Yes. I will be back."

Friedl nodded, and when Leo left he said shyly, "Please present my compliments to your lady."

He returned home and found her asleep, ignoring him. He felt abandoned, and his dependency frightened him. How had he deserved this incredible woman? How could he keep her, whose soul was great as Russia and whose beauty should be always newly adorned? He was afraid of losing her, he had no money to maintain her, his miserable self couldn't hold such a creature. He had forgotten his ugliness for a time but now, gazing at the beautiful sleeper, he saw himself as a monkey.

Her eyes were open, she was looking at him. How thin he was! Like a poor child of the streets. "Good evening, my darling," she murmured, and he came to lie down beside her without taking off his clothes. She embraced him and he lay in her arms trembling and crying silently. When he grew calm, she undressed him carefully and hung up his suit. He was already asleep when she returned to the bed, and she watched over him for a long time, anxiously and with premonitions, reading on his pale, sleeping face that he needed more than love.

"You haven't been writing much," she observed next day, "not for a while."

He understood. "My thoughts are filled with you and leave no room for imaginary adventures."

"And the sketches you were writing, after you finished *Maria of Austria?*"

"You mean those portraits of actresses? *Fake Ermine?*" She nodded. "They're nothing, I can do that any time."

"I know," she said sadly. "You must return to your work, and to yourself. Look at me, Leo." She cupped his chin and brought his face up level with hers. "Yes, you know that I'm right. You must go deeper into yourself, use your talent, risk yourself."

"As you did," he said miserably. He was insignificant as a fly compared to her. He was nothing. He would lose her—he was afraid of her. "I have no talent," he confessed. "It was a butterfly, nothing more. I have no gift, I can't even support us, I am worthless. . . ."

"Stop it!"

The command, harsh as a slap, brought him back to control. He looked up, she gave him her large, elegant hand to hold, and they talked of what should be done. At first he listened humbly, not daring to interrupt or dispute in any way as she rapped out suggestions. But eventually he understood that her words were those of a general, not an artist; she was telling him, basically, to stand straight, pull himself together, look to his work. What she said was right, logical, but resentment grew in him as he remembered his books. Her advice was like his father's—what could she know of writing? A pen was not a sword, and he no soldier.

He smiled, stroked her arm, and his thoughts retreated from her, edging to that steaming lake holding monsters and mermaids, if only he'd immerse himself. It was private, hidden, and could penetrate his flesh if he'd go into it. His body's mistress urged him to return to labor, leading him to where she held no dominion.

He dressed, made tea for them both and drank it with her. He rose and kissed her before going to the door. She clung to his kiss, returned it with ardor, and he perceived that her passion for him at this moment came through her assumption that she had given him something for which he would be eternally grateful.

He walked through the cool park, its mist rising, sunlight streaking the grayness to restore color to trees and flowers, giving back to the nuthatch its rosy breast, to the tit its bright blue cap. He walked through the Palace Gate and turned left, past the cathedral. The bakery at the end of the street always smelled more delicious to him than any other in Graz. Once, on a late morning in student days, he'd bought two rolls there and devoured them immediately. The woman stared, shook her head in disapproval and then gave him a third free of charge because he was so hungry. That had been kind; these random memories.

This city collected his life in incidents, like souvenirs. On his left, a cream-colored house with fine Renaissance façade. He'd made love here—which window? This, frothy now with lace curtains? No. That one there, third from the right, geraniums wild on the windowsill. Nanette. She'd made up that name, of course; raven's hair, voice like one too, with the claws of a cat. No poetry in her, but milky skin and small red lips would keep her on the stage another few years. Then, suddenly as a dropping bucket, she'd be old, probably fat, and would tell extraordinary stories of her theatrical past to aging gentlemen in coffeehouses who wouldn't believe her, but would welcome the company.

Actresses. He was writing about actresses. They had all been actresses, most of them anyway, creatures airy as whipped cream, the *schlag* of life. What would the world be without them, lovely women who live only to be beautiful and admired, whose reality is illusion and who accept role after role in hopes of finding the part that shows—is—themselves? Karl said they faded quickly when removed from the spotlight. And Joseph, who was now committed to the theater, whose ability to listen ensured that he would always be a competent, if not genial, actor, had said in a moment of inspiration (Leo smiled now, with affection and approval), "Actresses are like French geese, who must be stuffed with words and fantasies." They were delicious, though. Only the greatest of them (represented in *Fake Ermine*) invented their own characters; others, lovely ornaments with slim waists and slight talents, were kept in the play as a ball on a seal's nose. *Adieu, Nanette* (who spoke no French), *on a eu des beaux temps ensemble.*

He continued in the direction of the Herrengasse. What set designer could do better? he thought; the gentle Mur, the flowing Alps. *"La ville des Grâces, sur les bords de l'amour"*—who said that? A visiting monarch, French? Which? Witty. He made note of it by repeating the phrase as though uttered by a seventeenth-century king in opulent dress to his low-browed mistress on a small ship.

"La ville des Grâces"—Graz—on the banks of La M(o)ur. No wonder it abounds in actresses. A city of love, framed by gold leaf, set in courtyards intimate as *chambres privées,* peered at by the jealous eyes of Hapsburg yellow, the gold of egg yolk staring through crystal sacs of morning. The whole town constructed elaborately as the dreams of a mad czar: a place to act, with the stage set for extravagance.

He loved her, into her small recesses. Only in the first months had Graz appeared provincial to him, compared to Prague, in the months after Rosa's death. She could have become an actress, he thought. Rosa had that particular "radiance": an eager curiosity, tart vitality and a dewiness as though she'd just been born. The quality was unmistakable: very fresh and innocent, though at the same time other-worldly. Like a mermaid, but a good one.

Would have to be a German-speaking mermaid, he thought, not Galician. They were all evil, like the spirits of the mountains, plains and rivers. Does every landscape produce its own spirits? he wondered. Do hard landscapes, where people live close to their deaths, always present creatures of evil? Never a nurturing Virgin, or Minerva dispensing justice, or wise Beatrice offered in the way of hope? No, such places respond only to the dark side of man, leaving religion and culture to invent the light.

He told himself to channel his thoughts toward the mouth of inspiration, or to that hidden lake. His thoughts were all over. Come, thoughts; come, ideas; come, come, he articulated in his mind and smiled at his own childishness, and because he sometimes found himself amusing. Think about Woman, he said. *Cherchez la femme.*

Actresses and demons—were they the antinomies, the present form of Mary-Eve, Good-Evil, Mother-Temptress? In woman's nature we find our own. The witches of *Macbeth* speak to the heart, and the Lady's blood runs with the passions and evil of her time. In woman's nature we reveal our own. He hadn't caught the Powerful Woman yet, he knew, hadn't created her in the manner of a Lady Macbeth or Medea. But he'd known many strong women, was living with the strongest of all—why didn't she simply overtake his pages?

He entered the little Glockenspiel square, off the Bürgergasse, where for more than four hundred years the little figures swung out the doors of the clock twice a day. He had missed the morning chimes, but the clock stopped him.

Aunt Xenobia had a glockenspiel in the sitting room; a pair of children came out of it every day at teatime. Or maybe just once. He had only one recollection of it. A composite memory, or had he been there only once?

Through the clothes in the closet he saw her, dressed in white, black hair streaming down to ivory shoulders. She entered quickly, small purposeful steps in red boots, followed by a pale young lover. She threw off the cloak imperiously— brown fur spread at her feet. Then on the sofa, reclining, a clothed Maja; fair young man on his knees, kissing her hand. The door to her room burst open, her plump husband blundered in, his face steaming. (Were others behind him?) She sprang up, slapped him, seized a whip (from air?), beat him. Turned then to the young man, flogged him also, whipped them both out of the room.

Was it so? Was it so? He was breathing heavily. And now the child Leo, stifling among the furs, sneezes and falls out of

the closet. The magnificent Xenobia grabs him by the locks
—a Salome!—and throws him to the ground at her feet. The
child kisses the boot, the small red boot. It kicks him, she looks
down when she is kicking him, ice in her smile. Then she
raises him up, removes a pale stream of silk from around her
neck and whips him with it, a deep fragrance like earth exhaling after rain. She takes his face between both her hands, her
mouth comes closer, she burns his lips with her kiss. The
ground beneath him opens and he falls in.

He leaned against the wall with eyes closed, trying to
regain his breath. A passerby stopped to ask if he needed help,
but Leo smiled and shook his head, waving him on. When the
intense memory began to fade, he wanted to go back to it. His
heart was in his ears; the memory had been vivid as a dream
or nightmare that affects the body even when the images are
lost and tells the dreamer he has just been taught something
important about himself, if only he could understand.

Leo recovered himself and walked on, crossing the Herrengasse toward the quay. His excitement was strong but
controlled. It takes courage, he told himself, the courage that
Anna showed me by example. "Use yourself," she said. "Risk
yourself." She left her family, defied the world, and accepts
her stigma willingly because she loves. I have not been honest.
I've lied to my friends. I've hidden behind the respectability
of history in my work. I've always been a coward, and yet I
don't deny myself the satisfaction of my desires. But I don't
go further, I won't stand out against society because I am
afraid. I take no risks—Anna is right—and I do not declare
myself.

He felt that a truth had been revealed through the glockenspiel: the man and artist in him were both stimulated by the
same source. He must go deeply into that source, be afraid of
nothing, not ostracism, scorn or betrayal; he must allow himself to fall deeply into his own nature, and his work must be
fed by his own heart.

A weariness came into his elation. It would be better, he
thought, if I were different, if I were someone other than
myself. But then his new discovery raised him up again.
That's why courage is needed. My crime lies in trying to

129

ignore or disguise my nature. I must repent, and from now on acknowledge and express who I am, even though this may be distasteful to many, even to myself. The thought of his gentle mother unnerved him, and then he remembered Marika's restlessness, Anna's boldness, and he knew that life, which was also work, must be expressed fully and openly, that the artist must embrace the man whose self he inhabits; that the man must prove to himself that he exists as an individual.

He ran back to the main square, bought a large spray of flowers, hailed a carriage and rode back to Anna. She was still clothed as when he left her, in her moss-green dressing gown, her hair not yet dressed. He kissed the wild strands, her smooth cheeks, her open mouth, and then fell to kiss the hem of her robe. "You are my queen," he said. "You reign over me and teach me my duty."

Within an hour he was at work on a new novel, centering on a portrait of Anna, in her essence and complexity. Her individual nature would fuse with the force of Nature manifested in her, and the magnificent womanhood would reveal man to himself.

Her name is Anna von Kossow, and she lives as recluse in a ruined castle. One day a young man comes to visit, posing as a census-taker. His name is Sacher-Masoch; he has been drawn here by rumors of the beautiful hermit. She grants him an interview and eventually will tell him the story of her life. He learns that she left her husband and three children for a young lover. Society has shunned her, and now she is alone.

"Listen," he said when Anna brought him tea. He had written eight pages already and had just finished a paragraph that bathed him with warm pleasure in his own powers. "The narrator is commenting here: 'Our Christian society, in the first half of the nineteenth century'—that's when the story takes place—'had attained that perfection of delicacy whereby it would condone and even be amused by Anna's taking of one or more lovers, as long as she continued living with her husband. However, it would not tolerate her acting openly. Adultery could be charming; separation was uncivilized.'" He looked at her with triumph.

"You write well," she said dubiously.

"You understand, of course, that this is a book about hypocrisy, the intolerance of so-called 'civilized' people. The heroine lives in ruins, an obvious symbol for her actual life, made so by social disdain."

"I see," she said unhappily, wrapping her chest with her arms.

He left his work to caress her. She had never been so beautiful as now; he had never loved her so deeply before. She inhabited him thoroughly, through body, mind and soul; she was a part of him, the guiding principle, muse and mistress, and he existed through what she made of him.

She, who had lived thirteen years longer and had raised three children, could already glimpse a horror of emptiness but didn't mention it. In that moment, the outcome seemed inevitable: what had appeared to be her naked self, her inner being, turned out to be just another role, one she had never played before and so hadn't recognized. She would continue in it, though, with all her powers, despite this prescience that when the writer had his say, the last act would be performed, the stage swept bare and not a soul left in the darkness beyond.

She laughed lightly and pressed herself against him. They loved each other. He was brilliant and his talent would carry him high above other men and make him deathless. She was condemned to her beauty; she inspired him; her own immortality was now.

* * *

Estranged from her children through the offices of her mother-in-law, Sissi turned her attentions to herself. Acknowledged as the best horsewoman and the most beautiful crowned head in Europe, the young Empress devoted herself to horses and her own beauty. She bathed in warm oil and had wet rags placed on her hips to keep them slender. Her weight was not permitted to go over 100 pounds, nor her waist to exceed eighteen inches. Her life was a prison, she felt; she'd been given a life sentence of rule (but no authority), and she deprived herself of food in order to retain her only power. In the mornings, she was sewn into her riding skirt, that not a fraction of a centimeter be added to her waistline, and then she rode, fearlessly, violently, for most of the day, at speeds that took her breath away, riding into an unbounded freedom beyond state, court, marriage and self, where she need tolerate no caress but the wind's nor follow any rule except her own command.

She rode, and she traveled—to avoid her husband and his mother, Vienna, etiquette and her own uselessness. Her subjects complained that she was selfish, and she told her maid one evening, "I cannot help that; my training has made me so. People put themselves at my disposal. Why should I not make use of them?" Her maid nodded in adoration, knowing how very kind her mistress could be, and how much she suffered.

Others criticized her. Ludovica wrote, "My child, I am afraid you are the kind of woman who will never achieve what she wants. You are too uncompromising, and make no allowances for the exigencies of life. You feel you belong to the time of saints and martyrs, but my dear, you must not give yourself saintly airs or try to impress the world with your martyrdom."

Sissi cried, because her mother gave her no love, her husband was not a friend, and her babies were taken away. On horses and through books she could escape, through her beauty she could elicit homage, but her mind was ignored, she was very lonely, and she could find nowhere to place her heart except in her own safekeeping.

7

DISCOVERING HIS "vital source" wrought no basic change in Leo, though he paid even more attention to his feelings than formerly and was more ruthless in expressing them. At least, he tried. The new "honesty" couldn't remove his shyness or self-disgust, and with strangers he was as awkward, apologetic and deferential as he'd always been. He still felt a combination of contempt and fear in the presence of his father, and he was still happiest (outside Anna's arms) at the coffeehouse, where he could forget his ugliness as he held an audience captive or dueled with words. At the university, he ignored his detractors and called them idiots (but only behind their backs). He prepared lectures haphazardly, arrogant in his sense of genius, then went through agonies of nervousness, even terror, before he could deliver them. Students enjoyed his presentations, which his colleagues referred to as "performances." He was aware of efforts to oust him and remove his title and therefore resolved to stay, despite his disenchantment with teaching, which he felt took him too far away from his work, through demands on time and distractions of subject.

His mother was ill, and he went often to visit her. She was miraculously uninformed of his liaison with Anna, as though her maternal sense of hearing prevented any evil spoken of her children from reaching her ears. She believed he had taken rooms away from home to be close to the university and its library.

Each time he came, he brought a small gift—flowers or

little cakes, a volume of poetry, a bright ribbon. They sat in her room drinking tea from the samovar she'd brought from her father's house in Kiev. Their conversation was as gentle and delicate as when he'd been a child. They reminisced about occasions at home: the smells of Christmas, when the fat of roasting pigs hit the fire and Irina's cakes were brought out of the oven, suffusing the downstairs rooms with sweetness that made the mouth water; the day of the Three Kings, when the tree was burned and the cones crackled in the heavy smell of pine. They reminded each other of eggs painted at Easter, and hummed tunes from the churches or the countryside. He was alarmed at the thinness of her hands and the hollows under her eyes. She seemed too fragile to embrace, and he saluted her with a light brush of his lips on her forehead.

Sometimes he read to her and she grew drowsy, but she never fell asleep. "Impossible," she explained. "To sleep when my son is reading to me! What sort of mother would do that, I ask you?" Whenever she looked at him, a small frown of concern came over her face, making a delicate cross on her brow. She asked him if he thought of marrying, and he answered evasively, making a joke of it, "Not till I find someone like you, Mama."

"You need someone stronger than I, Lev"—she'd called him by the Slav form of his name ever since they had come to Graz—"someone more intelligent, who helps you with your work."

"I have never met a woman more intelligent than you," he said, believing it. In a woman, goodness and intelligence were the same. The quality was understanding, and she possessed it above all women. He thought a moment about having a wife: a beautiful, pure, delicate woman, created only for himself, who would love him always and unconditionally and would never betray him. Her image was tiny and perfect, held in the heart of a flower like Andersen's Thumbelina. Then the petals came up and closed over her.

Leo feared his mother would die and imagined his grief would be all-consuming. He terrified himself by visions of his suffering. However, Charlotte didn't worsen but remained

134

suspended in semi-invalidism, neither leaving the house nor taking to her bed. She had just passed her fiftieth birthday and told Leo she had "no intention of deteriorating until I see my grandchildren—*two* lots of them." Her younger boy, Charles, was just beginning to climb the bureaucratic ladder, and would for some years more undoubtedly move his energies in the direction of a position rather than a wife. She had hopes for Lev, though. He appeared less nervous than formerly, and his health seemed to have improved. He had learned to take care of his delicate nature, she thought, and no longer excited himself, as he used to, until he was feverish and delirious. He coughed only occasionally, and rarely trembled.

A particular aspect of himself came out at home, he thought, walking back to his apartment, as though his visits to his mother were a form of retreat. But with Anna, the implications of his "discovery" were showing themselves daily, always widening. He recognized, and told her, that he needed an affirmation of his unworthiness. She was a goddess; he, a mere supplicant. A goddess must have her god. Her eyes widened. "What do you mean?"

"That you must betray me."

"What! Leo, no. My darling—why should I?"

"To let me feel my love for you completely and absolutely, even through my pain."

"But I want no one else."

"Anna, my adored one, my empress. You have deep passions. You are too magnificent for one man alone to possess. I want you to express your lusts with a man worthy of you, noble and handsome as a Greek."

She protested, and for a long time refused to hear of it. But Leo understood that her betrayal was as necessary to him as her love, and he returned to it, persisted, though he sensed he was doing her an injury, that he was wounding her great spirit. But it had to be done, for himself and for the book. How interesting the plot would become!

First, however, he had to find the man. Karl was handsome, Joseph too, but he feared their ridicule more than their refusal. Leo had hinted to Karl that his ideas of love and lovemaking were out of the ordinary but could go no further when Karl laughed and said, "Next you'll be saying you like to be whipped!" Joseph had been more sensitive (because he was an actor?), saying thoughtfully, "Each man becomes a different animal in bed, and we can't predict how even our best friends behave." Leo had then mentioned pain, and Joseph replied, "It seems to me a woman's pleasure in love is always mixed. She desires what hurts her. She instinctively protects herself against the organ she craves, and moans her pleasure through her pain."

Leo was too innocent, or self-preoccupied, to reflect on the possible source of Joseph's observations, never thinking that another man could be endowed differently from himself. All he heard in Joseph's remarks was an indifference to causing pain in a woman, which disqualified him as a Greek because he would show no reverence.

The Greek was sighted, however, a few days later, playing billiards—a tall man, with the dark coloring of the Mediterranean, wavy hair and even features. From the innkeeper, Leo learned he was a Polish count, newly arrived in Graz and wealthy. Leo challenged him to a game, lost, and invited him to a bottle of wine. They talked amiably, and the count agreed to a return match on the morrow. The next day when Leo entered with Anna on his arm, he saw immediately that the adventure was as good as accomplished. The count's eyes took her in hungrily: the rich roan hair, the smoky blue, like morning light, of her eyes and matching costume, trimmed with ermine. Anna barely glanced at him, her disdain regal and provocative. Leo began to tremble, a sick taste came to his mouth, and heat pressed against his eyes. "Are you ready for the match?" he asked lightly.

"Certainly." The count bowed, never taking his eyes off Anna.

Later, having lost to Leo, he accepted with effusion the invitation to dine in their humble quarters the following day. He arrived with flowers and Anna took them, giving only a slight nod in recognition. Throughout the meal, the count was held in fascination, as Leo himself had been when he first met Anna, and she, though seeming to show him no favors, carried herself in the high way of women who know they are being admired. Her gestures revealed she was aware of being

looked at, and the small dance of her body was being performed, Leo knew, for the Greek.

He had wondered—last night, this morning—whether to
absent himself after dinner. He now judged it would be inappropriate. Despite the ways of her body, Anna remained
proud and stiff, and the count barely addressed her. Their
appetites, now awakened, had to be given time to grow before
they would feed off each other.

Indeed, when Leo had to leave for the university, Anna
rose coolly and gave the count her hand. His lips pressed it,
too hard for cordiality, and remained on her skin for the extra
instant that reveals intentions beyond politeness. Leo took up
his briefcase and accompanied him. "She is beautiful," the
Greek said. "A treasure."

Leo nodded. "You will come to see us again? You will
come often?"

In a few weeks' time it happened, Leo having feigned
departure in order to position himself in the closet, the door
slightly ajar (but unnoticeable), the crack permitting him an
unobstructed view of the bed—their bed.

He watched, in pain that sometimes blinded him, as the
Greek stroked her hair and skin, branded kisses on her arms,
shoulders, lips; he saw Anna's slow smile as desire stirred in
her, rose, heaved her body upward, ran trembling through
her limbs. The Greek murmured in her ear, he made love to
each finger of her hand, he raised her skirts. . . . When Leo
could bear to open his eyes again, she lay naked and resplen-
dent on the bed, the Greek over her on his knees, erect and
smiling. Her answering look was so perfect, full of desire and
blank at the same time, that Leo felt a mortal sickness, his
body burned and disappeared; his existence was only a shimmering pain.

When the Greek left, she remained there, perfectly still,
her nakedness spread. Leo opened the closet, staggered to the
bed and threw himself, weeping, beside her. She stroked him
absentmindedly, her eyes on the ceiling, focused within. So
they lay until, in a distant voice, she asked slowly, "Did you
mind?" She stretched and brought her limbs together with a
panther's grace.

"Oh, my darling, darling. I thought I would die. I wanted

to cry out, tear him from you. The torture!"

She turned her head to look at him, quizzically, as though she had just now noticed he was beside her. "Were you jealous, then?"

"Easier to die. I burned, Anna, consumed by love and terror." He began to kiss her; his body was feverish, his skin ached. He kissed her ardently, deliriously, his hands kneading her rich flesh, his body crucified into love, begging for his torturess, dying into her through his wounds and then rising again, coming again through her, into her, fusing with the strange nature, his only god, his murderess who delivered him, at the end, into a profound sleep, calm as a frozen lake.

She had never before known him to be so passionate, and he worked prolifically these weeks, on two books at once. The count declared his love for her and urged her to come away with him. He brought her a necklace of pearls and rubies, which Leo begged her to wear with him also, to ornament her nakedness. She had two lovers now, and no husband. Anna waited, like a temple constructed on a volcano, for the final judgment to destroy her or turn her to stone. She felt she had no will left. She was being carried inexorably on dangerous currents. She'd given herself to love, given everything, and had become love's creature, a thing without name or will that still decked itself in costumes, moaned under the body of a man, brushed its hair and placed a smile on its face. For love of Leo, she gave herself to him, but the love was not consumed and she was forced to give herself to another, for love of the first. She had defied society but now defied something much greater, and she waited—without fear or hope—for the dreadful punishment at the end.

It came through her body, and a dose of it was passed on to Leo. He first discovered the nature of his illness through a doctor and told Anna calmly, with kindness, that she carried this terrible disease. He then explained, against the thunder in her ears, that naturally their lovemaking was over. He suggested she go somewhere to find a cure.

She packed her things, her *kazabaika* and the pearl-handled whip, and kissed him good-bye. They both wept, and Leo vowed that he loved her still, had loved her beyond his senses and would always be true to her in his heart. Her other lover had disappeared, a flight that seemed mysterious until they learned through the Police Director that the "Polish count" had been a fraud, no count at all but an imposter wanted by authorities in Warsaw for embezzlement, who had disappeared from Graz leaving behind a heady stack of debts, the cries of his creditors, and silent Anna, the disgraced baroness.

Leo wept a long time after her departure and touched with reverence the objects that once had been touched by her hands. He lay in bed feeling her beside him, and after a few days of mourning when he did nothing at all, not even dress himself, he returned to his desk to continue working on his monument to her, his novel called *The Divorced Woman*, concerning an abandoned woman who leaves her family for a young lover and then betrays him with a bogus and infected count. The novel was different from anything he'd written before; he knew, even while writing it, that this was a major work.

PART III

Wanda (MATURITY)

You'll laugh at me, young friends, but I tell you: Where there is hypocrisy and lying everywhere, there truth appears as insanity!

—Leopold von Sacher-Masoch, "The Germans"

8

THE BATTLE of Königgrätz (also known as Sadowa)
marked a change in Austria's fortunes. The Prussian prime
minister, with his genius for subtly directing other nations on
paths carved by his own ambition, had led Franz Joseph to
war over Schleswig-Holstein. The Austrian Emperor, followed reluctantly by the peaceable young King of Bavaria,
Ludwig II, showed chivalry in defending the ancient honor
of legitimate monarchy against the disruptive, aggrandizing
schemes of Bismarck. At Königgrätz, horses tripped over
their own intestines and died; in one day 40,000 men were
killed, and in Vienna the crowds shouted for abdication,
jeered the Emperor, and called for his brother Maximilian.
To Sophie, who had always preserved a special, protecting
love for Max, the Viennese nevertheless seemed traitors to
Kaiser and country, sounding like the rabble that called for
Barabbas.

Her eldest son, who at nineteen had refused the crown
of German Emperor, continued his rule over an Austria
threatened by German weight. Observers commented that
Prussia had won through technology, her needle guns hitting
their mark before the Hapsburg soldiers had time to load
their muskets. Some disagreed, and in the coffeehouse of the
Erzherzog Johann, in Graz, men from the Styrian Hunters (a
regiment of volunteers) argued the case weeks after the cause
was lost. To the author Sacher-Masoch and his important
friends, they explained, "It wasn't the weapons at all, it was
our strategy. Our strategy was shit. The thick-headed generals screwed us up again."

"How's that?" asked the Herr Baron, drumming his fingers on the table.

"Those needle guns aren't accurate. At any kind of distance they just go *pop, pop* like firecrackers. Can't aim them at a distance, they go every which way. Our mistake was coming too close."

Another hunter took it up, to clarify for the gentlemen. "You don't fight hand-to-hand if your enemy has a knife and all you've got is a slingshot. That's suicide. You stand back, you wait for him, and then—*ping!* right between his eyes. He hasn't a chance. So much," he said scornfully, "for 'superior weapons.' "

The first repeated, "It was shit, our strategy. Our muskets could have taken them. Front-loading doesn't take all day; if we'd stayed back, we could've knocked those bastards off. But instead, these idiots order us to get on top of them. Who's got time to load? You're too busy getting killed. Numbskulls!"

"Who?" asked Joseph, the Herr Professor.

"Our generals, of course." And, dropping his voice to a whisper, the hunter added, "They should be shot."

Even his comrades were shocked by such outspokenness, and Karl rescued the moment by calling loudly for beer while jerking his chin in the direction of the door, where a charming woman was just entering. They all turned to look, nodded appreciatively, and buried the traitorous comment in a clinking of glasses and Prosits.

In Vienna, the coffeehouses had remained filled during the fighting. Gaiety continued in the theaters and restaurants; in the Prater, pretty girls rode on the carousel, reaching out to catch the golden ring.

His subjects were dancing, the dead horses had been cleaned off the battlefield. In the aftermath of Königgrätz, alone in his study, Franz Joseph was readjusting his sights.

* * *

As sun and moon share dominion, though each can reign only when the other is hidden, so now, when the Emperor's star had fallen, the Empress' rose. During the past year, Sissi had demanded autonomy of rule over all matters concerning

144

her children in an ultimatum to the Emperor. He signed with heavy heart, not wishing to offend his mother. But matters had forcibly changed priorities for Franz Joseph. Feeling his eminence threatened in the German-speaking world, he was now reviewing the concept of great Austria, a confederation of many lands, a multinational empire. Specifically, he hoped to be offered the ancient crown of Saint Stephen and become King of Hungary. In that venture, not Sophie but his beautiful Sissi, still remembered with affection by Hungarians who glimpsed her ten years ago, could be his strongest ally.

She spoke Hungarian fluently, and chose as her companion and lady-in-waiting one Ida Ferenczy, a country girl, friend to the revolutionaries Deák and Andrássy. Ida was a dedicated patriot of her country, straightforward and simple, whose candor of expression delighted the Empress. She won a warm place in Sissi's affections within weeks of arriving at the Hofburg and became her mistress's ally when most of the court expressed annoyance at Her Majesty's insistence on speaking Hungarian exclusively. Sissi ignored the disapproval, laughed at her husband's embarrassed reports of it, and continued speaking in the Magyar tongue, which freed her from dull Hapsburg pomposity in sweet assurances of friendship with Ida. When Sissi left for Munich, to secretly consult a doctor on the recurrence of old and dreaded symptoms, she missed her new friend and wrote her, *My darling Ida, I think of you a thousand times a day. I'm lonely, and long for your gay company. . . . God be with you, my dear, and don't marry while I am away, but remain true to your loving friend E.*

She was soon relieved from her loneliness, however, after reassurances from the doctor, when she traveled on to visit her beloved cousin, the young King of Bavaria, whose deep blue eyes, black curls and lips with their long cupid's bow made him the most beautiful man Sissi knew. Her subjects in Vienna gossiped about the Empress' affection for Ludwig, but she knew they were old hens who couldn't comprehend a bond as pure and strong as the two of them had. He was her twin, whose great spirit knew how to fly, and trailed hers along with him. She called him her eagle, and she was his gull. To Ludwig, there was no other woman; his cousin Sissi was the most beautiful of all, the only woman with understanding and a free soul.

They shared memories of childhood; Ludwig had often come to Possenhofen, where he had first heard a piece by Wagner, played on the piano by his uncle Max. In 1864, when he assumed the throne, Ludwig's initial act had been to call for great Wagner, and now Wagner was the Friend, the guiding spirit whose work he had pledged to support, whose rich music inspired his dreams and his reign.

Sissi and Ludwig flew to each other's arms and rested there awhile as birds will pause and perch during their migration. When they separated to look at each other, each saw the beautiful face, fine features and lips held closed over shared Wittelsbach teeth, their only defect, small yellowed traitors to their beauty. They both used their lips in the same way when talking—as sentries to protect the secret from view. Sissi reinforced their work by dabbing a hand or handkerchief in front of them. Her voice was soft, and people often could not make out what she was saying. Both had shy smiles, because their lips remained sealed.

"My eagle!" she said, and he answered, "My gull!" She sat with him while he ate in his opulent manner, ending the meal with fruit tarts and a large soufflé, washed down with sweet wine from Madeira. She ate nothing except a small bowl of ice flavored with violets.

She stayed with him at Hohenschwangau Castle for only a few days, spending her mornings alone, riding furiously into midday and joining her cousin in the afternoons. Ludwig was ruler of the night, known as the Moon King, who rode out into the mountains after midnight, tearing through the silver Alps, returning for a large meal in early hours of the morning, when he fed on quail and roasts, suckling pig and partridges, always drinking sweet wine, always ending the meal with cakes and a hot dessert. His teeth were rotting, he was growing fat, but he needed sweets almost as he needed the strains of Wagner. He needed pleasures, heroism, love and death, as other men need daily work to balance them. His rich fare gave him the energy to construct his dreams, to bring former ages back into being, to turn night into day.

Sissi returned from her visit reassured of friendship. He knew the intimacy between herself and Ludwig was secured forever, though constructed of the costliest, most delicate threads. Each understood the other's voluptuousness of soul within the body's chastity. Each lived for beautiful words, in a country of the imagination, where their brilliance created pageantry and they were artists of their own lives.

In the Hofburg, the Empress Elisabeth welcomed a delegation from Hungary with Ida at her side. Elisabeth wore Hungarian national dress and spoke to her visitors in their own language, with what seemed complete understanding of their problems and demands. Julius Andrássy looked at her with such open admiration that she felt herself blush. He was handsome and glamorous. He'd exiled himself to Paris after the revolution, and was hung in effigy at home by the Austrians. "Le beau pendu," as he was known by the fairest blooms of French culture, had found time enough, it was rumored, for numerous affairs, though none for illusions. He was now reinstated in Hungary, his estates and his rank as count again in his possession. He watched the Empress in fascination for her beauty and compassion, seeing her already as his queen.

*   *   *

"There he is! Move over, you—a chair for Our Author!"

"Good day, Honorable," said Hans, extending Leo's paper to him with a slight bow.

"How goes it?" asked Sacher-Masoch, placing an arm lightly over the man's shoulders. He liked Hans' open, reassuring face and his atrocious Styrian German.

"Come, Leo," called Franz. "Over here."

He accepted the chair, smiling at his friends. "All hard at work, I see. A quarter red, please, Hans." He put the paper aside. "What news, my heroes?"

"My apricot dumplings were overcooked," mourned Franz, whose place of work was too far from his brother Friedl's house to take dinner there.

"Time for a wife," said Joseph.

"They don't know how to cook any more, I've heard," said Karl.

"Then it's back to mother, Franzi."

147

"Oh, God," he lamented, thinking of Frau Zimmermann's lavish and overly filling feasts.

"Or change restaurants," suggested Leo.

"You see, you see," said Franz excitedly, pointing at Leo. "A genius, an absolute thinker!"

"Philosopher," agreed Karl, grinning.

"Full of imagination," put in Friedl.

"You will all be soaking wet in a moment, if you don't stop this quacking," said the author.

"But the fact is, my dear friends, I *can't* change restaurants," said Franz sadly. "I've gone there for so many years, I'm their only reliable customer. Mathilde would cut me up for stew if I deserted her."

"Ah," exclaimed Joseph. "There's always a woman behind it."

"Apropos woman," began Karl.

"Who's the lucky Lady of the Day?" finished Franz.

"I'm glad you asked. My friends and heroes, the Lady of today is a wild, lascivious brunette . . ."

"Ah," said Friedl happily, drawing on his pipe and settling as comfortably as he could into his chair. The others, too, looked happy and expectant. You couldn't be bored when Leo was around, the crazy Slav who always looked as though he'd just come from tumbling or sleeping in the streets.

"She's a tigress, and she hunts men. Let's call her Lola. She was born on the steppes one winter's night when the howl of the wind drowned the cries of the wolf. Foxes barked. The largest raven of the plain woke for a startled instant and flapped its great wings three times. These portents were noticed by the villagers, who lit candles and prayed, believing the infant girl was born under the Evil Eye.

"As it happens, their fears were justified. Within the seemingly gentle Lola ran a deep, dark streak of cruelty. She loved torture, even as a baby. At the age of two, she pulled wings off flies and then crushed their bodies. At three, she did the same with butterflies, and by the time she was four, she'd become an expert huntress of tiny birds, catching them with a net and then strangling them with her little fingers.

"As she grew older, she sought larger prey. She murdered cats and rabbits, then goats and sheep, cutting them up slowly, wrenching out one limb at a time, gouging out the eyes with her own hands. She committed her foul deeds at a distance from the village. The corpses were so horrible that no one suspected a human hand at all.

"By the time her first ripeness was evident in her breasts, Lola had become bored with her hunting. She looked for greater challenge. At the same time, she kept a modest and kindly demeanor, having understood the necessity of deceit from the time she was in the cradle."

"Terrible creature," muttered Friedl.

"Don't worry," said Karl ironically, patting his arm. "It's only a story."

"Then how did it get into Leo's mind? It must exist."

Leo nodded. "Of course. In Galicia and Little Russia still survive a number of sects that worship a strange and bloody God. To accomplish His will, these fanatics kill and mutilate, then offer their God a heart or a limb. Sometimes He demands abominable suffering, until death."

"Why should such things be, even now?" asked Joseph.

"The members of these sects—they are forbidden by law, of course—are simple people who feel the existence of Evil so passionately that they can think of nothing else. In their zeal to destroy Evil (and seeing themselves as carrying out God's will), they can conceive of Goodness only in sacrifice and suffering. Such people have existed elsewhere, in the Americas, for instance—"

"Aztecs?" offered Karl.

Leo shrugged. "Whatever they're called, and wherever they exist, such people take literally the admonition to give one's heart to God. In Galicia, they hide their bloody work in fear of the authorities, but they persevere and think of themselves not as evildoers but as avengers, who will return man to innocence through terrible suffering."

"Gruesome," said Joseph. "Who are their victims?"

"Chiefly young people, young men especially, whose joy of life and enthusiasm are regarded by the sectists as arrogance and contempt. To their ears, laughter is the sound of defiance. Life is sorrow, a period of suffering to be relieved only by the grace of death. The leaders of these sects are usually women. The demon priestess offers the blood and screams of her victims to the all-powerful, vengeful God she serves."

"And Lola?" asked Franz. "Did she become one of these?"

Leo nodded, not yet sure how the story would develop. He finished his wine, allowing himself the interval before the new quarter liter was brought to reflect upon his heroine. A name could echo and reverberate in the imagination until it produced a character. So Leo's inspiration worked, from a word at the beginning. "Give me a name," he might have said, "and I'll show you the woman!" His audience waited attentively. He felt his power—a storyteller could pull the world by the tale. No wonder his was the oldest profession; humans needed stories to acquaint them with their own reality.

"I won't bore you with details of Lola's initiation—"

"It's not boring," began Friedl, but Leo knew that certain narratives—those grounded in actual facts—had to be worked out on paper or they would provide inconsistencies. He overruled the interruption with a wave of his hand.

"Enough to say that by the time Lola was in her sixteenth year, in the first blossom of her womanhood, she had been duly initiated and accepted as a soul-snatcher. Her cleverness allowed her to catch men on the hooks of her words, and her victims, taken in by her beauty and seeming sweetness, never struggled until it was too late. She invited them to meet her in the privacy of a grove or arbor at midnight, some distance from the village.

"Then the handsome young man, the lovesick fool, would keep his appointment, and in dark secrecy, or in sight of the moon, he was gagged, bound and chained, and led to the priestess. She was always veiled, her voice deeply disguised. She would tell him of his sins, call him the lowest worm that ever crawled on the belly of the earth and order him to repent, to ask for death, his only salvation.

"If he seemed to dispute her, he was lightly stabbed about the heart and head; wounds that couldn't kill but brought his own blood dripping into his eyes.

"Her voice was deep as a man's and cold as death. Hardly ever did she find a victim abject enough to be permitted to live, and if such a one was found, she was inevitably a woman. Then that victim was initiated and became a follower of the priestess. The men who showed humility were always discovered to be hypocrites, their pretended enlightenment rising from cowardice, their pleas for death only a ruse to protect their miserable lives. Then she ordered the tortures intensified—fear of death was the most repugnant of all traits—and her assistants hacked off parts of the victim's body while she told him of death's boon. His entrails would be placed in his own hands—"

"Enough," begged Joseph. "No more details."

"Ah," said Leo, raising his eyebrows at Friedl, who meekly accepted the implied chastisement.

"Well, then. In time Lola became the priestess. Now, the people in her village and those in all the surrounding countryside lived in fear. Young men who drank and talked merrily in the tavern walked out the door before midnight and were never seen again. Their disappearance was frightening enough; but when gristly human remains were found outside the village, mothers began to watch over their grown sons as though they were babies and fiancées kept vigil all night beside the sleeping forms of their beloveds. The fear was great —of bandits, the Evil Eye, and soul-snatchers. The tavern closed its doors early, and men carried pistols or knives when they ventured forth.

"It came to pass, during this time of fear, that a group of hunters were caught in a storm and lost their way. When night came, they took cover, to be roused at midnight by muffled screams, reminding them of a pig in slaughter, and then a low, cold voice. With the stealth they used in stalking deer, they crept further along in the bushes. Each from a different angle heard and witnessed the vicious mutilations and murder. When it was over, and the torturers had gone away, the hunters remained in place, petrified by what they'd seen.

"In the first light of day they found their way into the village and presented themselves at the police station with their grisly story. They described the executioners, all except the leader, who had been completely veiled and wore a long mantle of fur.

"Before the sun warmed the rooftops, all the soul-snatchers save one had been apprehended. And she, the proud priestess, who desired only to shed her own blood and die for the glory of her God, was told in a vision that she must continue her sad martyrdom of life for His sake.

"So Lola accepted the next man who proposed to her, a certain nobleman of Styria whom you are all acquainted with. He had come to her village during a hunting trip and fell in love with the beautiful young woman at first sight. She accompanied him to our gentle city, where she bides her time in silks and ermine, waiting to be called again."

"Wonderful!" said Franz when he finished. "And where did you meet her?"

"Do you think I would tell you?"

"She's his tigress," explained Karl, "and he's keeping her claws to himself. She's always scratching at you, isn't she, Leo?"

"Who?" He had a moment's confusion, thinking Karl meant Anna.

"This one or another. Lola or Judith or Salome, or whatever you call her—the Queen Bee who kills the male after mating."

Friedl said, "But Leo's such a good-natured fellow! These are only stories from Galicia."

Joseph Meyringer, who had recently turned from acting to directing without giving up the former, was developing his natural ability to see the whole play, viewing each character as itself and also as a function of the entire work of art. "Lola has two sides," he pointed out. "She's lovely and gentle and 'admired by all,' while at the same time being a gruesome murderess."

"Yes," said Leo excitedly, giving his friend a look of affectionate gratitude. "If you'd meet her, gentlemen, you'd think her the most charming, witty, completely *civilized* woman in Graz."

"So," said Karl, who enjoyed contrasts whenever they

contained paradox, "she expresses the most atavistic urges of cruel Nature under the cloak of our proud Austrian Culture." In his studies, he had sought out antinomies of law, collecting all laws that contradicted themselves, discovering in the body of law so many conflicting rules that he formulated Eggendorf's Theory: "Man is a contradiction unto himself, reflected by his laws. Within every 'Thou Shalt Not' lies another prohibition that invalidates the first. In transgressing against his own transgressions, man expresses the priorities of his nature. When society breaks its own laws, it is asserting itself against history . . ." and so forth, summed up in the phrase, "Every law gives rise to its own prohibition." His "Theory" was not taken seriously by professors, but fellow students bowed reverentially (and ironically) to Eggendorf the Antinomian, enjoying (and often believing) that law was basically self-contradictory and therefore could be individually interpreted.

Leo smiled. "Yes. Our Culture, our European Civilization, with its wit, pride in literature, developed philosophies, scientific progress—ah, progress!—intricate architecture, our finely structured modern minds—all this deprives us of instinct."

"Emotions?" asked Joseph.

"And fear of God."

"But 'civilization' is something we have invented, dear Sacher, to placate God," Karl pointed out.

"Why should we do that?" asked Friedl, feeling he was missing something.

"Because God is a stranger, who yet has a mysterious power over the events of Europe. An *éminence grise* behind our affairs of state and otherwise."

Friedl looked at Karl in bewilderment. Leo, enjoying his witty friend but not wishing to give pain to the Zimmermeister, tried to clarify. "I see it as Nature, a female force. We try to subdue her, in our towns and cities, but we ignore her and avoid intimacy. We plant flowers and tend to our gardens, we make Sunday excursions with alpenstocks, and tell ourselves we've come close to Nature. But she's too powerful. Her gentleness masks her cruelty."

"Men belong to nature," said Friedl simply.

"Precisely. And we are cruel. When I was growing up in Galicia, the well-educated, 'cultured,' 'refined' gentry treated peasants worse than animals. There have been new laws since then, but man's nature remains the same. Those who are in power now in Hungary were condemned to death not many years ago. Their comrades died, many through brutal torture committed in the name of His Imperial Majesty. And what of Königgrätz? Forty thousand men in a single day—how does that show our 'progress' or 'civilization'?" Leo was becoming extremely agitated.

Joseph said, "Nature is also the mother, who feeds us and cures our ills."

"Life is pleasurable," said Franz and, hoping to sound more "scientific," added, "sometimes."

Joseph agreed. "Life is pain and pleasure—"

"But we mustn't try to avoid pain!" Leo broke in. "We must accept it, embrace it, if we want to understand life."

"We hate and love," said Karl. " 'Odi et amo'; we destroy and create."

"Schopenhauer," said Leo automatically.

Karl nodded. "Naturally. 'Sexual love is compatible with extreme hatred for its object.' "

Leo grunted his assent, and Friedl cleared his throat meaningfully. The others turned to him, and he fidgeted in embarrassment at their attention. "My friends," he began, regretting now that he interrupted the scholars at their work, "In all due humility, and though I'm sure your finer points escape me . . ." He paused and took a strengthening draft of fruity wine. The others waited. "It's all nonsense," he blurted out.

"How so?" asked Leo, delighted.

His brother Franz was encouraging him with his eyes. Friedl decided he was among friends. "You say life is this, life is that. It's one thing and then again the opposite. But life is just life. A table's a table. There are many different kinds of tables, yes, but they all have legs and they all have tops. Every life may be different from the others, but it's life just the same. This one has a little more happiness in it, the other more suffering. Nothing to do about that. If the grape harvest is bad one year, we drink sour wine. Next year will be better.

"And this love and hate—nonsense! You either love a woman or not. With all your great thoughts, you're still bachelors and have to get your meals in restaurants. Marika makes dumplings that bring tears to the eyes. How could I hate my Marika? When you bachelors find a good woman, like mine, you'll see your philosophies fly out the window."

They were all in high spirits when he ended. Leo embraced him. "When are you inviting the bachelors for a meal?" he teased.

"You can all come home with me now. Nothing much, I'm sure, but there's the remainder of a wonderful plum cake Marika made for dinner, and she would be very happy to welcome you."

"Done," said Joseph. They called Hans over, paid him, and left the coffeehouse, walking arm in arm like students.

*　　*　　*

Marika was still flushed with pleasure after her guests left. When Friedl had arrived with the four men—her beloved Leo!—she'd laughed her welcome and rushed away to put on her pretty blue blouse and the flounced skirt. Quickly, she gave her hair fifty strokes and pinned it up. Corals around her neck—and she flew back to them before they'd drained their first glass.

Marika loved company and bloomed through it like crocus in spring rain. She fed the men and they laughed with her, flirted, told her she was pretty as the Empress. Karl had danced with her, grasping her waist more tightly than was proper, and then Friedl claimed her and spun her so quickly that the room was still turning when she sat down.

Now they were gone, the plates and glasses cleared, the children sleeping in their beds. Her rosy face, pale gleaming hair, and the soft blue of her blouse were the incarnation of loveliness to him. And she smiled so warmly that Friedl wanted to fall on his knees in thankfulness. He loved to see her happy; when her face glowed like this, and her eyes sparkled, he felt himself the most fortunate man on earth. Her happiness was rare as a four-leaf now, and so wonderful that

155

for a few moments he could say nothing, only gaze at her with thanks and lightness in his heart. She rose and lifted him from reverie. Her skirt was wide and soft as a cloud. "You are the Queen of Heaven," he told her.

She shook her head prettily and protested. "That's going too far."

In answer, he sang:

> "I remember the ladies,
> Marika the best,
> Under her petticoats,
> A warm little nest."

"Go away!" She slapped him playfully. He caught her wrist, whirled her around and pulled her down to his lap. "You're still the best," he vowed, kissing her on her little mouth and pinching her nipples.

She broke loose, stood over him with hands on hips and asked flirtatiously, "How would you know, you bumpkin?"

"Bumpkin, am I? We'll soon see. I have something to show you." He rose and led her to the bench by the stove. He went to close the door, in case the children woke, and returned, loosening the string at his waist, letting the trousers fall.

Marika laughed. "It's not well brought up," she said. "Look how it points."

"On the contrary," he answered, pulling up his wife's skirts, "it is brought up very well—by you."

A few minutes later, her heart light as the down of their featherbed, Marika was lying beside her Friedl, feeling life had given her more than it ever promised, in this good man, the warm house, friends and children.

The following day, Leo traveled to Vienna with a pretty woman. She was a young actress, similar to the others, lovely and pleasant, who could excite him only through her narcissism, the mildest form of imperiousness. They were both free on Saturday and Sunday; Leo had proposed the journey and she accepted eagerly. For him, change was always stimulating. The motion of a train rocked the mind to passivity and there, inevitably, a scene or story took root. He had a theory that the cradling movement of train, boat or carriage restored fantasy—the earliest form of experience—and permitted the imagination preeminence over intellect.

His lady friend had no theories but loved to travel. Her pleasure came from a changing backdrop, before which even her old wardrobe appeared as fresh costumes, and the audience was quite new.

They dropped their bags at a small hotel and took a fiacre to the Prater. The evening was warm, and as they strolled a light breeze played with her pale yellow skirt, wafting it to and fro to set off the tiny waist bandaged tightly in chiffon. She was proud of her dress, an actual Paris design, copied faithfully by the "chic-est" dressmaker in Graz with fabrics from Vienna. Unhappily, she saw that Leo made his usual impression, as though his clothes were wearing him and wearing themselves out.

He smiled when, passing two young officers in brilliant uniforms, she slightly widened the distance between herself and him. "So you're ashamed of me, Kitten?"

Immediately she took his arm, frightened by his sensitivity and remembering that he was an important author. Leo sighed at his own weakness; these pussycats were all the same, no danger in them, no true elegance. Yet in the past two years, since Anna—as in the years before her—he'd found no woman to engage his soul. But one needed a woman from time to time. If there was no tigress, a kitten would have to do. This lovely child was faceless; it was difficult to remember which name was hers. He was true to Anna in his heart. Magnificent Anna, mistress of his soul, who had disappeared completely (Switzerland had been only a stop, and then he'd lost her) but still inspired him, the image no other woman could dim. Shortly after the identity of the "count" had been made known, Baron von Kottowitz and his household moved away from Graz. He left no address behind. The little girl would surely look like her mother one day. Perhaps she would read his book, *The Divorced Woman*. He wondered if she would admire it.

Kitten sighed, and he suggested they rest awhile, have

coffee at one of the tables and watch the Prater's activities. Old men sat in the corner at cards. Children accompanied by governesses spun their hoops down the path and were told to stop. Young ladies ignored them and turned melting eyes to their cavaliers, who looked straight ahead, erect and proud in military dress. Without doubt, thought Leo, they outshone everyone, with their gold buttons, tight tunics and long slim trouser legs. He'd always loved soldiers, dressing them in paper uniforms he cut out of books. They were different now; he once could tell each regiment of the Austrian army by its clothes.

A young cavalry officer, large medals pinned over his heart (Königgrätz? too young for Solférino) was bowing to a lady at the neighboring table. Leo liked her face—a handsome Jewess, with the typical strength of Jewish women. His Kitten looked very soft. Slavs and gypsies, too, like the Jews, showed character in their faces. The persecuted, the oppressed—these were the folk who understood life through suffering. Her husband and even the little boy had faces that set them apart from other Viennese. Jews revealed an understanding all their own; they had sucked at life's breasts and been given no milk. They'd made bread from stone.

The little Jewish boy had run off and now was returning to his parents' table with old Otto, a familiar figure in the Prater. He composed verses on request, for a fee determined by the number of lines (never less than two, naturally, since they had to rhyme), always on the subject of the customer himself. Leo directed her attention to him. "That's Otto, Kitten. When he was a young man he dreamed of being a poet. He wrote feverishly through the night, ready to starve for his art. He composed odes and paeans to his beloved and then never dared send them to her. She was too magnificent, he felt, and he an unworthy poet. So he married Bertha from next door, who had her health and carried his child, and he supported them by working on the railroad. Now here he is." Leo made up the story as he went along, feeling that it must be true in essence. The Jewish father gave him a few coins and told him the child's name. "Hush," said Leo to Kitten, whose high, sweet noises now irritated him. "I want to hear."

Old Otto stood beside the table, holding himself like a soldier. He cleared his throat and began declaiming:

"Here among the linden trees
In the lovely Prater,
Sits a little Viennese
With *Mutti* and with *Vater*.

"Mark my words, he'll make his mark
As he grows wise and wiser.
Little Sigmund Freud will be—
Minister of the Kaiser!"

The pretty Jewish woman clapped her hands, and her little Siggy twitched on his chair with pleasure. "The first stanza is free," said Otto, bowing. "My small gift."

Ah, the poor were noble! Leo saw with pleasure that Otto was invited by the family to a *schnaps*. The boy regarded him in admiration. Perhaps Otto's prediction would come true. Would the boy then remember the old man? Irina predicted great things, and some have already come to pass. "A magician"—perhaps, who could conjure the future?

She was making the same sweet sounds. Night was coming on. She would stroke her own long-limbed body until the warmth flowed through his. In the fiacre she mewed against him. Each would take what was there, to avoid being alone.

But next morning he felt dismay. Strange hair on the pillow emphasized the parody of intimacy. He dressed quickly and left despite her protests. He breakfasted alone, then strolled on the newly opened Ringstrasse where the Opera House was being erected, nearly completed. Anna naked on her furs—was she fated to be the only one to possess him?

He gave silver to a beggar, who stared at the gentleman suspiciously. Leo felt worn out, as though life was already behind him, as though at thirty he already had begun to live in imitation of himself. His university lectures were repetitions; so were the women. His historical writings had ended with *Kaunitz*, written six years earlier, and his novellas were easy, without enough weight. It seemed he had already passed his moment of destiny unaware, and it had been no brilliant flame, but a small candle lit to an ideal. Now he lived on reflections.

He entered a building opposite the outer gate of the Hofburg, where the Emperor, troubled about his brother in Mexico, had already been working four hours (two of them on Maximilian's behalf), surrounded by paintings and statues of his absent wife. Leo walked up the majestic marble staircase under the painted cupola, past pearl-gray columns to the special exhibition of paintings in the Hapsburg collection. Many were Renaissance, his favorite period. Each Madonna revealed a woman who'd lain in the painter's arms, self-absorbed after love, unwittingly posed for a portrait of beatitude. Behind her, a tiny landscape, precise as in dreams.

In a small room, Correggio's "Jupiter and Juno" made him gasp. Juno, heavy in her naked flesh, her large body arched back, buttocks tensed, head thrown to one side, her feet and hands rigid. Jupiter, a great blue-gray cloud, penetrates her. She cups the air as though it had form, gives herself to him, it, with ecstasy. Yes, he thought, there it is—the great act performed through the hands of a master. The goddess in her abandon filled herself with mastering Jupiter, clutching the air, frozen in her lust. The painting brought him greater excitement than he'd felt beside the naked Kitten. His condition was so acute he was embarrassed by it and walked quickly into the next room.

He waited on a bench until his voluptuous response to the Correggio eased and he was able to take in other paintings. He walked past walls hung with Rubenses almost without glancing at them. Not Rubens, not now. Though he admired the artist, his lush women were too rich and soft, nearly obscene. Leo's sensuality needed more sober paintings, simpler lines, less romanticism. Only art could meet his despondency, draw him up into genius where he could confront the Ideal.

In a bright room of Titians, he found her: "Woman in Furs," a young, full-bodied woman with dark eyes and auburn hair, braided on her head and roped with pearls. From her ears hung delicate pearl pendants, and a string of pearls lay loosely at the base of her neck. She half wore, half carried a deep purple velvet coat lined and trimmed with sable, her left arm drawn through the short gold-embroidered sleeve and lying across her waist. Her right hand held up the coat, and her right side was bare, the pale pink nipple of her breast outlined against her strong upper arm. She looked out at him with archness, with defiance, her cupid's-bow mouth lightly puckered, the slightest suggestion of a *moue*. When he first looked at her she seemed surprised, as though she had thought herself alone. But when he matched her gaze the fine scorn showed itself, the conviction that all who gazed on her beauty were inferior to it.

She was the one, though captured nearly three hundred years earlier. She was here to guide him, to mock and scorn him and despise his efforts because he would never be able to possess her, could never even touch her. He stood before the portrait for so long that they exchanged natures. The image took on life and he became only a reflection of reality.

He left the building with his mood radically changed. The "Woman in Furs" had shown him a path. She'd beckoned him, and he would follow until his arms and words could embrace her.

*   *   *

Franz Joseph was worried about his brother. Maximilian, greatly loved by the Austrians for his kindness, liberal sympathies and the respect he showed toward social aspirations of nationalities, had signed a waiver renouncing his claim to succession and, against his brother's wishes, accepted Napoleon III's offer of the Mexican empire. He and his wife Charlotte went misty-eyed to the golden land of Cortez, taking the family eagle to meet Quetzalcoatl. He was in sympathy with the New World, fascinated by the romance of the Americas, and, in the same spirit that would make the English Queen Empress of India, Maximilian entered this lush garden bearing the fruit of civilization, that it would ripen into progress—the only palliative against suffering and poverty.

But to the Mexicans, the Imperial Eagle signified only imperialism. Mexico had been created at the spot where their eagle swooped down on the serpent and crushed it. Now they would have to rout the European snake in the grass, and though Emperor Max could not be disliked personally, he was an emissary of France, a speaker of German, a threat to Juarez.

Maximilian's wife, Charlotte, was free of political sympathies. She wanted to be an empress—who wouldn't?—be crowned, wear sumptuous dresses, live in splendor and be admired for the kindness she would then bestow on her subjects. Charlotte was a delicate, fine-featured woman, nearly a beauty, with sloping shoulders, long fingers, pale skin. She and her husband made an impressive couple, her dark hair set off by his blondness, her sculpted chin contrasting with his thick beard. She was elegant and sensitive as a racehorse, and took fright just as easily.

Rumors were enough. They led her to fears, visions and, finally, obsession. She was convinced of Napoleon's duplicity; she knew he had sent them as sacrificial lambs. She begged her brother-in-law for help, but he answered that Mexico was, and always had been, out of his domain.

Her nights became frazzled, her days disintegrated like worn-out silk. She couldn't eat or sleep; she started at every sound and shied from her duties. She prayed but received no answer, and the candles she lit showed nothing beyond their flickering. Her husband was busy, her ladies correct. There was no one to turn to except Rome.

She journeyed there, and the Pope was happy to see her again, though he immediately recognized her pallor as a sign of starvation. He listened, sadly, to her words, skittering like leaves in an autumn wind, bright words (her eyes brilliant with hunger), words that flew up, scattered, fell and were carried into the air again. Despite his compassion, he couldn't make out what she was saying, though he acknowledged her hysteria.

He called her "my child," this terrified Empress, and assured her he would do all he could, but now she must eat. Cakes and wine were brought before her, but she would have none. Setting an example, His Holiness took a small tart and munched it slowly. Her eyes devoured him, fastened greedily on his mouth, but she refused all nourishment and brought up again her words of terror: killing and murder, hanging, shooting. The Pope resolved to send a message to Franz Joseph, asking that she be put under a doctor's care.

It was time for His Holiness to say evening Mass, and the audience was over. But when the secretary approached Her Majesty, she saw in him the Executioner, let out a shrill scream and threw herself at the Pope's feet.

A bed was prepared for her in the library and she was carried to it, the first woman in history officially to spend the night in the heart of the Vatican. A bowl of fruit was placed beside her. She stared at it, the orange orb, thick shiny dimpled skin holding fresh juice inside. She couldn't take her eyes away, couldn't shut them, and then she snatched it, pulled at it with her long fingers, tore the skin with her nails and ate the whole fruit, skin, membrane, flesh and pits, cannibalizing it in delirious hunger.

Next day Franz Joseph had her taken to a family villa, still and contemplative, where she could rest. Her husband didn't join her. He was led out from his study by Juarez, walking behind the Mexican like a captured lion, with his big blond beard. As a soldier and a Hapsburg, he asked not to be blindfolded. His last request was to be shot through the heart at close range, that no one see a Hapsburg writhe in agony.

The soldiers were so awed by the majestic prince that they fired too soon, not in unison, and a bullet smashed into Maximilian's face, tearing it apart but leaving the man alive. "For love of Mary!" shouted Juarez, grabbing the closest gun and shooting straight into the heart.

* * *

Charlotte von Sacher-Masoch died in the same manner as her daughter, Rosa, drifting in and out of visions until they locked her permanently, and, believing herself to be a small yellow bird, she twitched the wings of her shoulder blades and was carried off to death in the strong arms of her husband. She left behind two sons, no grandchildren and the memory of her gentleness.

9

SACHER-MASOCH's letter stated he was resigning his *Dozentur* because he felt he no longer represented "the aims and outlook" of the university. The faculty was happy to accept his resignation, though a few cynics pointed out that he would have been asked to leave within a few days in any case. His teaching was not considered to conform to Graz' high academic level.

It had been a stone around his neck for some time now, which he carried only for the sake of the distinguished title. It had dragged him down, however, through tedium and academic infighting. It required him to serve a History that contained no rustling skirts or flails at harvesttime, and it meant that shortsighted professors looked down their long noses at his books. Now he was free to devote himself to his talents and temperaments with no distracting obligations. He'd become his own man—through the image of a woman —and would follow his star wherever it led.

* * *

In the Royal Palace of Buda, above the dark silk of the Danube, she was being dressed for the Coronation. Over the lace underclothes, over the dozen petticoats, her dress was lowered, a white-and-silver silk brocade embroidered with jewels, trimmed with lace. The velvet bodice was studded with pearls and gems, laced with ropes of small pearls from which hung large pearl tears, seeming to spill from her bosom. Her neck and shoulders were bare except for a collar of diamonds. The designer Worth, in Paris, had created the gown for Her Majesty, retaining the lines of traditional Hungarian dress. On the rich hair of the Empress' head rested a crown of diamonds, delicate as ice crystals, trailing a veil of lace like marbled window frost. When her husband entered her apartment at dawn in his gleaming white uniform, he forgot himself. Dropping all reserve, he took her in his arms, despite her attendants. She shied away from him by instinct and then, as though ashamed, moved forward and touched his hand lightly before he left the room.

A few minutes later Andrássy, the imminent new Prime Minister, came to see if all was ready. He, who thought he knew himself to the core, discovered that the core was a false bottom and, gazing on Elisabeth, he fell through. She blushed and shivered in the embrace of his eyes, feeling for the first time an emotion as contradictory as the meeting of two rivers in a seam of waves. Neither could speak, until Ida Ferenczy broke the spell. "This day," she said, "is an emotional one for us all."

They thanked her, these two that she adored, with their smiles. "I hope I don't cry," said Sissi.

"The tears of an empress," Andrássy told her, "turn to pearls." She expressed surprise. He smiled. "I thought even Bavarian princesses learned that."

"Oh, my good friend," she said merrily, "give me your hand. Today our efforts will be crowned." The three joined hands. Ida embraced her mistress first, then Andrássy, and each of them returned her embrace doubly in the way that a woman, gazing at her lover, will bend and tenderly kiss the child on her lap.

"Are you happy, Erzebet?" he asked softly, for her ears only.

"So happy I could die, Gyula," she answered. "I used to think freedom was a small white bird that had escaped me, leaving only the cage. But today the bars are invisible, and the bird is singing." She said it softly, her fingers lightly barring her lips, and she nearly wept, for the fragility of this moment when her own words seemed to flutter like a halo around her. Elisabeth was of that strain of people for whom truth and beauty lie in words, these words then mirrored by the external world. He kissed her small white hand and took his leave, to join her again in the cathedral.

At seven in the morning, the procession left the palace while the bells rang from every steeple and priests gave their sermons of joy and union. In the countryside, villagers were already dressed in their feast-day clothes, the festive breads were taken from ovens, and even the most recalcitrant peasant boy had been bathed from head to toe. This day would be the happiest in memory, when Austria married Hungary and the Austrian Emperor became the Hungarian King.

In the city, each house flew two flags, arrays of blue and white flowers honored the Empress, and, long before they caught sight of the procession, the people were shouting *"El jen!"* ("Long live!"). Representatives from all over the world had gathered here today, and reporters would telegraph back the news in wasteful, irresistible adjectives. *"La spectacle la plus éblouissante de notre siècle,"* *Le Figaro* would declare, and Fleet Street would echo, "Most glittering spectacle of our time." The American ambassador would telegraph Washington that he "never saw anything like it— even jewels on the horses worth millions. Their Majesties greatly loved."

Six hundred men, clothed in the native dress of fifty-two regions, were outriders. On a snow-white horse, in his brilliant white uniform, the Emperor looked every inch a king. Behind him rode Austrian history, horsemen dressed in costumes of the middle ages.

In the Matyas cathedral of Buda, they were anointed— he on the forehead, she, as prescribed since ancient times, under her right armpit. The sacred mantle of Saint Stephen, which Elisabeth had darned with her own hands, was placed on his shoulders. Andrássy held the crown over her a moment, then placed it on the head of Franz Joseph. (Observers said later that Elisabeth seemed greatly moved and was crying.)

They stepped out on the square as the crowd launched its cheer. Cannons saluted; gold and silver coins were scattered among the populace. Then the King took to horse and rode across the Danube to Coronation Mount in Pest, where he would take his oath. On the "mount" lay soil gathered from each Hungarian province. Franz Joseph drew out the sword of Saint Stephen from its opulent scabbard and pointed east, south, west, north, swearing to protect the frontiers of Hungary from danger in any direction.

He was King, Elisabeth Queen, of Hungary. Old Austria was dead, long live the new Austria-Hungary, the Dual Monarchy of two free and equal partners. The four-hundred-year-old saying of Matyas was being reenacted, as Happy Austria married once again:

Bella gerant alii! Tu, felix Austria, nube;
Nam quae Mars aliis, dat tibi regna Venus.
(Let others make war; Thou, happy Austria, marry;
For those realms which others receive from Mars are given to
    you by Venus.)

Then the *Eljens* burst upon the air: *"Eljen Erzebet!" "Eljen Ferenc Josef!" "Eljen Andrássy!" "Eljen!" "Eljen!"*

He stood behind her and saw that she trembled with emotion. He whispered, "My Queen." She wanted to let go, fall back against him, but she held herself straight and proud to prevent the crowd from noticing the shudder that ran through her. She was ruler of her beloved country and of its leader, whose eyes were black as a gypsy's and whose voice reminded her of when she danced barefoot.

Her new subjects asked her to bear a child for them, in the name of Hungary, to inherit the throne. She didn't return to Vienna, but remained at Gödöllö, her castle in the country, where she rode furiously, played with her dogs and children and entertained special visitors. The year after her coronation, a child was born for Hungary, black-eyed Marie -Valerie, no heir, just another small daughter, who became her mother's favorite, a child of love.

*   *   *

"Nature is neither good nor bad, neither altruistic nor egotistic, and it operates through the human psyche as it does through crystals and plants and animals, with the same inexorable laws." So Leo wrote, in his old dressing gown, in his old rooms near the university. It was time to stop now, dress and go out in the still middle of the day, the *Mittagspause,* when shops were shuttered and the town took a breath while its inhabitants dined and later napped.

He was rewriting, a task not necessarily easier than the original act but more controlled. The phrases were set down already but had to be reshaped, reorganized. Many had to be omitted, despite their intrinsic beauty or justice, because they were out of place, had wandered into the wrong book, and, no matter how charming or true, the brilliant words, masterful speeches, had to be exiled to wastebasket or buried under a thick black line of ink. Often, the fault was extravagance, since the first draft had been dictated in the heat of passion, like the still-beating heart of a victim on the Aztec altar. Now, in cool aftermath, art could plane the unnecessary peaks and quiet the jagged signs of vitality that disrupted formal order. This would be his best work, he knew, possibly a masterpiece, generated in the same way as *The Divorced Woman*, though with even greater dedication, allowing art to subsume life and letting the writer Sacher-Masoch direct himself as actor while he jotted his notes. At times, of course, the actor had improvised and lost his script, but now in second draft the experience could be viewed as a whole, contained within philosophy and aesthetics, actuality informing art as, during the adventure itself, art directed life.

The last lines before dinner ended a speech of Severin, the novel's hero. Severin's visitor, struck by the beauty of the woman in furs in a painting over the sofa, asks his host who she is. Severin replies by telling his friend (the author himself?) his extraordinary adventures with her. He speaks of "Wanda" and the time when he lived as her servant in Italy; his confessions, down to names and objects, will duplicate the experience of Leopold von Sacher-Masoch and Fanny Pistor (née Koch). The novel will take its title from the portrait, *Venus in Furs*, executed in the style of Titian.

The contract was drawn on the eighth of December. Fanny, henceforth known as "Wanda, Baroness von Dunajew," is granted total power over her slave Leopold, henceforth known as "Gregor." Gregor must serve his mistress in any and every way she requires; he hereby signs himself over to her for a period of six months. She has absolute and total control, the only stipulations being that she not require her slave to do anything dishonorable to himself as citizen and gentleman, and that she leave him a minimum of three hours daily for his own uninterrupted work. With these exceptions, he is hers completely, a slave who begs his mistress to show cruelty.

They traveled to Florence by rail, she riding in first class, he and the baggage in third. At the hotel, a salmon villa sitting on a meadow of camellias beside the ochre Arno, she took a suite of charming rooms, all heated, for herself, and a miserly, cold attic room in the servants' quarters for Gregor. A bell connected his mistress' suite to this tiny space, and she rang for her servant mercilessly, marvelously, her whims calling him from sleep and food. He brought her whatever meals she desired, bottles of champagne, and delicacies of exotic fruit, intricate pastries, chocolate creams, nougats and mints for her delectation. He carried in the tray, placed it down, bowed and backed out of her room to leave her in privacy. After serving her, he went to take his own meal, kindly supplied by servants of the hotel, and invariably, as he took his seat, her bell tinkled and he was forced to leave his plate untouched. In the middle of the night, she summoned him to stoke the fire in the fireplace, roll her a cigarette, place a shawl around her shoulders or comb her hair. The Italian servants referred to her as "La Donna Malvagia" and commiserated with Gregor, whose contentment in servitude convinced them he was an imbecile. Wanda sent him on errands for special bonbons and tropical flowers. He was famished, exhausted and very happy. This adventure was costing all his savings, plus additional money he'd borrowed from his father under false pretenses, but Gregor/Leopold/Severin felt only the exaltation of those who stand in grace. Calvary was priceless.

He served her and she whipped him for each mistake or clumsiness. She was strong and the whips were heavy. They'd bought them together, telling the Florentine whipmaker they needed the largest and most cruel ones he could devise for use on the lady's vicious mastiff.

She did it for him, and through her own adventurousness, her egotism, cruelty, and her desire to play the role of baroness. He dressed her in forest-green velvet lined with sable; in blood-red silk lined with ermine, trimmed with the tails. He'd had the *kazabaikas* made for her, with wide Grecian sleeves, a fastening at the waist, holding it small above the rich folds that parted and fell to the floor.

She was monstrously beautiful, his goddess, his Wanda. She stood in her *kazabaika,* whip in hand, and made him kneel. She kicked him and placed her foot on his neck. When she treated him this way and he lay under her heel like the most miserable untutored peasant, his excitement became almost uncontrollable. But he always controlled it, to be ready to serve her as soon as she commanded.

She demanded this service often. After the punishment, the beating and vile words, she raised him up into her arms, kissed his face and tears, his shoulders, chest, his whole trembling body. She moaned in her lust like a she-wolf seeking her lost brood, and when he entered her, she was magnificent, a bursting seed-pod, a shudder of the earth.

She had come to him through a statue of Venus. Severin, the young nobleman and dilettante of the arts, enters an arbor at midnight and is hypnotized by the pale gleaming marble in the light of the moon. This Venus is more than a goddess; she is the incarnation of Woman, to be doubly worshiped. He falls to his knees before her. Next night he comes again and finds a sable draped over her cold marble flesh. Now he realizes she is naked. He reaches out for her and hears distant laughter. He faints and is revived again in his room, where a beautiful woman sits shivering in her sable fur. She tells him he has brought her to the world of men through his love, but men are cold, she says, particularly in the north. They don't understand love. It is only possible to love something greater than oneself; but men wallow in sensuality and have a "dog-like nature," unworthy of ideals. He protests and says that to him sex is sacred, the only sacred thing. Woman in her beauty is the personification of Nature and man is her priest, her slave. Woman's beauty is divine and Woman's task—the continuation of the species—contains the meaning of the universe. She laughs, calls him a "sensualist" and disappears.

But she returns, his Venus, his Wanda, and offers to teach him love as no man has ever learned it. Later, she cries, "You will corrupt me, slave!" and tells him she feels like "a large cat—a dangerous one."

She reclined on an ottoman of red damask, in a room lined with red damask. Above her on the ceiling was painted the scene of Delilah shearing the hair of Samson. "After she betrayed him," he wrote in his attic room, "he gave himself to her another time, to be betrayed again." He kept a pelt beside him when he wrote. Others used a human skull as *memento mori;* to him, fur represented the world's savagery, of which death was only a part.

She reclined, her auburn hair streaming loose and her *kazabaika* parted to reveal the soft flesh of her thighs and the fur between them. "I stand mute and stare at her," he wrote, "and again I am gripped by indescribable nostalgia, and I long to escape." He knelt, kissed her foot, ankle, calves, and was stopped by her hand shoving him away roughly.

Severin's nostalgia is partly explained by the author through his hero's memory of an event in childhood:

> When I was about ten, a distant aunt, Countess Sable, came to visit us. She was a majestically beautiful woman with a charming laugh, but I hated her because she imposed herself on the family like a tyrant. I behaved as badly and sulkily as I could with her.
>
> One day when my parents were out, my aunt decided to use their absence to teach me a lesson. In her *kazabaika,* she entered my room, followed by the cook, kitchenmaid and chambermaid, a lovely kitten of a girl whose advances I'd rejected. Without saying anything, they grabbed me and bound me hand and foot. Regally, but with evil laughter, my aunt raised her arm and proceeded to strike me with a large whip. She whipped me until the blood flowed and I screamed and begged for mercy. Then she lowered her arm, had me untied and made me go down on my knees before her, to kiss her hand and thank her for the punishment.
>
> Under the whip of this proud and beautiful woman, who seemed an empress, there awoke in me for the first time a desire for Woman.

Gregor begs his mistress to betray him; she answers with a look of scorn. That evening, peering through her jeweled lorgnette from her box at the theater, she finds her Greek god in Salvani, a wonderfully handsome actor. They have only to look at each other, this Venus and this Mars, for their eyes to acknowledge the passion they would perform. She in *kazabaika* and he, in white silk blouse and trousers, shared a knowledge more important than any other: that they were beautiful. Gregor watches them with agitation, daring to hope they would soon play the scene that would annihilate him.

The actor called on Wanda next day, and Gregor trembled so in taking his clothes that he allowed one milk-white glove to fall. "Clumsy oaf!" shouted Salvani, and boxed his ears. He strode to the bedchamber as though into his own lair. A few minutes later Wanda called for champagne and her servant brought it on a silver tray to the fierce, proud pair reclining on the bed, their clothes loosened, their eyes feasting on each other.

While he poured, they grew bold. She opened her mouth, and her tongue slowly circled her lips, leaving them wet and parted. He stroked her cleavage, bared her breasts, cupped them, pinched the nipples. She moaned, he grunted softly.

Gregor was trembling violently and spilled champagne. Now they noticed him. "Idiot!" called his mistress. "Come here."

He shuffled toward her, holding the tray in both hands. "Set that down, you stupid cow. You deserve a whipping for your clumsiness." Then, in a sweet tone, she added, "Don't you? Don't you deserve to be punished for your clumsiness?"

He nodded meekly.

"Answer me. Tell me you need the punishment. Go on your knees and beg me to punish you." He did as he was told, and the Greek's eyes sparkled with amusement while he caressed Wanda's hip.

"Get the whip! Bring it here!"

When Gregor placed the whip in her hand, she gave it to Salvani. He rose slowly, stretching his powerful limbs like a lion after his nap. He raised his arm and brought the whip whistling down over Gregor's shoulders and chest. The pain was horrible, and it joined with shame into a sense of such humiliation Gregor longed for death. She urged the Greek to

172

beat faster, and they both laughed as he brought down the whip again and again. Then abruptly he threw it aside and sprang into bed beside her. The two fell on each other with dry lips and burning faces, clawing into their debauch.

She had done as he desired, fulfilling every hope of the contract, which stipulated she must deliver her servant to her lover. His skin lacerated, his bones aching, Gregor stood in reverence as the majestic creatures tore at each other, mating with loud cries, copulating like great hungry cats. After roaring climax came silence. Then the lioness crouched and began to lave the body of her mate with her tongue. When she finished, she dressed him slowly, taking infinite care, covering his beauty with garments to shield it from unworthy eyes. Finally, when he was clothed and sitting on the bed, she knelt naked at his feet to help him into his boots. Gregor closed his eyes and a wave of pity rose, cleansing his shame.

He'd been half mad with jealousy during the act, but in the servant's quarters, pen held suspended over paper, he realized she would never play the game through to its end. She would torment him again, in her voluptuous passions, in her magnificent selfishness, her beauty, her warm flesh, but —he foresaw—would never betray him completely because her vanity urged her to retain the furs and the title of baroness, at least until the contract expired.

She still jingled for him in the night and sent him on errands to satisfy her whims. She performed with her Greek and later gave herself to him, Gregor, who inhaled the smell of the other man's body rising from her skin. She brought him to a mindless, overpowering sexuality that she could never appease, that grew even while they were making love and abated only for a moment, only physically, after the act was consummated. He longed for her even while taking her, and in his quiet hours at work he knew that by placing himself in the fires of his own perversity, he would be expiated at the end, purified through sex into compassionate love for all men, and formal order.

In the third week, he was returning to their villa with two large bags of groceries in his arms, containing also the pomegranates and scented bath oils his mistress had ordered.

He caught sight of a familiar face, an old acquaintance from student days, and tried to hide behind the bags. But the young duke, former law student, recognized him, and now was crossing over. "Hey, Sacher!" he called out cheerfully. "What's happened to the state of literature? Not supporting you too well, I see; turned you into delivery boy. Never mind, come along with me, we'll—"

But Leo ran off, dropping the pomegranates in the street, giving no sign of recognition. He ran to the villa, up the stairs to his little room, threw off his wretched clothes, put on others equally wretched (he'd taken nothing decent along— why hadn't he thought of all possibilities?), left an envelope containing all his money except what he needed for the journey home and fled to the railroad station. His honor must not be touched; his shame must be kept secret. A woman could torture him to death, but he would not tolerate being made a fool of.

"Woman," says Severin, "has no character." He is ending his narrative. After Wanda has beaten and betrayed him, she meets a German artist. He paints her in her *kazabaika* and is consumed by the painting. This is his masterpiece, but it uses him up; he paints as though with his own blood. He loves her, it; and the love first tortures, then destroys him. When he finishes, he lays down his brushes forever. Severin points to the canvas above his visitor. He'd bought it from the German. His tale is ended; he is cured. The terrible episode is closed, the pale Venus still gleams in the arbor, the painting hangs in the sitting room, and the story has been told. The hero is wiser now, having confronted his own nature and willingly undergone the torment of his obsession. He asked for the punishment he was given and now has returned to a contemplative life with no woman in it except the young housekeeper, whom he treats roughly and who is devoted to him.

When the book was published, Leopold von Sacher-Masoch was considered a "poet." The nostalgia and decadence in his strange love story shocked no one who reviewed the novel. An Austria that considered Hans Makart, with his nudes in delirious orgy, as its greatest painter could hardly object to *Venus in Furs.* The Viennese were civilized and cultivated as black orchids. They waltzed to Strauss, swayed to Brahms and Liszt, were sirened by Wagner's Rhine maidens and praised the intricately wrought silver prose of Sacher-Masoch, seeing in it glimpses of Byron and Turgenev. A few critics, commenting on the aridness of German literature over the past decades, hailed Sacher-Masoch as "heir to Goethe." In the parable of Wanda and Severin, readers could discover man's yearning for beauty through the complicated web of sexuality that held him from birth. Echoes of Schopenhauer, theories brought to life in this modern story, where passions proceeded from the frieze of art (the ideal) and eventually returned to it. In the coffeehouses of Vienna, the novel was summed up: *"Ars longa, vita brevis."*

*　　*　　*

. The Empress was interested in matters of the spirit, particularly when they took form. Special reports on the Trojan excavation were prepared for Her Majesty. Though she'd not yet begun her intensive (some would say "obsessive") study of Greek that would lead her, in the company of a hunchbacked scholar, on a pilgrimage to every spot described by Homer and eventually to constructing her own Achilleion in Corfu, the Empress Elisabeth was far more concerned with Schliemann's discoveries of Troy than with the events or outcome of the Franco-Prussian War. The ancient city, residing so long in the world's imagination, was now being dug up and exposed to light. Under that city lay another, and under that a third, and yet still another, like generations of buried madness or the spirals of one's own self, widening through the years to show more of the hidden and unknown nature.

. The Empress shared her fascination for the Trojan discoveries with her cousin Ludwig, in letters rapturous as wingbeats. He, who was building two castles, at Neuschwanstein and Linderhof, with Byzantine motifs gauding their Wagnerian splendor, wrote that this was an age for great dreams to become manifest. He planned a moorish kiosk at Linderhof, with a giant peacock throne of lapis lazuli. He also ordered the building of a grotto of Venus, a cave held closed

175

by a large rock at the entrance, rolled away by means of a secret button. The guest, the wakened dreamer, would board a white swan boat and be carried through a tunnel of shimmering stalactites to a still lake. The ripples of the lake would be artificial waves generated by the cranking of machines below, and on one side of the cave would be painted a giant scene from *Tannhauser,* to be illuminated by a display of changing lights, ending with a rainbow and an aria of light. Sissi would love it, he wrote, for she herself was the woman who actualized the goddess in her own lovely form.

Sissi was enchanted by his letters. He was the one who remained her intimate friend, the only man who understood her and shared her dreams. Gyula was exciting, and she'd lost her heart to him for a while, but he was becoming just as tedious as the others, with his concerns of state and his criticism of her for neglecting her "duties." But the duty of a mother was far more important, she knew, and she adored her Mutzerl, little Marie-Valerie. Let public men attend to public matters. Their prosaic natures were at home with war and politics. Poets of life fulfilled their destinies in the construction of dreams to feed the hungering fantasies of generations now and to come. Each Troy rose up under a later Troy, to reveal what Homer sang, and still was singing.

10

IN BRUCK AN DER MUR, a town north of Graz where Karl had taken refuge from an "embarrassment" with the mayor's niece, the first mail arrived so disturbingly early that Karl arranged to pick up his letters himself at the post office. In any case, he enjoyed having daily tasks to perform. Life in Bruck was pleasant but dull, more suited to couples or families than a single man. The village was charming, founded a thousand years earlier in a cup of the Alps where the river Mürz flowed westward, emptying into the Mur. But it was too small, the girls were all chaperoned, widows were not gay, and the only evening activity offered by the town was a game of billiards in the Kornmesser coffeehouse. With its clear air, two rivers, and ring of mountains, Bruck was perfect for convalescents. Karl needed some recuperation from a life made nearly sleepless in the acrobatics of juggling four women at once, but after a few days in the village he became restless. He took long walks and ate pastries in the afternoon; he sketched landscapes, read, wrote a few short, witty essays applying literary standards to written law, another essay on the Prussian character—but nothing held him for long. He corresponded with his friends in expansive, speculative letters, and composed billets doux for his sweethearts, transcribed in triplicate and sent to all except the niece.

To Leo he wrote that he searched for a theme, something to occupy his energies, a fulcrum for his thoughts. Leo, who came up to visit Karl twice in the first three weeks, saying, "If you've run away from home, you need your friends with you," had brought along the novellas he was working on. Karl read and made comments, earning Leo's praise for his understanding. A week after Leo's last visit, Karl received a letter which pleased him by its trust more than by its very dubious offer of a theme:

> My Dear Karl,
> As my cycle of novellas on sexual love nears completion, I realize that its title—*Song of Songs*—is inadequate. While trying to devise a new, more revealing title, I came upon the idea of doing something other than I'd first planned. You remember, we talked of it: this cycle was to be followed by another, on "property." But I feel now I should embark on something larger, a whole series of cycles that represent—within the limitations of a novelist—the entire existence of man. Yes. I'll explain. The idea inspires and terrifies me. Please don't mention this to anyone at all. I'm superstitious, you see, and mistrustful, though not of you, my dearest friend, or why would I confide in you?"

Karl smiled as the words brought Leo to him directly. His epistolary style was totally natural, as though spoken instead of written. The critics who praised him for "complete lack of affection" in his prose should read his letters. Karl ordered a coffee and slice of Linzer torte, smiling at the buxom girl whose large brother watched her like a sheepdog. A sweet thing, she was, but too young for discretion. He returned to Leo:

> I want to lay out my plan to you in detail because, even if I work well, at maximum capacity, I'll need at least three or four years to complete the work. My health has always been delicate, and I must therefore remain aware that I may not live to finish my labors. If time and strength are not given me, then my planned work becomes a legacy for you.
> The completed cycles will bear the title *Legacy of Cain.* Six entire cycles will be comprised under that heading, each a collection of stories, novels and novellas. The six will be Love (essentially sexual love, the cycle I have now almost finished), Property, the State, War, Work, Death.
> Central to all the cycles is the idea that humanity will never find happiness until moral laws—true morality—govern state and society. (When that happens, our so-called "great

178

princes," "great generals" and "great statesmen" will end on the gallows or in prison in place of today's "common criminals.") As the world spins now, it is imperfect and evil; existence is a form of repentance, a painful test, a sad pilgrimage, and everything that lives on this globe lives off death, off the plundering of others. But enough; there is a healing light ahead. I return to my outline.

The State: misery and mismanagement as functions of absolute monarchy; the lie of constitutionalism; the healthiness of democracy; the United States of Europe; world government.

War: fear of war; recruitment; the wretchedness of permanent armies; fire, pillage, rape, famine, stealing of corpses. Obligatory military service for everyone prepares disarmament.

Work: a voluntary tribute to existence; protects man, brings happiness. The rich man seeks to work as little as possible. Society removes the indolent and parasites, provides just division of labor for all.

As epilog, a novella enclosing the entire cycle: "Holy Night." Birth of Christ, not Jesus-Christ-son-of-God, but Jesus Christ the Man on the Cross, who remains the eternal symbol of deliverance through renunciation of egotism; love of men; Christ the man, with no sexual love, no property, no country, no quarrel, no work, who dies voluntarily. He personifies the idea of humanity and carries the message: Take up the cross of mankind.

The above is a crude outline, with Love and Property omitted because we discussed their broad themes already. A crowd of ideas, stories, forms buzz around me and I will soon seize them, to develop my plan. Then I'll work on the *Legacy of Cain* and undertake nothing else until I've completed it.

Will I be granted the ability to develop the great thoughts that haunt and inspire me? That question is at the forefront, and worries me into creating.

Take what you can from this, speak of it to no one, and always remember you are very dear to the heart of your faithful

LSM

Karl smiled sadly, disapproving of the envy he now felt toward his friend's enthusiasm. To have a theme, however impossible, gave impetus to the day and a seeming integrity to

179

one's life. The envy persisted, and, to his own dismay, Karl discovered he was telling himself that Leo wouldn't undertake the task, at least not yet. His friend needed a taskmaster, or rather taskmistress, and ever since his bizarre secret affair in Italy and then his astonishing, wonderful novel, Leo had contented himself with abstinence or banality in regard to women. The little girl he had now would never put his soul in danger, and only from that precarious position could he write.

Leo, however, basked in his spring love, convinced he had exorcised himself and could now enjoy the pleasures common to other men. Like Severin, he believed it was necessary only to churn the waters of oneself, bring the hidden darkness to light, to be then granted ease, the calm surface. No one had learned of the adventure itself, in a foreign country. What he had enacted served for cure and creation. The story of love-cruelty-betrayal could be seen as a parable with roots in the historic mind of man (Samson-Delilah, Judith-Holofernes, Salome-John, Adam-Eve) and in individual memory (a mother betrays her child with her husband). By structuring his life formally, to accommodate art, Leo had loosened the devils within himself and placated them. He had offended no one and abided by society's unspoken exhortation to do nothing that would disquiet its members. While he was still mildly astounded by the discovery of his own bizarre eroticism, Leo was proud that he had exposed himself completely—honestly —without bringing any dishonor on himself or his friends. He was his own doctor, who had prescribed art and brought about a miraculous relief from the disturbing symptoms. The cure had a life of its own, as *Venus in Furs*. He amused himself with the thought that the novel was a homeopathic remedy.

Like baptism in icy water, this event needed no repetition for efficacity. Leo had returned from Italy, revised the book and immediately started the next. His cycle on Love was completed, and he strolled along the Herrengasse arm in arm with pretty Jenny Frauenthal, a distant cousin, an actress and his fiancée. She was sixteen, fresh as new grass, dew still bathing her large, serious eyes as she turned them on him and questioned him about the universe. He had followed his demon and now, with Jenny, he could walk through the woods and smell the moss. They overturned old rocks and found new life squirming underneath. He brought her bluebells and heather. It seemed that his darling Rosa was reincarnated in this charming girl.

His friends teased him with the nickname Romeo. He was delighted and called his Jenny "Juliet." She kissed him chastely, seriously and yet lovingly, wove garlands of flowers, plucked daisies with concentration and sang in the morning like a small finch. She honored him, believed him and never questioned his advice or decisions. They played together and he showed her the games of his childhood. He was blithe as a peasant boy with his sweetheart, brought her small gifts and flushed with pleasure at the joy they gave her. He could picture rosy-cheeked children, plump cherubs hanging on the skirts of their little Madonna-mother.

His companions were disappointed. "You've become boring," said Joseph. "A contented bourgeois."

"No more Lady of the Day," mourned Friedl.

"A fine lot you are," teased Leo. "Other men have friends who desert them in adversity. Mine can't bear to see me happy."

When Karl crawled into Graz one day, to escape what he called the "screaming silence" of Bruck, he challenged Leo's claim to happiness. "You're treading water, keeping afloat among the lilies of the lake. A charming child, yes, but your mind is becoming flabby."

"Perhaps," said Joseph, dispensing strange hope, "she's not Juliet after all, but Gretchen."

"Then," said Karl significantly, "we are about to enter the Second Part."

"With all the demons?"

Karl nodded, and despite the bantering tone, Leo felt a premonition. He shooed it away. "I'm no Goethe, I'm still young, I can make my way alone."

"See?" said Friedl to the others. "He still has it, still the old word magician."

Karl turned stiffly and, drawing in his upper lip, announced, "Sacher, you have a call to duty. Except for you,

German literature is in a deplorable state—stiff as a virgin, no getting into it."

"I'm Austrian," said Leo modestly.

"God knows what you are. A Slav for sure, but also a Jew, a German, Bohemian, Magyar. . . ."

"*L'empire, c'est moi?*"

"Why not? It takes a man born in Lemberg of a Ruthenian mother and an Austrian police director, who spends his puberty in Prague and then comes to Graz, who reads seven languages and speaks at least five fluently, to call himself an Austrian and to understand our life in the Monarchy."

"More," Leo said softly.

"More what?"

"I read more than seven languages."

"Braggart."

"Show-off," echoed Franz, thinking that crazy Leo could always restore them to good humor.

"Besides," said the polyglot, "even our dear Empress speaks five languages."

"And has nothing to say in any of them," declared Joseph.

"Hush," whispered Karl dramatically, glancing at Hans, who was bringing their order of five mochas, "we may be overheard."

"Ich spreak fiftzeen lingwiches, Dgerman das best," commented Hans and received a round of applause.

"The difficulty," Karl resumed, "is conveying the richness of our 'multilingual' German."

"Dialects?"

Karl nodded. "On paper they look like disguises."

"A false mustache," offered Joseph. "Though they're no trouble at all when spoken."

"I know." Karl winked at him. One method of remembering which one he was with during his period of multiple liaisons had been to adopt different manners of speaking. In the dark, he vowed his love in elegant phrases and knew it was Lisa; or he blurted his passion crudely and knew it fell on the ears of Brigitte. Such tricks relieved him from the boredom of repetition. He might call on one of them later this evening —but no, it was safer to take the train back.

Leo admitted the problem, saying that, though formal German was universally understood, it almost inevitably rang false. "On the other hand, a dialect, or many dialects, might turn the reader away. If I write, "Night draws nigh,' it's understood in Berlin as well as in Innsbruck, but the phrase is gray and lifeless. Yet if I write, 'It's gettin' late,' the salon ladies of Munich will put down the book for fear of soiling their gloves—or ears."

"Nestroy does it," said Joseph. "He throws all dialects into the one great stew of his play, and the audience finds it wonderfully tasty."

"Because it's comic," said Karl. "Think of Shakespeare's clowns. But what if it's not comedy, and your characters are Tyrolean or Bohemian or Moravian? How can they talk on your pages as they do in life? And a Viennese—my God! Just think of the absurdity of having a Viennese as tragic hero, with his incomprehensible slang and the words all coming out through his nose!"

"But literature is only an approximation," said Leo, "nothing more. Art isn't life and life isn't art."

"Are you sure, Sacher?"

Leo avoided his eyes. "Each is a symbol for the other; everything is metaphor."

"Art?"

"Is the emblem. Metaphor is life, always changing. Then art takes up the metaphor, condenses it, removes the fashion and shows us the form."

"Are you saying," asked Joseph, "that we never perceive directly, that we never go beyond the metaphor?"

"There is no beyond," Leo stated categorically. "Metaphor is life."

"And life metaphor?"

"Certainly."

"But that's rubbish!" exclaimed Friedl. "When I make a cabinet, I make a cabinet, not a metaphor."

"Of course," Leo said kindly. "But what kind of cabinet are you making? How does it appear in your eyes and in the customer's? How will it look in a few years? Is it simply a cabinet, or Friedl's cabinet? Is it a construction of wood, a receptacle for objects, a piece of furniture? Or perhaps it's a work of art, and its form and patterns are more important than its purpose. And how will it be regarded through time? Will it be used by people in the future, will they discard it as a thing of no importance, or will it stand in a museum?"

"Interesting questions," said Friedl, shaking his head, "but they confuse me. I build a thing for use, when someone comes and orders it from me. Then I sell it, to get the money we need to live."

"No, Friedl," said his brother. "You don't value yourself highly enough. You're an artist—everyone knows you're the best cabinetmaker in Graz."

Leo smiled. "Do you see now, Friedl?"

"You mean," he asked slowly, "are you trying to say that there's nothing absolute, even in my cabinets? That every person looks at something in a different way?"

"Yes," Karl said, enjoying Leo's explanation of his own creative process and his manner of historical interpretation, "and the same person can see it differently at different times. If he's actually using it, the object will mean something other than when he's simply looking at it in your shop, or calculating how he will try to haggle down the price."

"That means," Friedl continued, "that even if something is there, it's always changing. When Leo said 'metaphor' he meant a thing is itself and it also stands for something else." He felt a sense of accomplishment, as though, after extreme concentration, he'd been able to jimmy a locked door.

Karl and Leo signaled each other to stop. When they would return to this topic later, they would tug from opposite ends. Karl had gone over to Leo's side now only to help hoist up Friedl. The two Zimmermanns would be bored or, worse, embarrassed, by a continuation of the discussion, and their warm geniality was as tempting as the petticoats of philosophy. Joseph's position was something like mediator; he seemed an engineer of ideas, showing respect for them as materials only so long as they were useful.

Karl nudged Leo. "Walking through the door now is no metaphor, though perhaps a mirage." Leo turned and saw Jenny, her rosy face framed by her pale blue bonnet. He made his apologies quickly and went to her, kissed her lightly and escorted her out. Though at other times he sat with her in a coffeehouse, plucking her sweet interest, it would not be proper for so young a girl to join a company of men.

The glove-maker, hurrying along with her packages of white kid to deliver to imperial officers, stopped dead when she saw them. She recognized the lean man with the shuffling gait, that pinched face and sorrowing eyes. He was the famous author Sacher-Masoch, the Police Director's son, who used to pass their house on Merangasse when she was a little girl. She felt nostalgia, as though she'd once known him well, but naturally she hadn't, she'd only thought about him, made up stories around him, invented him. He'd belonged to her, once, on the second floor of the sand-colored house where they lived when her father was still with them. Up the marble steps with the wrought-iron balustrade, smelling everyone's dinner when she came home from the cloister school. The sculpted lions' heads on the façade once used to frighten her. She could open the pea-green shutters and look out on the street. In back of the house was a small garden, adjoining the elegant garden park of the yolk-colored ducal villa. She'd dreamed about the duke and thought of marrying him or, if he had one, his son. She wanted her own house, not the corner of a room, and yet the corner had seemed palatial when she'd been given a bed of her own, at last, and no longer slept in the drawer that opened out from her mother's bed. In that drawer she had nightmares, terrible haunting images that plagued her during the day. She'd lie quietly, hearing her mother's sobs and her father's sad reassurance as he told her they had only to light a fire in the oven and close all the doors and windows. She was three, perhaps, crooned to sleep by the soft words and sighs of her parents planning their deaths.

She invented stories to amuse herself, forming her characters out of actual men and women in Graz. At the cloister, the sisters accused her of daydreaming, but they couldn't stop her, and even as a grown woman she continued fashioning her tales, often with herself as heroine, married to someone titled or famous and wearing beautiful clothes from Vienna. Because she used her imaginative abilities in the service of her own aspirations, she was convinced she had literary talent. One day the world would hear of Aurora Angelika Rümelin, and her name would be spoken with reverence by counts and artists in coffeehouses. This in itself became a theme for stories or scenes: herself as famous writer. What she would write was never specified. As a girl, she'd planned to become a saint. Now, at twenty-six, with only the arms of poverty around her when she woke each morning, Aurora's dreams, though changed, were still bright enough to lead her.

Leo passed with Jenny, feeling the firm warmth of the girl's body beside him. He was explaining to her that the world's imperfections had their source in greed, and she was listening to him with such gentle seriousness, her head bent forward, that he wanted to take her in his arms, forget his sermon and speak only of the goodness in her clear eyes. He didn't notice the woman in black who gaped at him and his fiancée. Aurora gave the girl a hard look, taking in her youth, her clothes and the way Sacher-Masoch held her arm. She'd been given everything and was probably just a silly goose, who could never comprehend the man beside her.

Now if that woman were herself—why, then, they would share immediate understanding through their literary inclinations. Aurora had read some of his work, in books given or loaned to her by a neighbor. An avid reader of love stories, anything from mawkish to heroic, she found his work "inspiring." As Sacher-Masoch and the girl turned out of view, Aurora's main desire was to return home quickly, to be able to tell her neighbor that she had seen the author.

She walked with quick, nervous steps, stopping to deposit packages of gloves with the officers' servants. She left the inner city by Paul's Gate and headed north, to the dingy industrial outskirts where she lived with her mother. It was a long and fatiguing walk, four kilometers from the gate, and, once she was out of the City Park, the houses became dirty and uncared-for, the streets were not swept and the smells of rotting garbage and frying grease sickened her. She hated Graz, the long filthy trek that hurt her feet and destroyed her shoes. To ride home would be nonsense, of course, since she would be wasting the wages—so difficult to collect from officers!—that they needed for food. But in a carriage, it wouldn't be so bad; at least one could avoid the smells. The air was heavy with smoke, and soot always settled over her clothes and hair like a gray veil.

She hurried back and stopped first at her neighbor's door, to give her the news. Frau Frischauer, who had a widow's pension as well as a wage-earning son, was materially well off compared to Aurora and her mother. Frau Frischauer's son worked at the theater, was a friend of the Herr Director Meyringer and knew Sacher-Masoch personally. He sometimes brought his mother books autographed by the author, and she then lent them to her literary friend, the young Rümelin.

Frau Frischauer had two rooms and too much time. All her life she had schemed, though she always remained on the skirts or outskirts of action, as now she lived in the outskirts of Graz. At forty-one, her face suggested that she'd once been beautiful, though at eighteen she'd had the kind of plainness that promised to ripen into beauty later—and so she'd passed from girlhood to mature womanhood, her appearance drifting from possibility to memory with no true substance in between. She was still pursuing the life that always eluded her. Determined to be a heroine but never finding someone to write her part, she spent her days plotting. In her son, this tendency led him to the theater, but she carried her own stage with her, embellishing in the manner of untalented playwrights who substitute spectacle for form. The great scenes she planned and later described theatrically had never gone beyond shabby services performed by and on her in the dark, in return for a meal at a restaurant, a shawl made of reliable but inexpensive material, a blouse cut too tightly or too loosely and once an adulterous weekend at a spa, using disguised names in a second-rate hotel.

She and Aurora were close friends. The younger woman was handsome, quick-witted, with a flair for scheming ("invention," she called it) and was, like Frau Frischauer, a natural liar. This shared characteristic confirmed both women in the belief that they were creative, particularly in a literary direction, since literature was simply a way of twisting words.

"His shoes were unpolished," Aurora was describing,

"and he had an air of distraction. His hair needed brushing, and the melancholy of his face revealed that his thoughts were on deeper matters than his appearance. When he passed, our eyes met and my heart leapt up. His intense gaze pierced me, and in that instant I could feel our souls meeting. I lowered my eyes and when I raised them he was gone, with the girl in the bonnet."

Frau Frischauer laughed. "It won't last with that one. I've heard she's a real innocent. A man like Sacher-Masoch needs a woman who dominates and makes him suffer. This child is just a plaything of the moment."

"Isn't he engaged to her?"

Frau Frischauer shook her head, wise beyond rumor. "It will never be—mark my words. He needs a woman to put a leash on him and beat him."

Aurora expressed astonishment. Her own knowledge of men was limited to characters in fiction, a few encounters with officers (usually after they'd been drinking) and common soldiers, none of whom deigned to reveal more of themselves than what she could hold in her hand, and an unwavering hatred of her father.

"I understand men," said Frau Frischauer, who, after all, had been married to one and raised another. "I know Sacher-Masoch seeks a cruel mistress."

"But that's impossible," protested Aurora, who believed her friend completely.

"I'll prove it to you," said the widow, her eyes brightening to the new plot, "and we'll have a glorious time."

Next day Frau Frischauer had composed, and Aurora edited, a letter to the author expressing deep admiration for his work, particularly *Venus in Furs*, a book that compelled this correspondent to write, despite her natural reticence, since it "expresses so clearly my own feelings." Sacher-Masoch "captured the soul of Woman, whose nature demands slaves. No other book has so mirrored her essence." (Aurora was unsure about the mirrored essence, but could think of nothing better, and let it stand.) The letter was signed *"Wanda von Dunajew"* in quotation marks—the alias explained as a necessary precaution since the correspondent was a married woman.

Aurora posted the letter and began imagining possibilities. Like other unmarried women, particularly those living with their mothers, she could not meet, hear of or read about any bachelor without immediately postulating herself as his wife. This was true of criminals and men who had met with accidents, as well as of gentlemen and artists. She didn't visualize actually living with them, sharing a bed, meal or conversation; rather, she simply replaced her own last name with whatever his happened to be, placed a "Frau" in front of Aurora, and thought of the gold band gleaming on her finger as she signed the dressmaker's receipt. She was afraid of the male species, which she didn't know, but more afraid of poverty, which she did.

When her father walked out—simply down the stairs and out the door, never to return—there was no one else to care for them, and they had no skills to exploit. They'd sold the furniture, then the clothes (keeping one dress each), and found a miserable hole in the north of Graz where they lived in poor health and took in sewing. On some days there was no work and nothing to eat. At times one or the other was so sick she couldn't leave the bed, too weak even to sit up, and then the stronger went to neighbors, begging soup or bread for recovery. Weakness never left them or the other people who lived here, all of them desperately poor. Crime hardly existed, with neither opportunities nor energy for it. Someone was always at home, guarding the miserable possessions that might be used later in barter for something more necessary. The Rümelins and their neighbors existed listlessly from day to day, making meals out of what would be simply a side dish or garnish in a middle-class dinner, cleaning their rooms and themselves repeatedly and ineffectually, hoping to remove the stains and smells that marked their disgrace.

Enervation prevented crime and sex, and after Frau Rümelin had sold all she possessed, she didn't offer her own or her daughter's body. Sex was unmarketable in a neighborhood composed mainly of abandoned women and children and old people, where work itself was a luxury given only to some, and members of a household took turns going out on the street in their one set of clothes. So, through lack of opportunity and health, Aurora was kept honest.

Now the worst years were over. Mother and daughter had moved to a slightly larger apartment in what to outsiders appeared the same area, though inhabitants knew it as a "prosperous" street. Here some bright flowers showed among the weeds, a few cows and goats grazed, and often sweet breezes from the hills completely masked the pungent latrine. They had enough to eat, with milk as the major staple and sometimes also cheese. Both regained their strength. Since they had lived relatively well before the time of poverty, the lean years left no lasting mark. With strength came reassurance. Though Aurora had never lost faith in the powers of her mind, there were times during the bad years when her mind was almost separate from herself, its messages hallucinatory. She knew she was cleverer than most, and that her strong chin, high breasts and round arms were commendable even by aristocratic standards. She didn't look or sound like a poor woman, she knew, and therefore was confident she wouldn't remain one. Her expectations of the "Wanda" adventure hadn't yet crystallized, though she hoped the letter would serve as catalyst for a solution that would at least bear on her situation.

The following day brought a reply, expressing gratitude for the letter and admiration of its author and her literary skills. He begged for the favor of a response.

The correspondence continued. Sacher-Masoch suggested "Wanda" might be exaggerating her own character. He teased her, writing that "women generally are as weak in evil as they are in good." He admitted he was tantalized by her, however, and added that he had no intention of being seduced by an unknown correspondent; he insisted on a meeting.

Leo told his friends about the strange woman, obviously a disguised aristocrat, a baroness or perhaps a countess, who wrote him letters that sounded like his own creations. He was charmed by her audacity and by the magnificence of her candor. His only doubts lingered on her age and appearance, though her basic self, he said, was exactly "what I would have created, were I God making a woman."

"She sounds interesting," Friedl admitted, "but somewhat hard."

Joseph said nothing and wondered what would happen to Jenny. She was enchanting, really the loveliest girl at the theater, probably in all of Graz. Now that he was getting to know her better, as his leading lady in Sacher-Masoch's *Our Slaves*, Joseph was uncomfortable in Leo's presence. He dared not gaze at Jenny as he wanted to, or talk privately to her, or press her hand. He watched Leo's behavior toward her with a mixture of resentment, hope and jealousy. Leo was not attentive enough, not properly loving—and yet Joseph was glad of this, trying to read in Jenny's eyes an indication that she was losing interest in her fiancé.

For this production, Joseph had resumed an actor's role, since Leo wanted to direct his own play and insisted Joseph was perfect as leading man: "I need a man so handsome all the women in the audience will fall in love with him on sight— and that's you." Joseph regularly received the determined attentions of many women but was afraid of them, not know- ing what to do when the woman led. He felt more at ease with girls, very young and pretty, who were independent of him through their infatuation with their own youth and recently discovered powers, girls who took the admiration of men for granted and didn't waste their time trying to make conquests. Such girls—Jenny was one—were rare as sapphires.

"Tonight after the play," said Leo, "I want you to come for supper with me and Jenny. She's extremely fond of you, you know. She told me she never knew men so handsome could also be so fascinating."

Joseph flushed, an encouraging sign to Leo. Jenny's quiet ways and touching devotion were, unfortunately, beginning to bore him. He loved the girl as a brother or father, as he'd loved Rosa or Marika, and he recognized that his unwilling- ness and inability to make love to her meant they could never marry, never even be lovers. The spell he had entered with her had been wonderful, refreshing, like a bath of innocence, but his own painful looks were brought back to him when- ever he touched her firm, smooth skin, and he appeared to himself so disgusting in their relationship that he could feel not even the slightest eroticism. She was the heroine of his play, Joseph the hero. They were both beautiful, and together they'd be a pair out of a fairy tale.

He watched them at dinner, their eyes avoiding each other, their bodies each aware of the other's presence. Jenny barely touched her veal with mushroom rice, and Joseph left half his chicken on the plate. Leo ate and drank with more appetite than usual. He told them how pleased he was by their performances in his play and said, "I've found that if two are suited to each other in art, they are also suited in life." He had told Jenny that Joseph adored her and, because her sense of virtue would never permit her to respond to another man's attentions, he had been suggesting to her gently, over the past few days, that they should reconsider their engagement. He was twenty years older, he pointed out. He loved her tenderly, he said, but his work was his mistress. She understood his meaning, her eyes thoughtful. Last night she had been sad but now, in the Erzherzog Johann restaurant, her cheeks were pink and her breathing rapid.

After the meal, Leo suggested Joseph take Jenny home. Their eyes thanked him, and he watched them walk across the main square, their faces turned to each other. He felt no jealousy, only regret and a touch of fear, because he understood he would never be happy with goodness. He would return home and write a letter to the mysterious countess. Look at you, he told himself, going right back to your Wandalust. He smiled because, though he was able to disappoint himself, he could also be quite amusing.

He had to meet her, he wrote.

The pair that was Wanda were afraid to refuse absolutely, since he might see it as an act of bad faith and terminate the correspondence that brought adventure to their lives. A solution was found: "she" could both show herself and not be revealed at a masked ball, which Frau Frischauer attended in a large blue domino, heavily veiled, only her eyes, hands and shoes showing from the blue covering. He believed she was a married countess; he bowed over her hand and didn't compromise her with his conversation.

Next day he wrote that he was more fascinated than ever. Frau Frischauer laughed with Aurora. "It passed wonderfully. I didn't mention to you that I'd thought it possible my son would be at the ball. He wasn't, praise the Lord—he's growing very religious these days and probably disapproves of such 'frivolity.' " The mother chuckled at youth's ignorance. "Sacher-Masoch looked properly awed, and now come read this letter. He's practically in my pocket."

But victory was short. Again he insisted on a meeting, one in which he would be able to speak to her. (He meant look at her, for he still was ignorant of the lady's age and facial features, though her figure was majestic.) She answered with reminders of preserving her honor and reputation, but his ardor made him insistent and ingenious.

He felt he must know her at all costs, this woman whom destiny had devised specifically for him. He was obsessed with thoughts of her, he lived for their correspondence and he had no other woman in his life. His friends teased him about the "countess" and accused him of inventing her. He'd shown Joseph the last letter he received. In his new happiness with young Jenny, Joseph was unable to understand the letter, with its cruel and lascivious language. It revolted him, but his love and gratitude for his friend made him hold his tongue, and he merely laid the letter down on Leo's desk, shaking his head and smiling warmly.

Then the correspondence stopped. Leo, whose belief-hungry anticlerical soul made him extremely superstitious, reviewed all events for portents. He should never have shown that letter. He should never have visualized a meeting with her, or allowed himself to think of her calves and ankles.

He was as ignorant of the real cause as of his correspondent's identity. The letter he had shown Joseph remained lying on his desk at the theater while the two went for a walk and later to the coffeehouse. Young Frischauer, looking for Joseph, had entered the room and noticed familiar handwriting on the envelope. Wondering what his mother could be writing to Sacher-Masoch, he allowed himself to transgress and stealthily removed the letter. Then he turned white and a scream froze in his throat.

Hours later, Aurora found her friend incoherent. Eventually, after many ejaculations of horror met by reassurances in Aurora's embraces, Frau Frischauer described what had taken place. Her son had called her a whore, worse than that.

A terrible scene, out of *Hamlet* or the Greeks, and she'd been forced to promise, at the end, that she would terminate the correspondence immediately. Now she worried what Sacher-Masoch would do with the letters. If he never again heard from her, he might think her dead or banished from Austria and would show the letters around. What scandal!

Next day Aurora wrote to Sacher-Masoch for the first time, a formal, businesslike letter stating that she was a friend of his correspondent and that unfortunate circumstances demanded the immediate return of all letters from her in his possession. The letter ended with a diffused threat of "scandal," "higher persons" and "infamy." It was signed *Wanda von Dunajew*, as always, though the handwriting was different. With this act Aurora Angelika Rümelin was to enter a new existence, and her real name would be buried under a fictitious one.

Sacher-Masoch responded like a gentleman, promising to return every one of the letters. This would have to be done in person, of course, and he named a coffeehouse (one he never frequented) where the friend could meet him to receive the package.

She recognized him as she entered, though he looked older than when she'd seen him on the street, the lighting inside the room hollowing his face with shadows. He was much too thin and pale, she thought, and the excessive sensitivity of his aspect suggested that a loud noise could shatter him like a hammer on glass.

He rose for the heavily veiled figure in black who came toward him without hesitating. He played along with her game of "friend" and "circumstance," knowing she was the same woman, Wanda of the letters, who was wearing this shabby dress to disguise her position. He handed her the package first, ordered her a coffee and reached out to lift her veil. She shrank back. He decided to go more slowly. She talked of his books, his ideas, and he wanted to explain himself totally to her, to be known completely by the mysterious Wanda in the short time he feared would be all he could have with her.

"My double ideal of woman is united in her physical

being as heaven and hell are united in the mind. First is the truly good and noble woman, pure and elevated—but she no longer exists. Society corrupts her with its half-truths, false education and the immorality of convention. No matter how wild and generous her soul could have been, every woman is violated by her upbringing into faintheartedness and miserliness of spirit. She confuses goodness with its parody, duty. She loses her meaning in the universe, which is procreation, and denies the intrinsic holiness within sex and in giving birth. Once, a truly good woman could exist, but now she is false, ravished into propriety, ornamented with platitudes."

She forgot his ugliness as soon as his resonant voice began its gentle swells. She couldn't take her eyes from his lips, and she was thrilled by the warm steady flow of his words. He spoke earnestly, from his heart, as though it were important that she receive his phrases. No man had ever spoken to her like this before.

"Wanda—may I call you Wanda? I must—you should know that nothing in creation sickens me more than falseness. No cruelty, no evil, is more disgusting than the distortion of truth, which is a betrayal of reality. And so I come to my second ideal, the truly bad woman who refuses the lies of society and is guided only by her own selfishness. She's cruel but passionate and exists in nature." He looked at her with such seriousness that she was confused. What was he expecting from her? why making this confession? why presenting to her his silver prose? "Wanda, I will admit to you that I'd prefer being completely destroyed by a woman who is a demon than to live with a so-called "virtuous" woman and be killed by boredom while she concentrates on ironing out my spirit until it's as flat as hers."

She nodded, perplexed and excited. A man, a famous author, was presenting her his philosophy as a private gift. She felt both unworthy and powerful. The waiter passed with a tray on which rose a rich, creamy slice of Malakoff cake. She pretended to take no notice. Leo was watching her, waiting for her to speak, his face deathly pale.

"I think I understand," she began slowly, realizing she hadn't tasted a Malakoff cake in ten years, "but my words are inadequate. I am not accustomed to speaking in such a way, forgive me." The waiter stopped at their table to see if everything was in order. Sacher-Masoch asked his guest if she would like anything else, some cake perhaps, but she shook her head, saying she was fine. He understood that the pastries here would be inferior to those she was accustomed to. "I agree with you, though—I myself have felt the corrupting forces of society, seen my passions wasted and my longings unfulfilled." She felt the inspiration pass from him to her; she was speaking like an author. "When I was little, I held glory tight in my fists—until I was forced to open my hands. Yes, you are right. The bad is more valuable than the good if it is true."

He listened in amazement, overwhelmed by this meeting of souls. Her manner of expression was literary; he applied no judgment beyond this, since critical standards couldn't be used in regard to women. He longed to lift the veil. They spoke of her "friend," and now Leo suspected there might indeed be two women. This Wanda seemed younger and slimmer than the other. Was it the dress? When she entered, he'd been so convinced she was the same that he hadn't looked for signs. But this Wanda had softer eyes, less merry, warm brown as a cow's eyes with glints of the cat's. Perhaps the changed handwriting really did indicate another correspondent, not merely a disguise. Whatever, this woman, masquerading in black, was his real Wanda. Under the veil was a nose, cheeks, a pair of lips. Her breasts were high under the simple dress; wisps of hair suggested the rich darkness of sable. He must lift the veil—he dared not offend her—he begged for one glimpse.

The eyes were thoughtful, considering his plea. Slowly, she brought her hands to the hem of the veil and lifted it carefully, like a stage curtain.

"Wanda," he breathed. A faint smile had played on her small lips before she lowered the cloth. He felt the strangeness, the recognition of desire when, after long dearth, the body girds itself for an object, flowing toward the stranger who has opened the locks in oneself. He recognized the condition of his body, though he hadn't felt such physical need for someone since Fanny. His own mind had been feeding his eroticism, but now the woman was before him, as real and mysterious as Titian's painting, exciting his blood through a fever for possession.

She agreed to correspond with this strange man who put a spell on her when he spoke. He assumed she was married and belonged to the highest level of society. It was best so. Frau Frischauer had said that, for Sacher-Masoch, women started with baronesses. He wanted to look up; she would allow herself to be raised to the highest pedestal he could build. An unmarried woman might frighten him through expectations of attachment; Frau Frischauer said he'd been engaged many times, though he was still a bachelor. Men desired what was out of reach; they became quickly bored with what they could have—so she had learned.

Aurora took on the role of Wanda with the natural ease of a great actress, whose talent derives from having a poorly developed sense of self and who can therefore assume new identities as easily and comfortably as other women put on a new fur. Until now, she had written all her own scenarios, but a greater writer than herself offered her an exciting role, and she couldn't refuse.

Next day, she received from him a package of journals and books, accompanied by a long letter. His heart was hers, he wrote; it was their destiny to have met. He had felt an overwhelming sympathy between them. She answered the same day, thanking him for all the reading matter. He then wrote that her manner of expression was so interesting and excellent it was a pity she denied her gifts to the general public. If she would be willing to trust him, he would be honored to read any examples of her prose and ensure their publication.

With her next letter she enclosed an essay, and before the week was out she received ten florins in the mail and a receipt from a Viennese journal. Her mother looked at the money distrustfully; but when the next piece, a longer one, brought thirty florins, Frau Rümelin smiled, regarded her "new" daughter with admiration and told the neighbors that Aurora had always shown great creative promise, even as a small child.

Their correspondence continued without interruption,

and Wanda began to write in earnest. She sent in a few pieces each week, then started work on a novella and refused all further orders for gloves. Her stories were heavily influenced by the work of Sacher-Masoch, love stories written to the popular taste, with a dash of the exotic. Her novella brought three hundred florins. Her writings were accepted because they carried the recommendation of the well-known author, and payment was no problem to publishers in 1872, when coins were stamped and banknotes printed in a steady stream, inflating wallets and rolling quietly to the crash that would tumble the stock market in the following year.

She wrote him gratefully, *My talent never developed until I knew you,* and he answered, *You are my fate, as I am yours.* Through the summer they corresponded, while she wrote stories of sultanas ruling their harems of beautiful young men. In fall, his daily letters stopped suddenly and she learned after a few days that he was ill with pneumonia. On hearing the news (through her neighbor), Aurora/Wanda smoothed her hair and walked rapidly into town. The garden in front of his house sprawled with luxurious color. Scarlet roses spilled petals like fresh blood on white stones; fuchsia trumpets and tight knobs of zinnias crowded the marble fountain. Birdsong, in the fading morning, sounded a chorus as brilliant flashes cut the air between trees, above the nervous butterflies. She handed a note to the porter and waited for an answer. He returned within minutes. She gave him a few coins, unsealed the paper, and read, *This evening, at five o'clock, I shall become the happiest man in creation.*

* * *

To find one's ideal in another person, after the age of first love, is rare. Such discovery requires receptive ground, as grace is rumored to come to those who wait for it, or as a burst of inspiration appears only when hidden rivers of thought have flooded and their pressure breaks the constricting layers. Sacher-Masoch found his Wanda (whom he had invented) in a glove-maker with literary pretensions. King Ludwig of Bavaria found his God in Richard Wagner and built temples to the gospel of his music. Emperor Franz Joseph worshiped Elisabeth, but he was a prosaic man, dutiful (drab?), whose adoration abided in himself like an uncomfortable secret and was expressed only in daily letters to his "beloved angel." She, the Empress, with a capacity for adulation as great as her cousin's, had been able to fasten it on no one but herself, becoming supplicant and priestess in one. She starved herself, for her greater beauty, keeping the shrine perfect so she could throw herself on it. She accepted the Emperor's homage as a self-evident part of existence and showed him kindness at times of personal distress.

When Sophie lay dying, she returned to Vienna, and those who saw the beautiful Empress at the deathbed called her a "ministering angel." Sissi wept and prayed in the sweet spirit of forgiveness; Franz Joseph himself didn't show more signs of grief. His mother's hair had gone white after the death of Maximilian. The murder had unhinged her, melted her iron, stilled her voice of command and transformed "the only man at court" into a bereaved mother. Sophie looked at the lovely girl weeping beside her bed and remembered that she herself had been lovely and fair. The young French duke had soft blond hair, he'd read poems to her and his eyes worshiped her. He'd been a prisoner in the palace, once King of Rome. He was slim, beautiful, melancholy and he died young. After that, the word "love" referred to an act performed quickly and rarely in darkness, to ensure preservation of the seed. Franzi had been a beautiful boy; Max too, in whom some saw a resemblance to the duke. One of them was dead; it didn't matter; she had no more to say, she'd done her duty.

After the funeral for the Empress Mother, Sissi returned to Gödöllö with her darling Mutzerl, to her beloved dogs and horses, who carried her through the day. She was waiting to meet her Ideal with a speed that took the breath away. In Bavaria, her cousin sped through the Alps in a sleigh in moonlight, feeding off night's austerity before the breaking of gaudy day. It was said that the Wittelsbachs had strains of madness, but pedestrian minds consider beauty, extravagance and slavish devotion to an Ideal or to genius as mad.

* * *

They were plotting the next step in the Rümelin apartment. "A child brings a great sense of responsibility to a relationship," said Frau Rümelin significantly. She prided herself on refinement; it was best never to come out with something directly. Suggestions, innuendo, circumlocutions made the point more emphatically than bald statement. Like other women of her upbringing, she'd been taught a picador approach to life, which allowed her to disdain responsibility for possible later violence. She'd brought up her daughter as well as she could, by example and admonition, according to the same time-honored principles she'd learned as a girl. Though her gentility prevented her from comparing men with bulls, she knew one played with them before spectators, that they were dangerous and dumb, and that even the biggest of them could, through flourishes and careful timing, be brought in for the kill.

Wanda looked at her mother blankly, annoyed by the obviousness of her remark. Leo was planning their glorious future. He urged her to divorce her husband, then worried that six thousand florins a year would not be enough for the two of them to live. (Wanda's mother had laughed for a full five minutes on hearing that.) Obviously, her true situation could not be discovered until it was impossible for Leo to extricate himself. But she wasn't a silly girl, she didn't need advice, and she hadn't menstruated for six weeks.

Frau Frischauer laughed. "Marie," she said to Wanda's mother, "you're innocent as a newborn lamb. No one thinks that way any more, at least none of the gifted set. If Sacher-Masoch married every mother of one of his children, he'd go to prison for polygamy." She chuckled at her own wit. "Pregnancy isn't a reason for marriage any more, except perhaps among the peasants, and those men usually have the sense to wait until the child is old enough to see if there's any resemblance. Just a few days ago, I was talking to a friend in the coffeehouse"—she said it in the tone of one who spends her life in coffeehouses—"and asked if he had children. He answered, 'Probably.' " This time the other two women joined in Frau Frischauer's amusement. Then she dropped her voice to a dramatic whisper. "Sacher-Masoch is the same type. The Clairmont's daughter is his—but of course you know that." Wanda didn't, and avoided her eyes.

The Clairmont, one of Leo's former kittens (before *Venus*),

200

had left the stage of Graz for Vienna, where, with a new name (Mademoiselle Clairmont had been merely Fräulein Lichtberg in the provinces), new hair color (a revolutionary henna from Paris) and a new figure (the birth of the *enfant* had added measurably to her *poitrine*), she began a new career as soubrette of the Theater an der Wien and became a household *nom* among the readers of family magazines.

The two older women looked at her sympathetically, remembering when they too were unmarried and the whole laborious performance was still ahead of them. Frau Frischauer had snared her Otto at nineteen through a temperament described as "bubbling," which intoxicated the loyal accountant. She then skillfully wove together a tangle of compliments from admirers and landed her man in a net of jealousy with no escape except marriage. Marie Schubert, the Moravian girl who became Wanda's mother, caught her Wilhelm through sex. A God-fearing man whose idea of outrageous pleasure was listening to a military band, he had followed her exposed white ankle straight to the marriage altar.

Wanda didn't want sympathy. If Leo hadn't told her about The Clairmont and daughter, it must be simply that the affair had slipped his mind, not because he wanted to withhold anything from her. He'd given her a ruby brooch that had belonged to his mother. He'd brought her breakfast in bed. He possessed money, reputation and the promise of a title to inherit. Also, he adored her to such a degree that even the act itself didn't sicken her with him. She remembered proudly how well she fared, taking it like a soldier after the initial phase as general. "He adores me," she told the women. "He throws himself at my feet as though I were a goddess. He tells me I am everything and he is nothing. He would let me tread on him—and he is the great man. I feel humbled by his homage."

Frau Frischauer started to laugh again, but Wanda's look stopped her. She was losing favor with her young friend, who now obviously considered herself too grand for common folk. Maybe the little vixen would manage it, but she'd better hurry; her chin wasn't getting any firmer, nor her breasts either.

"I wear furs when I'm with him," Wanda went on. "He has a collection, and I slip into any one I fancy." She didn't mention that she hadn't the choice of remaining unfurred.

"As a bed jacket?" asked Frau Frischauer maliciously.

Wanda glowered. Two days later, returning from her assignation, Wanda stopped at Frau Frischauer's in a black velvet cloak lined with marten and trimmed with blue fox. She came by merely to say "good evening," but the other woman understood and kept her own counsel afterward.

Leo shuffled in with such haste that he banged his nose opening the door. But nothing could annoy him. He smiled at his clumsiness, put one hand over his bruised snout and triumphantly waved a piece of paper with the other. "My heroes," he called excitedly, continuing his fast shuffle to their table, *"le jour de gloire est arrivé!"*

Friedl had to lean back as the paper flapped before his eyes. Leo spoke so quickly he nearly babbled. *"Voilà!* They are printing one of my stories—'they' being nothing less than the *Revue des Deux Mondes,* simply the most important literary journal in the world, the supreme accolade for French writers, *l'honneur superlative;* and that means, my heroes, that means *après moi le déluge,* or rather, that a following in France means I will conquer the world. You see before you a shabby writer locked in eastern Europe, singing from his open grave. And yet, the wings of fame come fluttering from the west. Today France, tomorrow England, America and who knows? Around the Pacific through China and Persia to Petersburg and home!"

Karl grinned at his boyish enthusiasm. "I'm exhausted already, and quite seasick," he said. "We need champagne. Hans!"

Leo wanted to hug them both in his delight. He was a child at Christmas, so excited he could hardly remain in one place. Other successes had brought him pleasure, of course, but didn't extend his fame beyond the frontiers of the Monarchy. The French honor gave him to the world; all frontiers would melt at his name, and Sacher-Masochian prose would be read in French, English, Spanish—even in the jungles of Brazil.

"To Sacher-Masoch," said Karl, raising his glass, "the Gallic Galician with a nose for success."

"To Leo," said Friedl, "the latest Paris fashion."

"To you, sir," said Hans, who'd been invited to join the celebration, "my congratulations on your achievement."

Leo spilled the entire contents of his glass down the front of his suit. He laughed, dabbed at it with a napkin, and held out his glass for Hans to refill.

"You are wet," observed Friedl.

"Quite right, my dear Zimmermeister, one hundred percent correct."

"You will drown in happiness," remarked Karl with sarcasm. His friend's extravagance embarrassed him a bit.

Leo noticed the faint disapproval in Karl's tone and tried to become more sober. "You too are conquering the world," he reminded him. "Your essay will be published soon, won't it?"

"In part—the part that is completed."

"How far along are you?"

"Enough for the first installment," Karl said casually. The essay frightened him as much as anything could. It was monstrously difficult to write, and he often cursed himself for having undertaken the project. At its inception, all seemed clear, and Leo had encouraged him, discussing the theme with him and making him believe it would be as simple to set down the argument as to talk about it. But fingers were more intractable than the tongue, and everywhere obstacles rose up between the mind and the flunky hand, incompetent to convey its messages. Karl had started the essay when he returned from Bruck, the day after he received a note from Leo informing him that the mayor's niece was betrothed and the wedding imminent. Karl was pleased for the bride, relieved for himself and contemptuous of the groom, a weak creature to be so bamboozled, when the necessary haste was dictated by the consequences of Karl's ardor. He wondered idly how soon after the wedding would come the issue, and how the darling girl had managed to hide her belly. She probably retired into virginal modesty with the nincompoop, for whom only the wedding night would uncover the fact that he'd married not one but two.

Still, it meant he was safe, and Karl returned to Graz with new energy. Joseph had his Jenny, Leo his Wanda, but Karl wanted respite and chose to engage himself more at his desk than in boudoirs. His essay took its theme from the work of the Englishman Charles Darwin, whose second book, *The Descent of Man,* had been recently published, a dozen years after the one that made people turn red or white, called *On the Origin of Species.* Karl was attempting to equate the evolution of social behavior with biological evolution, through arguments demonstrating the phylogenetic history and development of social theory (including law) and manners. His greatest problem was in measurement. Atavisms (the "throwbacks" of Darwin) occurred constantly in the process of history, which had to be regarded as progress. The neat development, the biological chain from caveman to civilization, became difficult to plot through increasing population, the growth of cities and, in recent times, the introduction of machines. Epidemics diverted and even reversed the tide of progress, and at times Karl felt he must abandon his attempts at accuracy in favor of a truth revealed through the generative energy of a society or in the impulse behind an event. He thought of composing his essay as Leo wrote his history—but then it would be characterized as fiction. Perhaps later, when Leo's exaltation faded, they could discuss the problem.

"You know," said Friedl, smiling shyly, "I too have a small accomplishment to report. Very insignificant compared to your great labors, but pleasing none the same. It's this: You remember I told you the mayor ordered a cabinet for his niece as wedding present? He promised to pay twice the usual price if I could finish in time for the wedding. I did, and he has paid me already!"

"Wonderful!" Leo put his arm around Friedl's shoulders. "What will you do with all the money, you millionaire?"

"Oh," he protested, but couldn't stop grinning, "it's not so much. I haven't decided. I wanted to order a beautiful gown for Marika, but"—his happy expression changed into an anxious one—"she says she would rather travel. Is that . . . can she . . . what I mean is, do you think it's proper for a wife to travel alone?"

Leo tried to hide his alarm. "Of course, naturally. Every-thing's proper now. She actually suggested that—going alone, I mean?"

Friedl nodded unhappily. "She is so restless, my Marika. She tells me she feels imprisoned. She says there is a large world outside and she wants to see some of it before she dies. But of course she's not old, she still looks like a girl to me—so slender! Death is far off. And yet . . . and yet . . ."

"The children, who would care for them?"

"Marika thought they could stay with my mother," said Friedl in a soft voice.

Leo felt worried. Few women traveled alone, and they usually left their reputations behind if they did. He took out his watch. Time enough before darling Wanda came to his rooms, her face lighting at his news and later, her cool body granting him entrance. He put a hand on Friedl's arm. "Why don't we go to Marika," he said, "and celebrate with her? All our successes! And she loves champagne."

Friedl switched so quickly from despair to gaiety that Leo felt for a moment it was all a joke. But the "thank you" was said with unusual warmth, and Leo perceived how very worried his friend actually was and how very much he needed reassurance. Karl, who considered Marika virtuous because he had never made love with her, didn't feel the anxiousness of her husband or her "brother"; nevertheless, he understood this was some kind of family matter and said he would stay where he was and perhaps (pulling out a notebook) get some work done.

Marika welcomed him with open arms, but Leo saw her pallor and felt her trembling against him like a captured bird. Wild birds stopped singing when they were put into cages. "Lev," she said, with her old gaiety or in imitation of it, "your own presence is enough festivity for me. Why did you bring the champagne?"

He told her, in more subdued terms than an hour before, and she embraced him. "What wonderful news, my old one. You'll be known all over the world. And you will travel to see your publishers in marvelous places. You will journey to Paris, and then London, and even, maybe, on a large ship over the ocean to America." The place names animated her; she pronounced them with a hungry greed that frightened Leo.

"Not so fast," he said in a light tone. "They're only publishing one of my stories in one journal. They are interested in my prose. No one has given me even a kreutzer to see my face."

"Your poor face," she said lovingly. "It's so thin. Come, let me make you dumplings. We have fresh plums. . . ."

"Marika, my darling, sit down. Don't flit around all the time like a butterfly. Rest awhile. You, too, are thin."

"Yes," she said proudly, "my waist is nearly as small as the Empress'."

"Too small," he said. "If I embrace you properly, you will snap in two."

Friedl shook his head sadly. She was so fragile he hardly dared touch her. And when he did, when he came to bed with her, she trembled as though with chill, and her body was cold. He loved the lightness in her voice at this moment and the smile on her face. If only he could keep her smiling! If only he could make her happy! He would give his life for that, he was sure—except that the offer of his life would not bring her happiness. Her rare smile was almost unbearable for Friedl, and tears he would not permit to fall burned his eyes. He loved her with all his heart and had nothing to give her. He was losing her. He felt the sadness, the nostalgia, that comes with the first sweet-smelling breezes of spring, bringing intimations of past springs, mortality and fall. With heavy heart, he went outside, to leave them alone and to walk along the route his children would be coming down on their way back from school. Poor darlings, with the most beautiful mother in the world, to whom they could not bring joy.

"Little mama," said Leo, "for many years you took care of me and advised me and showed me what to do. Now it's the turn of your little brother to advise you. Tell me your troubles, dear. You are making yourself ill."

"It's foolishness," she said, trembling on the chair. "Foolishness and foolishness. My Friedl is such a good man, and I bring him nothing but worry. I try to prevent it, I do, Lev, but some bitter demon sits in my soul and tells me constantly to flee."

"Where to?"

"It doesn't tell me. Only to move, never to remain still, to travel, to wander. That is not good, my darling. I have my children, and I love them so much that I must creep into their room every night and look at them while they sleep, even though they're big now. They are so beautiful, still so innocent—and I sometimes can't believe they are mine, I can't believe that God has given me such healthy, marvelous children. And a good husband. I thank our dear Lord every day for him. Yet I bring Friedl much unhappiness, I sometimes think it would be best if I were dead."

"Don't talk that way!" he said sharply. It pained him to hear her, to see how she was suffering. The ways of the Lord toward His penitents were indeed mysterious, to afflict the pure, good soul of Marika, to take fifteen-year-old Rosa in delirium, and Mama the same way, who had patiently served all her life. He felt ill. His head ached and his lungs were heavy, resisting his breathing. He forced himself to continue their conversation.

When Friedl returned with Johann and Hannerl, who ran first to embrace their mother, then Uncle Leo, he could feel a change in the air. Something had happened. "Go to your room, children, and let us talk. I'll call you for your supper." The boy bowed, the girl curtseyed, both of them slender and elegant as their mother, and Leo thought how completely charming they were, how delightful it would be to have children of one's own.

They told Friedl what had been resolved, awaiting his approval. Marika would indeed undertake a journey, but she would not travel alone. She would take the children to visit Irina and their Uncle Yarko. Friedl would join them if he could and, if not, their trip would be short in any case, no more than a month. Leo insisted on contributing to the expenses, since Irina was his second mother and he wished to take part in offering her a visit from her grandchildren, a gift that would give her greater pleasure than any other.

Friedl listened mutely, not knowing what to say or even how he was feeling. He would be left alone, without his darlings. But they would be happy, traveling to her far birthplace, and in her native village Marika's fluttering soul could find peace. He agreed to the arrangement.

Leo came late and anxious to the apartment, but Wanda was waiting for him, having been let in by the porter, who recognized her. "Forgive me," he mumbled perfunctorily, feeling slight annoyance at the need for apology.

"You're late," she observed.

He frowned. "Important business." He thought that Karl might still be in the coffeehouse; they could have spent the evening together.

She responded to cues with a sensitivity close to genius. "Poor devil. You've had an exhausting time. Lie down; I'll make you tea."

"Yes," he mumbled, "I'm not too well."

She brought the tea and stood over him in a velvet *kazabaika*, firmly fastened at the waist. He took a few sips, put the cup aside, and kissed her hands. He curled the fingers under, rolled them into a fist. Her skin was soft, the small fist plump as a child's. He looked up at her face, strong and aristocratic, with firm jaw, straight nose, hair parted in the center. "Wanda," he said humbly, "you are too good to me." Her bearing was queenly, her eyes sharp, her lips dispensed the hint of a smile. In her magnificent presence he felt the beginnings of familiar faintness. He wanted to throw himself at her feet, lay gifts before her, beg her forgiveness. He'd spoken sharply to her; she should punish him, and already he felt the chastisement across his back, tension at his groin, the need spreading like ink on a blotter through his body, softening it to a liquid that could pass into hers.

He told her to move back so that he could rise from the bed. When his feet were on the floor, he fell to his knees, his face at the parting of her cloak. The odor was warm, overpowering, sweet and rotten as meat caught between the teeth or the fresh carcass of a slaughtered pig.

She hit him lightly on the shoulder. "You came late. You kept me waiting."

"Yes," he murmured, trembling, hoping she would strike him.

She laughed. "You're shaking like clothes in the wind. I've never seen someone shake so."

"Wanda, Wanda." He drew apart her cloak and placed his lips on her knee. He opened his mouth and began drawing a line up her thigh with his tongue. She rapped him sharply on the head and drew back, closing the curtains. "Tell me why you were late," she said.

"I was . . ." But he faltered. He desired her now so painfully he was unable to stand up, yet her question annoyed him. He would not account for his actions, though he longed to be punished for them. He wanted his skin broken, his spirit bled to voluptuous oblivion, freeing him from his sad, miserable body to glory, spilling light, orgasm.

She turned her back to him. He wanted her and couldn't possess her. "Marry me," he begged. "You are my whole life. I love you unbearably."

She looked at him archly, her eyebrows moving up.

"I know," he said, "but marry me anyhow, before no witness but God, in this room. Vow that you are mine. Give yourself to me, be my true wife."

"How do you mean?"

"I mean—oh, Wanda, you must do it, you must say yes —here, the day after tomorrow, on my name day, in this room, let me hear you vow to be my wife, vow to be true to me forever and accept my eternal fidelity to you. We will exchange rings and give our hearts to each other."

She agreed, wondering how soon the actual performance would follow the rehearsal. Her stomach was still flat; she couldn't risk disclosure till after birth. If luck was with her, it would be a boy. She hugged Leo tightly and loved him for his goodness, his fame and his complete devotion to her. She'd never felt so tenderly about a man as she did about him, and was glad to be carrying his child.

Karl found Wanda attractive and mistrusted her, as he did all the mistresses of his friends. He disliked women who assumed a proprietal behavior toward men, and though he had a horror of women who acted as though he were their belonging, he resented those who showed their ownership of a man who was not himself. When Leo proclaimed that Wanda was "magnificent," Karl merely grunted. He strictly obeyed his own prohibition against voicing unfriendly opinions about the lady friends of others; his own collection was motley enough to elicit scorn, and he scrupulously protected himself by never disparaging another man's woman, even if her jowls sagged and her breath was sour. Besides, he completely understood that "one man's meat is another man's poison," since even the game he had chosen for himself had occasionally turned so rotten that he couldn't find the slightest justification for having tracked it in the first place.

Leo couldn't contain himself. Though he'd been aware of Karl's unspoken rule since the time they were students, and had never transgressed it by either offering comments on Karl's affairs or soliciting any about his own, Wanda seemed to stand above all his other mistresses as Karl stood above other men. He hoped Karl would understand the nature of this love, as he'd hoped Wanda could comprehend the loving friendship he had with Karl. Yet neither seemed interested in the other. Karl's grunt reminded Leo he must keep his worlds separate.

They were walking together along the streets of their youth, and Leo had a comforting sense that life remained basically the same, that people neither "developed" nor "deteriorated" but simply went on different forays, returning to their original positions. They walked up the Schlossberg as they had always done, speaking when either thought of something to say and otherwise silent, without feeling the need to talk as a display of reassurance of interest. Leo sometimes felt he was more himself with Karl than when he was alone. A sympathetic fellow being brought comfort, removed his tendency to self-diagnosis, permitted him to clear his mind for any random thoughts and impressions that chose to occupy it. He didn't think of Anna on this walk. Too many years had passed, too many identical walks, the millions of steps eventually erasing painful images and memories of her that had always come to him here in the months after she left. When he thought of her, it was with gratitude and honor but no strong emotions.

"Old one," Karl said, "I need you to instruct me. This

devilish essay has me sleepless. How, in the name of all that's philosophical, do you manage to bring out the sense of an event or theory beyond a catalog of details?"

"Seems to me," Leo said slowly, "the details are what count. The event or idea are nothing without them." When Karl didn't answer, he went on. "It's of major importance to know what color eyes Catherine the Great had."

"What?"

"Oh, yes. That fact alone influenced her entire wardrobe, thereby decreeing the wardrobes of all the court ladies, which determined the wardrobes of common women in the following generation." He smiled at his own facetiousness; his last book was a collection of stories from Catherine's court, a diversion from his *Legacy of Cain* dictated by the need for money. "Although," he said, "her eye color is diverting. Catherine's eyes were blue, but her hair was auburn, and she dressed in jealous green."

"Trivia," Karl said, adding, "Our Empress wears white."

"She has sallow skin," Leo remarked conversationally, "but magnificent hair."

"And what's the meaning behind her white?"

"It's symbolic," suggested Leo.

"My thanks to you, professor. Is His Imperial Majesty's white symbolic too?"

"No, no. It's simply showing off. He never spills anything, you see. His mother taught him that, and he wants his subjects to notice how spotless he is."

"Without stain."

They were nearing the top. The restaurant was closed for the winter, and it was too cold to take a rest. They circled the little park with pear trees and began their descent. "I am the opposite of the Emperor," Leo said. "I must always wear dark colors."

"To hide your stains?"

"Precisely. I'm always spilling and soiling. If I had no care for society, I'd wear a rubber suit."

"You'd suffocate."

"But cleanly. Now, brave King Ludwig wears lapis lazuli to complement his eyes. He detests uniforms, I've heard."

"Because Ludwig's eyes are the color of lapis lazuli, Bavaria opens up trade with Afghanistan."

"An apt pupil, my dear Eggendorf. And that, my hero, is how the world turns."

"Sacher," said Karl, putting an arm around him, "I'm glad we don't share the same bed. You'd give me sleepless nights."

"And carefree days. The Prussians, however, love uniforms."

"Spotless too. You could eat off them."

"It may soon come to that, my dear," said Leo.

"Touché," answered Karl happily. "Well put."

As they neared the bottom, Karl asked, "Shall we?" and Leo nodded, because they understood each other and he, too, wanted refreshment.

As they entered, Joseph sang out, "Here come the comrades!" It was indeed a cause for rejoicing. For weeks now the quintet had been disassembled; in fact, they had all five convened there only a few times in the past year. Different lives, work and women kept them apart. Joseph rushed home with his Jenny, whom he was about to marry; Friedl often worked day and night on his cabinets (though he had a few assistants, none were capable of the finishing touches, and his orders had multiplied like rabbits); Franz was often traveling with and for wine; and the two "comrades" each returned to his desk after dinner, taking his wine alone or with a private companion in his study.

"A party," said Franz happily. "We'll have a party."

"Casks of wine," said Friedl dreamily, "a Tyrolean band—"

"And Tyrolean dirndls," said Karl, "tasty as dumplings."

"Who, the girls?" asked Franz.

"Of course the girls. How can you think of food when you're in the arms of a woman?"

"I'm not in the arms of a woman," he pointed out.

"But you wish you were."

"This is becoming ridiculous," said Joseph.

"Good," said Leo. "I'll drink to that."

"Me too," said Friedl.

"And me," said Franz.

When they set down their glasses, Joseph asked, "Is it true what I heard yesterday?"

"Probably not," said Leo, the skeptic.

Joseph was not deterred. "About the journal you've been asked to help establish. Will you do it? Go to Vienna?"

Since publication in the French journal, Leo had received myriad offers, the most remunerative of which was the invitation to help found a journal in Vienna. "In a few weeks," he said.

"With Wanda?"

Leo nodded. "She's due to have the baby in late May, weeks after the World Exhibition opens." The journal was to publish its first issue in honor of the Exhibition's opening on the first of May. "That's one reason to take on the position. We'll soon be three, and I need the money."

"You're too young to be a father," said Joseph, who had explained to Jenny that there was no need to think about having children for years. She had nodded sorrowfully, looking at him with her great serious eyes.

"It's still crowing time, old cock."

"For you it is," said Leo affectionately to Karl. "I'm getting old. A stone's throw from forty. Have you noticed? People are becoming very young suddenly. Everywhere you look, you see children. Remember when Graz was an old people's home? We laughed at the ancient decrepits. But where are they now? Everybody's nineteen. They drink wine, they chatter away like real people, and they don't have beards yet!"

"Ah," said Franz painfully. "The young ladies talk to you about their admirers as though you were an uncle."

"The tailor suggests more conservative colors," contributed Karl.

"A chocolate cream puff with *schlag* no longer brings tears to your eyes," said Friedl, joining in the spirit.

"A cigarette makes you cough," offered Joseph.

"You look in the mirror," said Karl, for whom the experience was still fresh, "and, though you know you've seen that person before, you just can't place him."

"I surrender," said Leo, laughing. "This round's on me. What's it to be, my heroes?"

"White," said Friedl.

"Red," said Joseph.

"Fruity," said Franz.

"Dry," said Karl.

"Red," said Joseph.

"White," said Friedl.

"The devil take all of you," said Leo. "Order what you like, I'm having a beer."

Before Hans could write down their orders, Wanda joined them, wearing the red mink-trimmed jacket Leo had given her as "wedding present." He stood and bowed over her hand, thinking that her new plumpness made her even more attractive than before—irresistible, actually. She gave off femininity like a stove its heat.

"Ravishing, my dear," said Karl, standing to hold out her chair. She threw him a long, intent look, touched his hand lightly and accepted the seat. Her eyes followed him until he took his own. This Leo observed, and felt the room spin while a shower of needles fell on him. He put out his cigarette viciously, stabbing it against the ashtray.

"Radiant," said Joseph, who was annoyed that Wanda should join them. Jenny would never even presume. "Your condition suits you admirably."

She wrinkled her nose at him and laughed deeply, like a cat purring. "If I could only stop getting fat, I'd enjoy it myself."

"One can never have too much of a beautiful woman," said Friedl, his atypical gallantry arising from his strong disapproval of her presence among them. She was broad and dark, an exaggeration of woman compared to Marika, who was leaving with the children in a few weeks—probably around the time Leo was going to Vienna. Marika would enjoy coming to the coffeehouse, but a woman was out of place in this company. "You must eat, to feed both of you," Friedl said to Wanda. "The cottage cheese cake is fresh and soft as a baby's bottom. No refusal. Hans!"

She thanked him. Leo was proud of his friends' obvious enthusiasm for her. They fussed over his darling, complimented her and spoiled her. She could have any man she desired, yet he was so thin, so shabby. Joseph was a beautiful man, his emerald eyes a prize for any woman. And Karl—his strong, broad shoulders, his blond hair and clipped mustache; Karl, his beloved brother, his other self—there was a match for Wanda, with her dark, regal bearing. Those two would be like a Grecian pair, an Adam and Eve, Mars and Venus.

On the way home (the others had left shortly after Wanda's arrival), Leo asked her what she thought of Karl. "I'm fond of him," she answered lazily, her arm through Leo's. "I'm fond of all your friends," she added. At no time before in her life had she caused a sensation by entering a room. These men were delightful; they all admired her.

"But Karl is handsome," Leo tested. "He is wonderfully handsome, like a Greek god, and I am"—he hesitated a moment before driving the spike in on himself—"I am ugly."

"But you're mine," she said, putting pressure on his arm.

He felt remorseful. She hadn't denied it, because she was honest. Such a woman deserved a beautiful man. "Would you like him?" he asked, with desperate lightheartedness. "Should I give him to you for your name day?"

"Thank you," she said, as though dismissing the exchange. They continued home in silence, with Leo puzzled and disturbed.

11

On such a day, Vienna was the crown of Europe, sparkling with fresh jewels. Her churches and cathedrals glistened, streets and houses were scrubbed, even the river and sky seemed polished for the occasion. The inner city was circled by the Ringstrasse, studded with the new buildings designed by Europe's greatest architects to serve as a legacy of Franz Joseph. A new Troy had recently been unearthed, and a new Vienna rose up amid the old, bearing the name of its emperor, whose reign would be the longest ever known.

It was a prosperous day, well-heated by the sun, scented through a melange of budding fruit trees, flowers and roasting coffee. In the Prater, exhibitors from all around the world were setting up their displays. The Americans included a bar and a wigwam in the seven hundred exhibits they had brought. In and around the Rotunda, the Monarchy and its guests gave signs that all was well as they paid homage to Industry, a word that now had as its primary meaning not a human attribute but a mechanical achievement. Throughout the city, new hotels, restaurants and places of amusement had been constructed to accommodate the expected millions of visitors, who would scatter florins and guldens into the golden seine of Vienna. Bright, gaudy blossoms decorated houses, parks and lampposts; trees and grass were richly green. Austria was booming and Vienna was in bloom.

New railway cars were being coupled to long trains. The Empress Elisabeth was being fitted in Gödöllö for the sumptuous gowns she had ordered, while complaining to her friend Andrássy, now foreign minister of Austria-Hungary, that the trip would be exhausting and boring. He reminded her that an empress had certain duties to fulfill beyond riding her horses, maintaining her waist and having her hair washed with twenty bottles of cognac. She turned so violently that pins cut the dressmaker's fingers. Her eyes blazed and he thought she would slap him for impertinence, but then her face softened, her fingers moved up to cover her lips, and she bestowed on him a sweet smile. In that smile lay a buried Eden, the bright fruit bowing down the branch. Looking at her, he had the strange thought that beauty was as necessary to the world as politics, and had its own laws.

In St. Petersburg, the imperial jewels were being shined with ashes in preparation for the journey of the Czar and Czarina. In Paris, Athens, Persia, Spain, wardrobes and entourages were being readied for Vienna, and gifts ordered for the potentates to bring to Their Imperial Majesties. The city itself lay calmly in its golden covering, dressed to receive all admirers. Wine waited in casks stamped with reliefs of Their Majesties in profile; jewelers and grocers had spread out their wares, Sacher-Masoch's journal was in the hands of the printer, and all the girls of Vienna displayed their dowries of charm.

On the first of May, 1873, the capital bursting with tourists, the Emperor and Empress of Austria opened the World Exhibition of Industry and Art, the Empress so ethereally beautiful in her white and silver gown that the Shah of Persia had to poke her with his stubby finger to satisfy himself that she was real. The Crown Princess of Germany, Queen Victoria's daughter, found her charming and intelligent. Mutual liking between the women eased the confrontation of their husbands, for the golden helmet of Crown Prince Frederick sent a sliver of Königgrätz into the heart of Franz Joseph.

The Russians had to be welcomed and entertained; then came Kaiser Wilhelm with his monumental Augusta, six feet of Biedermeier stuffing from Berlin. Elisabeth left the German Empress to the care of her husband, who accepted his duty with usual grace, but promised himself a later reward for his labors in the company of beautiful Eugénie of France.

The Prince of Wales was generally declared to be "charming," though his manners were peculiarly informal and he kept time so loosely that nearly any genial Viennese could steal it. To Crown Prince Rudolph (Edward's counterpart in the east), the Englishman seemed delightful. Rudolph, not yet sixteen, had his mother's beauty and sensitivity, his father's devotion to duty and a mind of his own. He studied and admired English democracy and had been eager to meet Prince Edward, whose informality suggested an egalitarianism not present in *gemütlichkeit,* and whose candor appeared to Rudolph as perspicacity. "When you, me, and my brother-in-law inherit our empires," confided Edward, "the time of princes will be over. You and I know that, but Frederick will still be strutting in his white and gold uniform, wound up each day by Bismarck and put through maneuvers that will make us both quake in our oversized boots."

Rudolph expressed his hope that the time would come when neither princes nor soldiers would be necessary, since the latter were only required to guard the interests of the former and would become obsolete when progress developed its cure for economic inequality, the infection recognized by its symptoms of self-interest, indifference to the common weal and moral disintegration.

Edward was astonished. "The Crown Prince of Austria," he wrote his mother, "possesses a clarity of mind quite remarkable in someone so young. He has graceful manners and is exceptionally handsome. You would be as taken by him as I am."

Rudolph's mother was interested more in personalities than in politics. Sissi's favorite among the royal and imperial guests at the exhibition was the bizarre and incredible Shah. In Europe for the first time, he regarded his surroundings as a stage set to be rearranged according to his whim. He traveled with many dozens of attendants and a stable of horses whose manes had been dyed pink. He consented to meetings or interviews only when his astrologer confirmed that the stars were propitious, and kept the grand vizier standing behind his chair during meals, to sample every dish brought to him in case it was poisoned. Elisabeth was the only person he asked to see, and she found in him a marvelous contrast to the tedious formalism of European rulers. He was self-willed and arrogant. He categorically refused to speak to any woman who was not beautiful or to any man whose face he didn't like. He told Franz Joseph bluntly, "You insult me with your little castle of Laxenburg. It is not good enough for me. I want Schönbrunn." To further announce his displeasure, the Shah ordered his servants to smash a few statues and windows in the inadequate castle.

He stared at Elisabeth and examined her through his glass. He prodded her and at last gave out his finding: *"Elle est vraiment belle."* The Empress laughed with pleasure. He was a fellow connoisseur of feminine beauty, who had collected magnificent women in his harem. She knew some of them by their portraits, smuggled out of Persia on her command by personal couriers. It was taboo for anyone to own pictures of the Shah's wives, but Sissi had a few of them now in her collection of the world's most beautiful women. The Shah demanded a portrait of the Empress. In return, he gave her a pink-maned stallion.

After the first week, Elisabeth was exhausted and planned to return "home" to Gödöllö. But she was advised that her presence would continue to be expected. There had been a crash on the stock market, she was told, people were fleeing the capital, and the wealth of her beauty was more necessary than ever.

* * *

On "Black Friday," May 9, 1873, Wanda went into false labor in their small furnished apartment many kilometers from the Prater. Leo's journal was one of the first tolls of the crash, to be soon followed by waves of bankruptcy and suicide. At the same time, Nature acted as though man were not capable of inflicting adequate punishment on himself and added her contribution in the form of cholera.

Leo and Wanda had been in Vienna since February, their money spilling and scattering at the touch like a *noli me tangere.* Leo had received an initial payment for his work on the journal, but the cost of their hotel, then the six months' advance rent they'd been forced to pay, took care of more than

219

he'd been given. The half-year lease was the shortest they could find, and the landlord removed the furniture as soon as he was paid, replacing it with cheaper stuff.

They couldn't afford restaurants and cooked their meals in the kitchen to which they had access. They ate in the shabby room they called their "salon" (the other was the "boudoir"), munching sausages and potatoes and dreading the visits of those who came to honor Sacher-Masoch and who would have to be served refreshment. They lived on small sums, the kind of nervous income that soon attacks the mind, allowing it no respite from thoughts of money. Leo, who had never been poor, was terrified of starvation and wrote in a frenzy, ignoring standards and considerations of art as he poured out the stream to keep them afloat. Wanda regarded this time as a phase and assumed that payments would come with enough regularity to keep them fed and clean. She herself wrote nothing, her literary career having been rendered in the warmth of furs.

Leo's play *The Man Without Prejudices* was being performed in Vienna in repertory, with The Clairmont as leading lady. He received a small commission from it, and on opening night they sat in the front row, where Wanda could see that the actress was "very pretty" but, as she told Leo during intermission, "unfortunately devoid of talent."

The journal was compiled and edited by the first week of April. Leo wrote short pieces, essays and stories, mailing them as soon as he finished, sometimes a few of them in a single day. "I keep the fires burning with paper," he told Wanda, whose resilience amazed him. He was humbled by her devotion and loyalty to him despite her deprivation. His abandonment of the *Legacy* seemed paltry sacrifice compared to hers, who should be in fine clothes and enter a kitchen only to give orders to the cook. Instead of Cain and man's burden, he wrote exotic romances, like *A Female Sultan*, tossed off in ten days and sent out unread to a well-paying family magazine which accepted it.

Wanda, who had never before been out of Graz, and to whom Vienna had promised pastry shops, ermine tails and respectability, controlled her bitterness to the point of poisoning her health. Unmarried, pregnant and without even a kreutzer to her name, she couldn't afford to complain to Leo, her only hope and devoted worshiper. But her body was no diplomat, and revolted against the pressure.

After the false labor, she spent more time in bed, though relaxation was impossible. The weather turned muggy, the better to hold and trap contagion. Leo didn't dare leave the rooms for fear of cholera, and she was forced to go out to do the marketing. Each day more doors were boarded and shutters locked as the tenants behind them died or fled. Life and money had become worthless in Vienna, though desperate citizens tried to hold on to both. Payment for Leo's stories arrived in batches; the inflated currency was obscene as a tumor. Guldens were florins, florins kreutzers, and the weight of money for a day's needs tore holes in the pockets. It was little comfort to know that the economic depression was spreading westward over the continent and would not stop at the Atlantic. Men with far less skepticism than Sacher-Masoch concluded that something rotten lay at the heart of the system. The wares available in the shops that remained open changed prices from hour to hour, and Viennese gallows humor had a flowering: "By the time you've smoked your cigar, you've stolen it"; "This morning's loaf is this evening's slice"; or, "When you've finished paying for it, you've bought only half." A riddle circulated: "Why is money like a mimosa?"; with the obvious answer: "It shrinks at the touch."

Death ran through the streets, and doctors were among the first to flee. Leo sat at his desk inventing beautiful monsters and cruel mistresses while wagons passed underneath his window piled with corpses. When he saw one, he became violently sick and had to abandon his work. He was unable to eat and could sleep for only a few minutes at a time. His thoughts skittered from money to cholera and remained there, poisoning everything with cholera. His memories were cholera, himself was cholera. He was afraid to stay in the apartment and afraid to go out.

Newspapers didn't report the epidemic, which was not in official existence on account of the visitors. Cholera was not permitted in the Prater, where the great exhibition commemorating man's progress still brought sightseers to gape, drink, eat and ride the carousel.

A knock on the door made Leo's heart jump. Wanda was lying down in the next room. Another knock, and then a voice he recognized, dear to him as health. He opened quickly, pulled Karl inside and bolted the door behind him. "The devil!" he said. "Don't you know there's cholera?"

"I believe someone did mention it. . . . Old one, how do you look?" Karl took Leo in his arms, hugging him and slapping him like a playful puppy until Leo had no breath left. Karl held him at arm's length and studied his face. "No, my dear, it won't do." He shook his head. "Not even a starving witch would eat you for breakfast. Come, we'll fatten you up."

"No use, no use." But despite himself, Leo felt sudden relief, as though hearing a ship's horn at last answer his distress signals. "And you, my hero—why are you in Vienna?"

"The kittens were showing their claws all over Graz," he said, but Leo didn't believe him. He knew why Karl was here, and tears came to his eyes because he wasn't worthy of such love. Karl didn't notice, or pretended not to. "I hear the journal's defunct; never mind. Here you are in gay Vienna, city of flowers and deflowering—by the way, is the child born yet?"

"Wanda's in the next room, I'll call her. No, we thought it was making an appearance a few weeks ago, but it turned out the little devil was just practicing—a false alarm. However, we expect the debut shortly."

"Karl!" Wanda stood in the doorframe, head to one side, smiling prettily. She'd heard the knocking and his voice, quickly applied some color to her cheeks, smoothed her hair, adjusted her robe and now greeted him with the pleasure women can always take, no matter how black their situation, in foreknowledge that they will be admired.

He went and embraced her gently. Her large belly touched him. She looked much healthier than Leo and had somehow managed to maintain the color in her cheeks. "I want to take this dreary devil out of here," he told her. "Fatten him up and get the yellow out of his skin."

She exchanged glances with Leo, who had refused even to open a window in weeks.

"I—" Leo began, but Karl would not permit refusal.

"Tomorrow morning I'll snatch you away. You may come voluntarily or under constraint. I'll stuff you with doughnuts and drown you in wine. . . ."

"Violent fellow," said Leo happily. Terror still staked its claim, but Karl had come this long way to deliver him— they'd see on the morrow.

Next morning Wanda gave birth to a squalling boy, slightly underweight but healthy, delivered by an aging midwife with large warts on her face, who asked only a small sum for her labors, and refreshment.

Leo remained in the other room while the birth itself was taking place, his ears stopped with cotton. When the placenta was cleaned away, the child washed and placed next to its mother, the midwife came to Leo and nodded that he should go in.

The baby was amazing, a perfect little piece of humanity with crumpled skin and hands tiny as a gold piece. He didn't dare touch it. He trembled, could not take his eyes from the infant even to look in the mother's face. Its eyes were closed, but the mouth moved blindly against her skin. She brought the little cargo to her breast and eased her nipple between the pulsing lips. Now he saw them, mother and child, her face calm and painfully beautiful. "You," he said softly, "look what you have made. A person!" Tears spilled down his cheeks. He fell on his knees beside the bed and sobbed deeply, in an attitude of prayer.

Even on the train, her children charming and gay as kittens, Marika felt anxious. The landscape sped by too quickly, shapes and colors meaningless as scattered pieces of a jigsaw puzzle. Objects jumped at her, shadows turned into wolves. She had lived with the demon for many years—now at least she was doing its bidding, and a terrible foreboding came over her that the demon was laughing at her, mocking her, because nothing she could ever do would chase it away. For years she had dreamed of traveling, and in that dream she could hold on to the belief that a solution existed, that she would be able to find peace once her wish was granted. Now it had been, and she felt restless as a caged cat. She was afraid of everything, frightened of strangers speaking to her and frightened that they would ignore her, would look through her and not notice she was there. As they passed a field, a pheasant flew up suddenly and she shied from the window, cringing in her seat.

Thank God, she thought, that the children and Friedl didn't understand how deep and wide the fear was. She was sometimes afraid that she didn't exist, that the shell of Marika was hollow, that—without noticing—she'd been transformed into her own ghost. Other times she was made aware of having a body, of inhabiting the strange, hateful piece of matter. Then she fasted and wore old clothes, in the crazy hope that she could make herself invisible.

When they arrived, the rejoicing that met them was fit for the Empress and her children. Irina cried and prayed, kissed the ground and thanked God for His goodness. She kissed Marika's hand again and again and held the children so tightly they struggled to breathe. Yarko stood grinning helplessly, and even the villagers who had never known Marika gave their blessings and thanks.

For days before, the village had baked and cooked; the schoolchildren had lain awake in their excitement, imagining the "Beautiful Lady" from a distant land and wondering which of their toys to offer her children. The musicians tuned their instruments, and the best tenor, a young man of eighteen, practiced:

> "My years, they are passing,
> And summer flies—
> Oh, I weep at the river—
> Happiness dies."

They had also prepared a German song as a special surprise for her.

Marika thanked all of them with her beautiful smile. She turned to her mother and wept a long time in her arms. Irina held her weeping child, stroking and kissing her hair, bringing her back to girlhood. The strange lady became her daughter again, and solicitude like pain entered into Irma's joy. At last she said, "You are thin as a spike. And the children too. May the Lord forgive me, but does your husband not give you anything to eat?"

Marika smiled, extricated herself and kissed the old, loose cheeks. "He is a good man, Irochka. He gives us everything and deprives us of nothing. The children are growing so fast that the fat rolls off like water from a duck, and I—well, I like being slender."

Irina muttered to herself and said nothing more, but her heart grew heavier when she saw that Marika left most of her food untouched. She needed nourishment, and besides, the neighbors would be offended. They had stuffed the geese and roasted potatoes with them, in the rich goose fat. They had made borscht from the choicest beets, collected mushrooms and chopped them for appetizers, creamed the herring and fried onions until the whole village had their tongues hanging out from the delicious smells. They'd baked meat pies and sweet tarts; Irina had made a loaf of her festive sweet bread for each of the children, their names lettered in colored sugar. Yet Marika was indifferent. It seemed she had lost her sense of smell; the wonderful odors didn't arouse her appetite, and the feast they'd prepared for so long in happy anticipation was flat and tasteless on her tongue. Her smile was charming, she still looked like a girl, beautiful as a princess, but Irina knew she was troubled and prayed earnestly for her daughter's peace of mind.

They had much to talk about. Yarko was now a strong, broad man of forty-five, his face heavily lined but his hair still thick enough to cover his missing ear and his eyes clear as ever. He spoke to his sister with pride of all they had accomplished since she left. Yarko's study of agriculture had resulted in rich harvests, first for himself and Irina, then, through his advice, for the other peasants. Their village became known for its productivity, and men who were unable to read were employing the latest methods of farming. As their yield increased and they grew more prosperous, they bought new implements, which in turn brought them even more yield. The livestock were fed a scientific diet and protected from disease. Profits were pooled, and the money was used to build a school, then an infirmary.

He told her there had been some troubles, particularly with marauders from the hills who, envious of their prosperity, had swooped down and attempted to plunder everything. But they had been repulsed, Yarko said, and the village soon recovered from their damage.

He didn't dwell on the misfortunes, now they were over. Marauding had been frequent; unexpected drought destroyed nearly all the harvest; factions within the village had formed, leading to violent quarrels and even a death. But eventually the bandits brought them together, as the men of the village forgot their disagreements and turned vigilante together, to rout the menace from the hills. He did not feel obliged to tell his sister all these stories; hardships were to be buried as soon as they ended. He asked her about her own life, about the city of Graz, her husband and his family, and the Sacher-Masochs. Irina grinned to hear of little Leo, now a famous author who still remained a dear friend to Marika.

Marika stared at her, could not take her eyes off the grin, the hollow mouth with only a few teeth, the senseless cavern filled every day with things to eat. She tried to continue, she told them of the death of Leo's mother, she said that Leo and her husband were great comrades . . . but her own words came from far off, and when Irina reached out to touch her hand, Marika pulled it away.

Two days later she floated on the river in her flounced skirt, her hair free. She had tripped and fallen in, the villagers told each other and her poor children, but there was fear in everyone's eyes, and to the old people's ears came a ringing, high and soft as the song of a *roussalka*.

12

FOUR DAYS after the birth, Karl managed to persuade Leo to come out with him. And, once he had kissed Wanda, stood a moment in silent tribute to the sleeping infant, Leo left the rooms and forgot his fear. He harbored the paradox of most hypochondriacs, who invent and nurture illnesses but become cheerful, even blithe, in the face of actual danger. Such people will instantly discover in themselves the symptoms of any disease that's mentioned (the slightest stomach cramp confirmed Leo's diagnosis of cholera, and he immediately foresaw his terrible end) but are cavalier, at times foolhardy, about their health. They'll continue to overeat after a doctor has told them this will certainly lead to gout or an attack of the liver; they will smoke tobacco though they hardly have breath left to pull it in. Like the elephant trembling before a mouse, or the war hero who dares not go on the street for fear of horses, these people (like Leo) terrify themselves out of their wits through their own imaginations. They are most afraid of death; they'll see it everywhere except at its true source; they use their terror in place of the awesome fact and replace the true face of death with masks. By complaining of and living through illnesses that prove to be insignificant, they can overcome what is at the end of illness; they have survived yet another battle, have placated the angry god (they suffered) and have once again forestalled the inevitable. For someone like Leo, each death is both his own and a protection against his death: the Grim Reaper has once more been assuaged and will not come this way again just now. Hypochondriacs are always superstitious, reading misfortune and death in commonplace occurrences. If the next person to walk out a particular door is wearing black, the day's work will be lost or the money won't arrive. If today's meat is overcooked, her love is not sincere—and so forth. But if such a person becomes really ill, he astounds those around him by his courage. Whatever happens is never so bad as the mind has prefigured; actuality is the relief from imaginings; the fact has occurred, terror is banished, and one is—amazingly—alive.

So Leo now accompanied Karl through the streets of Vienna, walking the long way to the Prater in good cheer without even the protection of a handkerchief over his nose or mouth against the germs. Leo wanted no protection; he felt invulnerable. He took deep breaths of air and pointed out the beauties of the city. He spoke rapidly and enthusiastically; his heart was brimming with goodwill toward all, and he saw every woman they passed as beautiful. He felt reborn into a deep understanding of life and nature, the cycles of existence, the meaning of love. In such a mood, he could write a masterpiece. He tugged at Karl's sleeve and spoke excitedly. "Most important of all studies is the relation between the sexes. In its end is the necessary aim of human life, its preservation and regeneration. . . ."

"Schopenhauer," said Karl drily. "Have you noticed, my dear, that the thoughts of this philosopher, sweetened of course, are offered up as bonbons by Viennese dandies to the pretty and bored young wives they meet in coffeehouses? I must tell you that, while I have nothing against philosophy per se, I do like to keep it out of the bedroom, where I much prefer garters and lace."

"But the *end* of a relation between man and woman—"

"Is rather costly, I've found, and generally unpleasant," said Karl airily. Then he grinned and put an arm through the new father's, and forgave him his stuffiness.

They visited exhibits at the Prater and stopped for goulash and beer. "Wonderful!" Leo exclaimed. "I've never tasted anything so delicious. The paprika—how good it is! What a beautiful color! And the rolls—listen to them, just hear the crack when I break them! This beer, quite extraordinary, definitely Bohemian—ah, my friend, what a meal!"

Karl smiled at this outpouring, thinking that Leo had been locked in too long, worked too hard, and that Wanda probably oppressed his spirit. The food was really only mediocre.

But nothing could interfere with his high spirits, not the disapproving look the waiter gave Leo when goulash landed in his lap, not the disdain of a pretty young lady to whom Leo bowed ceremoniously, flourishing his hat (and hitting a stout matron behind him, bringing on insults), not the economic situation, the political one or the epidemic. Leo was brimming and bursting with pleasure like a river breaking its banks or a cloud, grown too heavy, spilling its moisture.

They returned late, with Leo still drunk on life, to find Wanda in an agitated condition. The child was ill, hadn't eaten all day and was vomiting. She'd brought in the midwife, who examined the whimpering infant overtaken every few minutes by spasms and went out to find a doctor. She still hadn't returned, Wanda didn't want to leave the child alone, and the spasms were horrible.

"I'll find a doctor," said Karl, his hand already on the door.

"I'll come too," said Leo, who dared not remain in the apartment and didn't go to look at his son.

They went quickly through the dark, shuttered streets. Each door was locked against them and from behind each a voice would tell them, "Please go away. He's not here, the Herr Doctor is not in the city, he's away, he went away." They tried all doors, any door, whether it announced a doctor or was unmarked. But no one could advise them, no one opened to them. Everywhere they were told the doctor was away. The medical doctors had all given up in the face of their enemy, fleeing to the country and abandoning Vienna to cholera. Karl and Leo decided to double the search by taking separate ways.

At midnight, terrified of the dark uninhabited city, Leo returned. Wanda was white as paper and told him in a thin, cracking voice that the child could no longer vomit, but the spasms continued with dry retching and high, helpless sounds of pain. He could hear them, dimly; they were not human, they belonged to no living person. He huddled in a chair in the far corner of the sitting room, embracing himself while he shivered and sweated.

A few minutes later, Karl walked in with two policemen and a squat, fleshy man they called "Doctor." Leo saw him as the executioner. He walked into the bedroom angrily, examined the child in a minute and gave his quick, brutal finding: "No hope." He glowered at all of them and strode out. Leo was shaking violently; Wanda was stiff as a corpse. She said nothing, but her eyes looked on him pityingly.

Karl went out again, with the policemen, and returned quickly with a young priest, who baptized the contorted infant, then went to its mother, said a short prayer and made the sign of the cross over her. Then he blessed Leo and left with Karl.

The priestly rituals had calmed the violence of Leo's body. Wanda brought him a footstool and covered him with a blanket. She went into the other room, to her bed, placed the child beside her in the crook of her arm and hummed softly to it. The night was peaceful, until the false dawn, when it gave a high, dry rattle and was dead.

* * *

Gödöllö brought peace to Sissi after the stresses of Vienna. She embraced her dear Ida, her "sweet dove," and said that she'd been homesick. "The Emperor is constantly occupied, and the people at court are very solemn. Most of them are false, I believe; they evade the truth and cannot look you straight in the eye." The Empress had no friends at the Viennese court, except for her husband. Despite her spiritedness, she was a shy woman, but the Viennese believed she was disdainful, and in the Hofburg she was misquoted as having said, "Friendship is a broken reed that can never be relied upon."

But she had intimates, and was loving to those she cared for. She regretted that she could not be more openly affectionate toward Rudolph, but he was too much like her, and at times she felt uneasy with him. On her youngest child, she bestowed endless kisses and embraces. Her eldest, Gisela, was marrying Luitpold of Bavaria, a match for her correctness and pomposity—though of course, Sissi amended her thoughts, Gisela had a few pleasant traits. To be the mother of a bride was an unfortunate role, though in this case the Empress decided she looked no older than the plump Archduchess.

After embracing Ida, she went to greet each of her horses in turn, with her dogs Putzi and Spatzi at her heels. They adored their mistress, who kept pictures of them in her room. They were her favorites; large, furry, bounding up to her, always playful, their tails wagging for adventure. They were as indefatigable as herself, the only companions who could accompany her on the eight- or ten-hour walks she took at a brisk pace. She loved them, but neither could ever replace Zsusi, the dog Gyula had given her, Putzi's mother, with eyes so intelligent and loving it was impossible to believe she did not understand human language. Zsusi's picture rested in a gold frame studded with garnets, and her body was buried under the Empress' bedroom, her grave tended by Sissi herself, who brought fresh flowers and talked to Zsusi's corpse beneath the ground as she had talked to the dog in life.

*   *   *

After the death of her child, Wanda decided to confess everything to Leo. The birth was followed so soon by death that even her body could not adjust, and the milk waited painfully in her breasts for his hard, grasping mouth. The confrontation with mortality unnerved her. Life was short, brutal and generally in vain. In the child's fate she also read a punishment for her own lies. She would tell Leo the truth and hope that he (or God) forgave her.

He listened intently, not taking his eyes off her lips. She told him she was not married and had never been, that she'd lived in the disgrace of poverty with her mother after her father abandoned them. When she was born, he was an adjunct to the military governor of Graz, a Prince von Würtemberg, who so engaged her father's loyalty that he would work for no other military official after the prince's departure. He found employment at a small railway station south of Graz, on the Trieste line.

"I went to the cloister school. I loved God and His saints with all the great love I bore for my unfortunate mother. I was a brilliant pupil, though the sisters were not kind to me. I had difficulty taking communion; the wafer made me vomit.

"When I was thirteen or so I used to see you walking past our house. I knew who you were, even then." She smiled faintly but suppressed the temptation to flirt away her confession. "I came home one day after school and the door to our apartment was locked. Thinking my mother had probably gone to a neighbor's for something and would be back soon, I sat down on the steps to wait. They were cold, and I sat a long time. I became aware of sounds coming from inside the apartment, but before I could rise the door flew open and a young woman rushed out and ran past me down the stairs. I knew who she was, a vulgar woman from the floor below. I looked up and saw my father on the other side of the door. We looked into each other's eyes. I didn't know the nature of what had happened, but a feeling told me it was ignoble and ugly. I never again confided in my father or talked to him without a deep sense of shame."

He nodded gravely, and suddenly Wanda was confused by a feeling of remorse. Her father appeared in her mind as he'd looked when she was little, and they walked hand in hand up the Schlossberg on Sunday to hear the band. He always bought her an ice, and he let her sit in a chair all by herself when there was no other seat at the concert. He understood that she felt more important that way than sitting on his lap, and he stood tall and straight with a hand on her shoulder. At night she would wait for his kiss in the dark, making bets with herself to see how long it would take him to come. To Leo she said crisply, "He left us."

He was fascinated. Instead of a countess, he'd caught himself a stationmaster's daughter. The marvel of her disclosure hit him—she had deceived him more than any other woman, deceived him utterly, magnificently. He laughed and she looked at him with alarm. He thought of how cleverly she had dissimulated all this time to accomplish her own purposes. Through poverty (or natural inclination) she'd learned to be totally selfish, to care for nothing but her own survival. Only the fear of death made her honest, and he wasn't even sure he could trust her words now. While he'd agonized over her "deprivation" and abandoned his great work to support her, she had never even hinted that her previous life had not been one of wealth and privilege. He clearly remembered their first meeting, and the shabby dress he took for a disguise. It was probably her only dress! She'd taken him for a fool, and been proved right. Her entire being was deception. What small hands she had, and what disdainful flesh. She suffered his passion, nothing more, and her coolness made him covet her even while he was having her. He could never possess her, but he preferred to spend his life trying than to live even one day without her. He had sacrificed much for her already, and longed to sacrifice more. She was a stranger, a force unto herself, who with a slight look could make him forget everything in his desire for her. Her skin was always cool, and her scorn was magnificent when she placed her foot on his neck. She was an empress—a stationmaster's daughter! She had duped him, shown her complete contempt of him by lying from the beginning, through all their time together, and while carrying his child.

He fell on his knees and kissed her feet. "Marry me, Wanda." His eyes were full of tears.

She looked down at him in bewilderment.

"Please marry me. Allow me to give you all the things you never had. Let me work for you, slave until I can bring you opulence and luxury."

She smiled in pleasure. "But my humble beginnings— don't you mind?" She remembered his famous affair with Baroness von Kottowitz, that beautiful woman she'd seen on the Schlossberg. "I thought your ideal was someone like Anna—"

His expression stopped her. "You are my fate," he said abruptly. He didn't want to hear Anna's name from her lips. He rose and drew her up with him. He held her in his arms and thought that this woman was to become his wife, the most sacred of all names. He had committed himself to her before, in mock ceremony, not realizing how deeply he was being mocked. Now he committed himself again, in earnest this time, and wondered if she would advance from deception to betrayal.

She embraced him in a preoccupied manner, distracted by his good faith. She would never understand him, men were strange creatures, but he would provide for her, she would have a house of her own, she would be the wife of a well-known man, and she would be dutiful.

They left Vienna even before the lease was up, despite their prepayment of rent. The baby's death hung in the air, though neither mentioned it. The little cadaver had been removed and the rooms disinfected. Leo accepted Karl's words of sympathy with "Can't be helped. Maybe the poor beggar saved himself a life of sorrows." He tried not to think of the child and had not wept for it.

Karl urged Leo to leave the city and suggested Bruck an der Mur as a perfect place for restoring his health and Wanda's. He himself returned to Graz after a week in Vienna, saying, "See you over billiards at the Kornmesser."

Leo and Wanda took rooms at the Hotel Barbolani on the main square and breathed the contagion-free summer air gratefully. Behind them rose the Schlossberg of Bruck, a steep park of cypress and roses, abustle with wagtails, blue tits and bumblebees, its paths stained with the flesh of purple grapes grown too heavy for the vine. The good mountain air was a tonic to Leo, whose joie de vivre woke him early every morning with fresh enthusiasm for the day's work.

Wanda was still pale and tired. They would stay here until she recovered completely, then return to Graz to be married. He promised to have a beautiful trousseau for her by then. He began the second cycle of *Legacy of Cain*, "Property," working through every morning and then taking walks with Wanda in the afternoon, each day slightly longer as her strength returned.

He was sure he loved her, that she was his true mate, the cruel mistress he was destined to seek. His nature was formed the way it was. Pretty actresses with their commonplace love and no cruelty beyond their own vanity could not hold him long. He now believed his erotic destiny had been revealed to him in early childhood, giving him his theme as man and artist. He felt he was capable of greater passion than other men, deeper love—though until Wanda he had found no woman (except Anna?) to offer his heart to. Fanny had been magnificent, and he'd vowed his love to her again and again in Italy, but in the end she, too, was just an actress and the play was over. A woman could bring you to your true nature, though she could offer no friendship. But women were not meant to be like men. Their minds and souls did not develop as fully. They didn't, and weren't able to, concern themselves with questions of the universe, considerations of morality or art; that had been given men to do, and as men formed the world, women inspired it. Men made paintings and theories, music and engines and medicine, contributing to the progress of mankind through their minds and honor. Women's bodies brought life to the world, and in women one confronted death. Male and female together were the necessary union, the vital balance.

She smiled at him, sitting in the armchair in her furs despite the heat. She did it for him, he knew, and would willingly deliver him his death if he asked for it. In advance of her had been a stream of faceless pussycats and a few ignominious times when he lay in bed after a long womanless stretch, held his hard aching member, stroked it gently as though to calm it, and then was compelled to increase the pressure of his hand, to pull and jerk it while his mind hid itself, his breathing swelled like infection, the shame bore down on him even as he beat the offending limb until the hot liquid gasped out and he was relieved. Then he would sleep, to forget the disgrace of having been his own lover.

Wanda forgave him his clumsiness, his thinness, his gaunt face. She rose and went to select a whip. He trembled in anticipation, heat passing through his body like a current to electrify his senses. She came up to him in her long fur and told him to kneel. He fell forward onto his knees, and she told him to remove his shirt, then his undershirt. He did as she asked, clumsily, his fingers becoming stubby knobs in his anxiousness to do her bidding. He could see the expression on her face, queenly and contemptuous. She lifted her arm. "Sinner," she said. "You are a miserable sinner." She brought the whip down across his back. "You are wretched." She dragged

235

the cord slowly across his skin, then raised the whip and brought it down quickly, viciously. "You have transgressed, you have stolen from the earth." Again and again she brought down the cruel whip, biting into his flesh, lingering across his back in a strange caress, then cutting him again with even greater force. Her strength was magnificent. She never tired until he could see that her eyes were rich with desire, inflamed by her own power and cruelty. Then he called out, "Yes! Beat me like a dog!" and, smiling, she let the whip fall from her hand. Slowly, she parted the *kazabaika*. He kissed her boots and looked up into the great, warm mystery of her own fur. Slowly, majestically, she walked to the couch and arranged herself on it. He crawled to where she lay and gazed at her, spread like Leda after the swan's ravishment, at the strange body in an attitude of abandonment, with skin cool as marble, from which rose the command, "Take me." He served his mistress then, feeling small and insignificant on the proud monument of her body, draining himself into her, who lay with closed eyes and a faint disdainful smile on her lips.

"Wanda, you are mine forever. Through you I burn in all the fires of hell to redemption."

She smiled and stroked his thin head absentmindedly, wishing she didn't have to wear furs in summer and feeling tired from her exertions.

After resting a short while in each other's arms, they rose and she washed his wounds, covering them with an ointment of zinc and thin linen gauze. Then they dressed themselves for the afternoon excursion. The day was clear, and the black-red roofs of the town bright as blood. They passed the grain merchant's on the corner, where a small gray cat lay sunning itself on a large sack of grain. Leo stopped and stroked it, as he did every day. The little cat was always there when they went by, peacefully napping on the grain it appropriated. At Leo's touch, its amber eyes opened. He spoke to it cajolingly, and the little creature stretched and curled back into a warm ball, content with the admiration but showing no response beyond a low purring. The merchant smiled to see his cat with the author, thinking that even scholars could be kind, and that Sacher-Masoch must be a good man if he showed affection to dumb animals.

236

They walked across the Mürz, glistening a deep aquamarine, and out toward the Frauenberg. Leo felt at peace, with his woman beside him, a solid day's work completed and his legs moving him toward the cool woods. They walked for three hours, at a leisurely pace, and returned to find a note from Karl at the hotel, saying that he had arrived this afternoon and was waiting at the coffeehouse. Leo told Wanda he'd go straight away and bring Karl back for supper.

Karl was pleased by the change in Leo's looks. "They've stopped the digging in your cheeks, I see—good thing, too. And Wanda?"

"Well; getting stronger every day. She longs to see you and is waiting for us with freshly smoked sausages and a wonderful *schnaps* we bought today on the Frauenberg." When Karl looked dubious, Leo added, "We'll come back here later for billiards."

They left the coffeehouse on the square, the only one in Bruck, just across from the hotel. "Look at it." Leo prodded his friend. "The Kornmesser House—really something." The building (of which the coffeehouse formed a part), was long and sand-colored, with a rich façade of arches and columns that married Romanesque to Baroque, then laced them with iron filigree. "Built 1499," said Leo, "when they still knew how." Contemplating it, Leo could see a pageant of its inhabitants from the beginning to the present day, a procession more gorgeous each time it appeared to him. Old buildings that had weathered time, wars and marraiges and still retained their beauty always elicited this pageant, when history raced toward Leo with a rustle of skirts, explosions of gunpowder, bleeding lances, kitchen smells and golden crowns. Sometimes he noticed the sky above the building and the land around it, as it was and had been. There grazed the placid cows in pastures dotted with ladybugs and bumblebees, while the small mice scuttled under the ground in fear of the shadow cast on the field, and the hawk stood silently overhead, slicing the wind with swift wingbeats before its plunge. Then the peasant and his boy led the cows home, the herd blocking the road where a soldier of the king came speeding toward destiny. *Sic transit*, and so it would always be, the crickets playing their same song despite the hoofbeats, carriage wheels and changing national anthems.

Wanda greeted them, poured their *schnaps* and took a seat close by the window, where she could use the last light to crochet another round in her doily. She had changed into a loose dressing gown of oriental cut with pale figures embroidered on the cream brocade. Her head was lowered to her work, her neck bare and vulnerable. A swallow flew in the open window and out again. The pale light gilded her profile —"a Madonna," said Karl, and was embarrassed.

"Yes," said Leo thoughtfully. The dying light drew color from her skin: a marble head outlined with gold. He looked at his friend, a vigorous, handsome man, the sand of his hair now deepened to dark amber, fires in his eyes turning them blue-black. His profile could be stamped on a Greek coin. His chest had broadened above the still tight waist. "Kiss her," said Leo.

"What!"

"Kiss Wanda."

"In front of you? Why not behind closed doors?" His tone was forced.

"Later. Now kiss her behind the ear. Isn't she beautiful! And look, see the way she looks at you—her lips are trembling!"

Karl was horrified. "Sausage," he said. "You invited me for sausage."

Wanda put down her crocheting to get the food. They ate in silence, and afterward the men left to play billiards. They forgave each other without mentioning it—after all, it had been a joke, nothing serious, but each unconsciously stored future action.

Next day, when Leo stopped to pet the little cat in front of the grain merchant's, its owner came out and presented it to him. Leo was overjoyed, but politeness forced him to demur. "It would be an honor for me," said the merchant, bowing, "if the little puss here were to belong to the famous poet." Leo thanked him, gathered the ball of fur in his arms and went back to the hotel. He left it in Wanda's care while he went to the butcher to get fresh giblets and liver, then to the grocer's for milk.

They decided on the name Petey and christened him in a formal ceremony. Leo adored the animal in a way that perplexed Wanda. Because of Petey, they could no longer take their afternoon walks; the pussy could not be left alone for so long, he explained. It slept in their bed and lay on the desk while Leo worked, stopping to stroke the animal every few minutes. Its eyes were amber and its fur a soft gray mother-of-pearl. It showed its affection by placing itself near Leo, but otherwise displayed only sleepy indifference. Leo spoke to it with endearments, calling it "my darling," "my precious," "my sweetheart," and not even Wanda was permitted to give it food.

He doted so on the puss that Wanda was able to go off by herself for short periods in the afternoon, to walk up the Schlossberg or stroll through the town. Before Petey, Leo had never permitted her to leave his side. She thought the cat was sweet, but couldn't understand what seemed to her something close to adoration in Leo. His great love for Petey was, she thought, almost unnatural.

For weeks they lived like a three-personed family: man, woman and cat. Karl had not returned for another visit. Wanda was stronger, healthier than she'd ever been. Leo was shaping his *Legacy* with confident control, and Petey purred his spoiled contentment. Leo kept his mind on his book, desiring nothing more than what was given. He was sure of his work, suspended in the grace bestowed on him, where he was free of doubt, where fresh images, scenes, came to him daily and, after the morning's submersion into writing, he surfaced in gaiety on the afternoon. Evenings were soft and loving, with light meals (which Petey shared), games of cards or backgammon (while he watched or dozed) and early bedtimes for all three in the large bed.

One night Petey whimpered strangely in his sleep, waking Leo abruptly to a sharp sense of alarm. He sat up in the dark, his heart pounding, and waited: the whimpering came again, an unmistakable sound of pain. He got up, lighted the lamp and took Petey in his arms. He stroked the cat, called it his little darling, whispered soothing words, but the animal began to tremble, then vomit. Leo, who usually retched at the sight or smell of vomit, cleaned it carefully, took Petey in his arms again, on his lap, covering him with his nightshirt. The little cat shook violently, in spasm, and vomited again. Numb with fear, Leo again cleaned the small circle and again resumed his seat. He was crying now, and as he stroked Petey, crooned to him, he felt the tiny body tremble in his hands. Then the cat was calm and seemed to be sleeping. Leo hummed a lullaby, while tears he didn't notice ran down his cheeks. Suddenly the cat gave out a wild shudder, more violent than any before, ending suddenly in death. Leo screamed and Wanda ran from her bed to him. He didn't notice her, he went on screaming, he rocked the chair furiously, his face was covered with tears, his hands grasped the furry corpse, and his wild eyes focused on nothing.

Wanda was terrified. He wouldn't speak for a long time, but howled and keened his pain. Later, when the words finally came, they were incoherent. "This body, this boy. My son, my son . . . he died for me." Silence, and then: "Where are you, my darling Marika? Rosa, fair naiad? Mother, in your wildest dreams. You died. And Rosa, my son. Where is she, with pale hair streaming, a pistol waving freedom?" Wanda dared not leave him alone to go for a doctor. She made tea and brought it to him, but his eyes were still sightless; he didn't notice her.

He rocked in the chair, the cat in his arms, moaning like a wolf on the steppes. Then, his voice clear, he held his head erect and sang:

> "Down to the river
> My sweetheart goes.
> Who will find him
> When the water flows?"

When he finished, he turned to Wanda and said, "Marika, you must not be afraid, little darling. My mother will look after you." Then he fell into silence again. Wanda called him, but he didn't hear. Through the night he wept, sang and spoke in words so delirious she feared he was possessed. At dawn, he suddenly looked down at the dead cat in his lap, raised it, held it out to Wanda and said, in a normal voice, "This is not my child."

She herself wept then, in relief. Later they went out for wood, made a small coffin for Petey and buried him at the base of the Schlossberg between two poplars.

They remained in Bruck until Leo had finished two more novellas in the "Property" cycle, then traveled to Graz, where, on the twelfth of October, in the Church of Saint Blood on the Herrengasse with the bride and witnesses in black, they were married.

PART IV

Interim (DOMESTICITY)

I have the feeling of having been sold or of having bonded myself to the devil.
—Leopold von Sacher-Masoch, *Venus in Furs*

13

Retired POLICE DIRECTOR Sacher-Masoch didn't attend his son's wedding, and he died a few weeks later, bequeathing his new daughter-in-law a gift she fondled on her tongue, the small preposition "von" that meant she was now the wife of Leopold Sacher-Masoch, Ritter von Kronenthal. The elder cavalier left behind little beyond the title; most of the furniture went to Charles and his solid bourgeois family, and the small sum of money saved from a life of service and from his pension went to a fading but still-attractive widow in Graz in whose parlor the old man had often sat heavily after a good dinner, reminiscing about days when people were decent and civilized and bowed at the sight of him.

Leo and Wanda lived in Bruck, where they rented a large apartment for little money. Leo enjoyed the peacefulness of the village, and Wanda was happy to escape her native town, which she detested. She was soon pregnant again, but long before she came to term they acquired an unexpected child in little Lina, daughter of Leo by The Clairmont, who had not kept up her payments to the peasant woman employed to care for the girl. The woman brought Lina to the Sacher-Masochs' door and in great humility, addressing the writer as Your Excellency, said she must return the child. Little Lina was pale and very thin, with the long oversensitive face of her father. Wanda looked at her and saw infested streets, potato peelings that would have to serve as dinner, stains on dingy walls, and told Leo that Linerl must stay with them.

He was delighted to have a little daughter and played

with her sweetly while Wanda and Frau Rümelin (who lived with them) prepared nourishing soups and dumplings for her. The little girl resembled him and was very shy. She crept into his lap and put her two frail arms around his neck with the furtiveness of an urchin. But after a few days Leo wearied of the new toy, his illegitimate daughter, who rarely spoke and struck him as unintelligent. When he patiently explained something to her, a dull look would come to the child's eyes. She was always cold and she bolted, sometimes shrieked, at any sudden noise. An unfortunate inheritance, Leo decided: the looks of her father and the mind—if chameleon thoughts could be so characterized—of her mother.

Leo left her to the women: Wanda, her mother and Majinka, the sturdy Bohemian girl they'd hired as servant. Majinka had robust arms, a hefty build and long honey-blond hair. Leo called her Brunhilde and enjoyed teasing her about her strength. "I'm as strong as my brothers," she said proudly.

He admired the force in her. "Do you think you could beat me in a wrestling match?" he asked.

"But Herr Doctor, why should I wrestle with you?"

Leo smiled and read her one of his stories. She listened wide-eyed. Next day he read to her again, and when Wanda protested, saying the girl was not being paid to hear stories, Leo coolly informed his wife that Molière read all his plays to his servant.

In the evening, when Mama Rümelin and Linerl were out of the way, Leo played "Bandits" with Wanda and Brunhilde, who chased him around the apartment, laughing in their romp until they'd caught him and tied him up. Then Wanda whipped him, but lightly, all in the spirit of fun, and he asked Brunhilde to take up the whip, to beat him the way she would a bad dog, or the way masters formerly beat their peasants. She did as she was bidden, smiling proudly, and the blows she rained on Leo were strong as a man's. Next day she was dismissed by Wanda, who could not tolerate the scandal of a servant beating her master. Another girl was hired, although "Bandits" remained Leo's favorite game.

On the seventh of September, after a long and difficult

labor, Wanda gave birth to a healthy baby boy. He was christened Alexander and called Sasha. The child was beautiful as an angel, declared his father, a golden-haired cherub with eyes of love. This was the child of his heart, and Leo wept to Wanda in gratitude. A few weeks after the birth, Wanda received a surprise from Vienna, large dressmaker's boxes arriving at her door, filled with treasures ordered by her dear Leo, who had vowed to adorn her like a queen. A gown of black velvet, another of pale violet silk; a white satin dolman trimmed with black fur, a ball gown of oriental design, a white brocade. She tried each in turn, her face pink with happiness, parading proudly before her worshiping husband and applauding mother. She was the wife of a knight, and mother of a future knight and now had the wardrobe befitting her station. She was not pleased, however, when Leo displayed a cavalier attitude toward the bills that came from Vienna. They would be paid some day, he said, but Wanda was so agitated about money matters that he suggested she take over their finances. She wrote out a contract stating that all monies received be given to her, and Leo signed it.

Wanda was beautiful in her motherhood, and the child was breathtaking. Leo worked on the stories of his "Property" cycle, but at times he felt the fire going out under him. As mother, Wanda had grown more beautiful but more listless. Her cruelty and mystery diminished, and the life-giving terror he'd felt in her presence dwindled to a feeling not much stronger than nervousness, a banality.

He knew the fires could be fanned by her infidelity. He begged her to tell him about former lovers, other men. He asked for details of their bodies, their performances and all the ways and degrees in which she felt desire. She offered what he asked for, but he could tell she was lying. His memory was brilliant for such details, and he noticed that she often contradicted herself. He suspected there had been no other lovers, and that she invented details with the same plodding dutifulness of wives who recited their husbands' genealogies.

Wanda did as she was told and didn't question her feelings. Without being aware of it, she was beginning to feel a dislike for her husband, the kind many women live with all their lives, accommodating themselves to each new resentment as chronic sufferers will unthinkingly place their bodies in an attitude that brings least pain. She served him because they were married; the warmth she had felt for him through gratitude and hopefulness no longer existed. As his wife, she took her identity from him, and though she thought him peculiar and often found his commands unpleasant, she obeyed him and complained to no one. To admit his failures was an admission of her own conspiracy. She was glad, however, that Sasha didn't take after him, and that no one could suppose Leo was the father. By serving her husband, she ensured protection for her child. She would do everything in her power to make sure he was not deprived in any way, or deserted.

Leo begged her to find a lover; she pointed out that she was nursing the child and couldn't leave him. By spring, however, she was pregnant again and Sasha was weaned. Leo sent her to Graz to find her Greek (Bruck was too small).

As her train pulled away from the station he was winded by loss, and jealousy crippled his movements. He wrote her that he was burning, he missed her unbearably, counted the hours and couldn't sleep until she was back in his arms. She returned two days later, telling him she'd been attacked by a violent toothache as soon as she left, had spent her time nursing the pain in bed and had decided to come home. She'd not worn any of her beautiful dresses or gone to the theater, or even a restaurant. Her toothache, she said, prevented her from leaving her room.

On November 25 Demetrius was born, little Mitschi with dark fur on his scalp and a small frail body. Leo bent down and kissed Wanda. "A scrawny thing, isn't it?" he remarked of his new son, thinking that Sasha was the true child of his heart, fair and light as joy itself. This squawking little gypsy looked dark and terrified, emerging into life from a demonic underworld. His mouth was too wide, his eyes too deeply set. The mouth gaped against the breast. When it found the nipple, it clamped viciously, as though to bite it off.

Leo felt uncomfortable in the apartment and left his wife and new son to the care of women while he escaped to the coffeehouse. He ordered a small coffee and settled down to read the Viennese papers. Trash, he thought, as always, censored beyond the making of sense—better to leave politics alone entirely than to weave them into a child's fairy tale. On the inside corner of the third page of the *Tagblatt* he read:

> Young man, handsome, rich, energetic, eagerly
> seeks pretty, elegant young woman for mutual pleasure.

He gasped, straightened and, to the horror of the other customers, tore the newspaper intended for all. He ran out, tripped, righted himself and continued in haste, deaf to the calling waiter.

He ran up the stairs. "We have him!" he shouted. "The Greek!"

"Hush," said Wanda. "The baby."

He insisted on replying immediately. She transcribed his dictation and he rushed out with the letter. The answer came the following day, by return mail, containing a photograph of the sender—young, extremely handsome, dressed in oriental costume, signed *Nicholas Teitelbaum.*

"I'm tired," said Wanda, who had just given birth.

Her husband urged her to rest, and he himself waited on her in bed, bringing delicacies and a hearty Burgundy he implored her to drink to revive her strength. When Mitschi was nine days old, Wanda was taken to the railway station to catch the train for Mürzzuschlag, up the line at the bend of the river Mürz.

It was snowing hard, and on the ground the snow was already very deep for early December. Icicles menaced her from the station roof, the cold stabbed her lungs and the wind bruised her face. Her high boots and thick fur didn't prevent the icy wetness from penetrating her skin, her flesh, her bones. Her body was still swollen from pregnancy; she'd lain in bed for more than a week; the bleeding had stopped only four days earlier; she was vulnerable as the neck of a wolf in defeat.

On the train she shivered. The marbled frost of the windowpane impressed her as no delicate etching, but the frozen hieroglyphics of deathly chill. Her breasts ached and she was extremely thirsty. Her mind was chilled, and she had no thoughts as she pulled the fur tightly around her except that she must survive, must return somehow to her babies.

Teitelbaum met her at the station in Mürzzuschlag and brought her by carriage to the hotel. A fire burned in his room. She stood frozen and continued to shiver.

"Won't you at least take off your gloves?" he asked with gentleness.

She stared into the flames. He laughed softly and told her in a regretful voice that he must make a confession: he knew who she was, the wife of Sacher-Masoch. He'd seen a photograph of her in Vienna, at the house of a mutual acquaintance, and, taken by her beauty, had inquired about her. He greatly admired her husband, said Teitelbaum, and he hoped she would not be offended, but under the circumstances . . .

She had removed her gloves while he was speaking. Now she smiled and gave him both her hands, which he kissed fervently.

Dinner was served in his room, an excellent meal of marrow soup, roast stuffed veal accompanied by small onions and *risibisi* (rice and peas) and rich mushroom gravy, a salad made of beans, cabbage, lettuce and beets, and plum dumplings afterward, glazed with butter, sprinkled with sugared bread crumbs. They drank more than a liter of mild, fruity Tyrolean wine, and she felt warm, almost happy, though her breasts still ached and now she could feel the moisture seeping through the front of her blouse. She pulled her shawl over her and listened while he spoke of his life, his dream of being a writer, his inability to have relations with women he knew. He was more handsome, even, than on the photograph, and she decided she liked him. She almost regretted that he could not be her Greek.

Leo burned despite the cold as he waited for Wanda to return. When she told him what had happened, he wept. She believed they were tears of love, but he felt only loathing now for this woman, who so bitterly exposed him to ridicule.

* * *

The most beautiful woman in Europe still, or the most beautiful monarch, despite being a grandmother (an absurdity, she felt, a misplaced fact), Empress Elisabeth continued to ride, sitting erect on the horse's back, her slim torso rising from the billowing skirt like the upturned stem of a vase, her hat perched on gleaming chestnut hair, a crop in her gloved hands, narrow hands, fingers slender as a woodcock's bill. She rode to her heart's content, to her heart's urging, in England's misty air and over the turf of Ireland. She was the best horsewoman in Europe; no one could fly as she, and she sped all day, avoiding the invitation of Queen Victoria (who informed her advisers that the Empress of Austria was "badly brought up"), riding beside a man who understood her urgency. He knew little of court etiquette, but could speak to mares and raced with or against the Empress, taking mad hurdles, flying out into space and tumbling down, rolling in the turf or mud and coming up laughing at his own miscalculation, shaking his head with wonder at the still erect, gently smiling queen. He wasn't with her, though, when she fell from her horse in Normandy. At the news, the Emperor was deeply concerned and wanted to rush to her side, but she sent a telegraph saying he mustn't come, it was all nothing, she'd be home soon. And though it was a concussion, she didn't want her long, proper husband beside her but the stocky English captain who dashed with her, laughing, over the boggy turf and brought her into a tavern to drink Irish beer with the common folk. She was a creature of mind, soul and body. Andrássy, her old critic, belonged to the first; Ludwig, her twin, to the second; and Bay Middleton, the captain, was with her in physical strength, radiant health, body with body.

Rudolph came riding in England too, but she hardly had time for him, the heir of Austria who delighted Queen Victoria, who visited the Prince of Wales and won the affection of Disraeli. To Rudolph, riding was a pastime, as women were beginning to be; he loved hunting more than either, but mainly he was political; he cared desperately about the governing of nations and the lives that subjects could aspire to. He was stunning to look at, with a mind that set him apart from the ruling classes. He felt that all men, regardless of station, must earn their living by work. He was up in the morning as early as his father, had inherited his father's memory and attention to details, but had a quick imagination and a flair for writing. His father suspected him already, on many grounds, and his mother kept her distance. Sophie had adored him, but his own parents always gave him the sense of intruding. His mother, with her extraordinary beauty and love of literature, seemed the most perfect of women. His father was cold and insensitive, someone to be feared. He himself had grown up so quickly that he discerned a staleness before he was twenty-one, and already had glimpsed boredom waiting in the arms of women.

*   *   *

At times Leo thought he was losing his mind. Words flew up like flushed partridges and disappeared before he could bag them. Or else they marched as stiffly as soldiers, uniform and undistinguished, flattening his prose in drab conformity. The second cycle of *Legacy* was finished, and he feared his own lack of invention. At times, he felt he had written everything he had to write, and if he put pen to paper in the future, it would be only to imitate himself, to go on repeating like an old parrot the only words he had ever learned. He was ready to make the devil's compact, presented to artists in middle age or later when they feel their powers failing or have been given the terrible insight that their talent will not support the purpose they aim to serve. The compact is always the same: the artist offers whatever and everything he has in return for the gift of creation. The devil promises words and inspiration, taking as payment the man's life or his sanity. Leo was ready to commit himself to drunken existence, to live with obsessions and fetishes, no matter how ridiculous he seemed, because he was doomed to write, and his passage on earth was a painful expiration through offerings of words and phrases he could gather only at the edge of madness.

Wanda was forced to do as he asked for the sake of the children and the family income, which depended on Leo's writing. She had to sit in his room while he worked, dressed only in furs, a whip nearby to be used whenever he asked for it. "Wanda," he'd said, "don't be weak and stupid like other women. Please don't. Understand what I need from you and give it to me with conviction, with your whole heart." She understood only that he refused to write if she didn't obey his strange wishes, and when the writing stopped, so did the money.

The ritual became part of their lives, though a thing apart. He still hoped she would have courage enough to take a lover and betray him, but she'd never felt desire for any man, and resisted infidelity through both a lack of appetite and a suspicion that Leo asked her to do this so he could then leave her. She was willing to be an obedient wife as long as her actions remained in the family. She recognized that Leo was a good man. He worked diligently, supported her, the children and her mother, and could be a loving father, particularly with Sasha.

When Sasha developed a bronchial influenza, Leo abandoned his work to be with the child. He remained at the boy's bedside, reciting little poems and stories while Sasha regarded him gravely, too young to understand completely, but following the cadences and rhythms of his father's voice with deep satisfaction. Leo sang to him songs he'd learned as a boy, and soon Sasha sang along, his infantile lisp stumbling over the unfamiliar sounds of Ukrainian:

> "My years, they are passing,
> And summer flies—
> Oh, I weep at the river—
> Happiness dies."

Sasha accepted food from no one but his father, who spooned gruel and soup into the little mouth without interrupting his flow of words. Leo told Wanda, "If Sasha is taken from me, I could not live an hour beyond him." And the boy recovered. He became strong enough to leave his bed, and father and son walked out together into the early spring, each seeming to mimic the other's unsure gait, gathering flowers that had once been stars, Leo said, but fell to earth when they saw Sasha was ill, and bloomed for him.

On Sasha's second birthday, the family moved back to Graz, leaving behind Frau Rümelin, who had been invited to share an apartment with another woman and was encouraged to accept by Leo, who promised her a regular allowance. Leo hoped that the return to Graz would restore his productivity. Bruck was peaceful, but the long isolation from literary men and matters had dulled his wit and discrimination. When a number of people wrote inviting him to be in Graz for the celebration of the theater's centennial, Leo read this as a sign that the phase of Bruck had ended and it was time to return to literary circles.

When Leo arrived, Joseph presented him with an American silver dollar, minted for the centennial across the seas. It was a good omen, representing a widening sphere of influence. The *Revue des Deux Mondes* intended to publish the work of Sacher-Masoch with regularity; he had a strong following in France and a young Swiss translator who wrote him charming letters, so lively that he felt he could be in love with her.

PART V

Kathrin (DECADENCE)

I'm often so badly judged!

—Leopold von Sacher-Masoch, private
correspondence, November 1877

14

SHE STEPPED DOWN from the train in the Graz railway station, holding herself tall in her pearl-gray suit, showing that she considered all Styria, all Austria, all the world, perhaps, as her private audience. She pulled off her hat and tossed back the splendid blond mane in a gesture of finality, indicating that she'd reached her destination, or that the train journey had been a long performance for which she was now taking deserved applause. The porters and passengers stared at her, a magnificent young Swiss woman molded in pearl gray, her hair streaming, who stood on the platform as though she had just been newly and radiantly born.

Kathrin Strebinger, Leo's translator, held her hat in hand, her mane streaked by the sun coming through slats of the station roof, and cast a majestic, keen look over all those on the platform. Sighting her prey, she moved forward quickly, swooped down on the Sacher-Masochs, taking Leo tightly in her arms and kissing him full on the mouth. She stepped back to admire whatever effect she'd caused, then turned on Wanda and embraced her too—though in the French manner, kissing her left cheek, right cheek, then left again. She took each by the arm, gave another toss of her head to show the porter that he was to follow with the luggage and said happily, "I am welcome in Graz. It gives me great pleasure. Your work I find exceptional, I am translating too much of it—no, *so* much, is correct? Yes. You will believe I am not so intelligent when I speak your German, but in my French I am very intelligent, and give you a wonderful language in your works."

257

Leo felt his old shyness with women and could only grin at her hurrying dialog, each word skipping to dazzle and confuse the stream. Kathrin was tall and elegant, her lion hair contrasting with eyes dark as his own. Yet a pixiness played in the elegance; her snub nose mocked those who considered beauty to be in perfect features. Though the rest of her face conformed perfectly to contemporary standards of feminine loveliness—pale skin, firm jaw, straight eyebrows—that nose stood in the center, humorously defying anyone to take such things as standards seriously. He was overwhelmed by her energy, her vital force contained in queenly bearing, and was grateful that Wanda, who seemed equally enthralled, was yet able to take up their side of the conversation.

"You must stay with us," she said pleasantly. "We live on the Normalschulgasse, in the heart of town. I'm afraid we can't offer a large room—we have three children and the servant—but perhaps you will find the small one cheerful. It's light enough and generally quiet."

"Of course, of course, it's nothing," she said. "It will be very pleasing. And then perhaps I rest a longer time in Graz, and I will find someplace to live by myself. I enjoy to live alone—ah!" She sighed, as though living by herself were a goal almost impossible to attain. Feeling the slim roundness of her hips against his side, Leo thought that was probably the case, and wondered what kind of lover or lovers she was fleeing.

After she had settled in, by removing books and manuscripts from her luggage, taking off her jacket, telling Wanda that the servant must take care to hang her clothes properly —"I do not like my dresses to grow new shoulders, you understand"—and to place her sachets of lavender in the drawer with her underclothes, she came to join Leo and have "a good conversation now about all the great things you write and what kind of man you are and what you will be writing in future for me to translate for the French people."

He had never met such a woman before. Hips encased in pale wool, breasts rising and falling demurely under smooth silk, eyes darting over his face as she talked or listened as though to inflame the words, she was decorous as polished stone unmoved in fire. He discovered that despite her flickering speech, she was more perceptive about his work than almost any other critic. Over the days, their discussions progressed, reaching out from literature into society, history and theoretical problems. He was amazed at the range of her knowledge and by her interest in political affairs. She frightened him. This woman who belonged to neither of his ideals was beautiful, strong-willed and extravagant as a czarina. But her intelligence, which brought him almost as much pleasure as it obviously brought her, was a quality he'd never associated with women and considered unnatural to them, particularly if they were beautiful. Women could possess common sense, at least at times, but until now Leo had been convinced that no woman was ruled by her mind; she lived on her essential nature, her femininity.

And yet Kathrin was extremely feminine. Every look, every movement, even the way she shaped her lips before releasing her words emphasized feminity. She appealed to a man's senses while simultaneously making sense of difficult topics—incredible.

"You are looking at me with surprise," she observed. "How I can know many things. My lover has been Rochefort, who is of great intelligence, the pig. I have loved him deeply. I loved that pig more than all the others, I tell you. He is still only a journalist now, very much in the politics. He comes of the highest family, and all are saying he should become the Premier of France. If he marries me, he cannot do that because, you see, I am not a citizen and also my class is wrong. So I say to him, 'Good-bye, better I am friend of the Premier than wife of a journalist.' And then he is giving me a beautiful piece of jewelry—from his mother, he says, because he loves me more than everything else in the whole world, even his mother. And then I go to the jeweler to find out the value and he tells me the gold is only plated. Pig!"

Leo smiled throughout her narrative, baffling as a conjuror's act, transforming love to property. "The jeweler is a pig?"

"No, of course not," she said impatiently. "It is my lover."

"But he meant well, I'm sure. It was his mother's jewelry."

"In that case, his father is the pig, and he is the son of a pig."

And that finished the topic of her great love, at least for now. Leo noticed she never remained with any theme for long. Everything about her was quick, energetic. She seemed very much in a hurry, like those who are always attempting to flee from the present configuration of their personalities to another one, a trait often seen in highly intelligent individuals, whose thoughts race so far ahead they must employ all their powers just to catch up.

"Dear Leo," she said now, her hand resting lightly on his arm, her lips soft as the inside of a petal, "We must go to the theater, and I must be seen."

"Of course."

"And you will notice how I inspire you," she added, as though in prepayment for the seat.

"You do already, my beautiful Kathrin." He bowed his lips to her hand. He thought her the most dangerous woman he'd ever met, glittering and unknowable as a bottomless lake where monsters may lurk to claim the oblivious bather. He wanted to deliver himself into her hands for cure or destruction; he felt she could lead him to adventures so remarkable they would transfigure him. But when he looked up from her elegant hand into the deep brown endless eyes he felt his awkwardness and was sure she'd never have him.

"Then," she said happily, "it is settled. We will meet people who are interesting. The bores you will be pleased not to introduce to me. We will go—you, me and Wanda, and she will be all in her furs, no? Yes, it will be amusing." She stood up. "I shall now be amusing for Wanda," she announced, "and then we shall eat. Too much talking is not good for the stomach."

Wanda welcomed her company with an enthusiasm she hadn't felt in years, an excitement she'd known only once before for another person, when she was masking Aurora in the presence of Sacher-Masoch, and he bestowed his words on her like manna. With Kathrin, now, rose again that old sense of possibility; the presence of this woman drew Wanda out of herself, yearning toward the other, who made the world more interesting and sprinkled the dust of glory into tired eyes. Wanda loved to see Kathrin laugh; she felt pride that this glorious woman consented to stay with them, to be her friend. And because Kathrin served Leo's literary work and respected him, Wanda's old admiration was stirred as she looked on her husband through the beautiful young woman's eyes. If he found favor therein, then she, Wanda, had been wrong ever to doubt him. If Kathrin would consent to be his lover then she, Wanda, might be able to feel gratitude again when he shared her bed.

"Men are simple," said Kathrin cheerfully, watching Wanda prepare the meal, "and they are always surprised, like children. I would like to give myself to them all—they are so grateful. Each one is different, like magic boxes. I would like a new one every day, each more beautiful than yesterday's. Each smells and tastes differently—ah, dear Wanda, I envy myself! My life is a banquet."

"You never feel too full?" asked Wanda, smiling.

Kathrin considered this question seriously, as though she'd been asked to comment on a work of literature. She shook her head slowly. "I think not. You see, I never take too much at one time. I am no glutton." She looked down at her slim figure, directing Wanda's gaze there also. "I select what I want for the moment, nothing more, and as soon as I feel it is about enough, I stop. I like bodies," she added thoughtfully. "Only the souls make me feel fat."

Wanda, who had never desired the body of another, or even felt the warm curiosity of those pretty women whose passion lies in the expectation of being adored, heard Kathrin's words in the way that dilettantes listen to poetry, as charming patterns of sound with little meaning or consequence beyond the present entertainment. She couldn't understand that Kathrin's lust—compounded of acquisitiveness, admiration, danger and a sense of existence so picaresque that only constant experiments, graced by the term "adventure," assured her of being—was a powerful physical sensation, stimulated by the sight of a man, ruling her with authority so absolute (for the moment) that all her forces were marshaled to the one attack, and she could not think, eat or sleep until the driving lust had conquered and been subdued. Kathrin's desire was sudden and terrible as a tempest; by comparison, Wanda's mild sense (a few times in her life) of finding a man not displeasing was the thinnest trickle from a tap not fully closed. All life needs moisture, but whereas Kathrin gasped and raged for it, Wanda took in only the amount necessary to prevent desiccation. And yet, as the poet longs for the soldier and patient clay waits to be informed by the potter's hands, the older woman saw in the younger a moving force through which she herself could be inspired. With Kathrin in the house, everything seemed brighter and more vibrant. Food was tastier and the spring air had never smelled so sweetly in Graz before. Nurtured by friendship, Wanda bloomed. For Kathrin, whose originality required an audience to exhibit itself, Wanda provided the receptiveness that brought out her quicksilver charm.

The three dined together merrily, Leo and Kathrin giving up their dissertations for Wanda's sake, Wanda and Kathrin abandoning their talk of men for Leo's. When the children were brought in to join them for dessert (apple strudel with *schlag*), they ran to embrace their Aunt Kathrin as though they had always known her, their favorite big person, magic and beautiful as a fairy. She stroked them all and made each child feel he was her special pet. Lina pressed her lips fervently to Kathrin's hand in the hopeless dream that someday she could resemble her. Sasha threw his arms around her neck and kissed her cheek noisily, while little Mitschi gurgled and drooled his pleasure. Leo was proud that he had brought them a fairy queen, and Wanda's heart was full of gratitude for Kathrin's goodness.

Within a week of her arrival, word of the beautiful young Swiss had spread through the town. Leo's cronies begged to meet her, and he invited Kathrin to join him in the coffeehouse. She didn't arrive at the appointed time, and half an hour later she was still not there. Leo assuaged his friends' restlessness.

"A beautiful woman arrived one day in the Galician

town of Kolomea," he began, "no one knew from where. She was young and blond, with majestic bearing and the clothes of a noblewoman."

To Friedl, such a story brought back the old times, and tears filled his eyes, grief so nearly stopped his ears that he had to force himself to listen, over the roar of an old death, to a story of Galicia.

"A young lieutenant, the handsomest man of Kolomea, was so much in love with her that he could think of nothing else. One day she granted him an audience. He threw himself at her feet and swore that his life was worthless without her. He beseeched her to have pity, to set him any task in return for even a ray of hope.

"Her voice, soft as the rustle of aspens, told him she would be leaving Kolomea soon, to return to her own castle in a distant country. From there, she said, she would call for him."

Leo's audience had changed its appearance over the years. Friedl had aged measurably, with deep wrinkles and gray side whiskers. His pate was bald, his nose red, and yet his face held an authority it never exhibited before. Kindness still characterized his eyes, and the loss of his wife and separation from his children had engraved a patience or wisdom on his features, as though he were deeply acquainted with the earth and familiar with her cycles. It was a face one trusted immediately because, though it contained no hope, it was equally free of fear or anxiety. The face was the man, masking nothing and showing the configuration of the soul. By contrast, Joseph had grown fat, his face puffy through indulgence in too much sweetness. Pretty Jenny fed him kisses and endearments until the taste of them brought surfeit. He needed more spice, a bitterer sensation, and he was away from home more and more frequently as he sampled the tarts of Graz to mitigate his wife's honey.

Leo's voice and the rhythms of his speech were as hypnotic as ever. His eyes were deeper, his lips more narrow, but when he wove his tales he was the same spinner he had always been. "The following spring, a magnificent blond woman dressed in widow's weeds appeared in the town of Sniatyn and lived in seclusion. Those who saw her from a distance were captured in an instant and were ready to die of love for her. When the dark and passionate son of the manor lord obtained an interview, he, too, threw himself at her feet and vowed he loved her. In a voice sweet as the fresh spring she told him she would be leaving the town soon, but would send for him from her own castle in a distant country.

"My friends, Galicia possesses many strange and evil spirits who dwell in the forms of magnificently beautiful women. Each lovesick young man who came in sight of the stranger's castle was seized and bound by her servants. He was brought into a round chamber of marble studded with sapphires and rubies, where his mistress lay on a golden couch dressed in a sumptuous fur, her loose hair streaming with diamonds and pearls. She rose as from a dream and slowly began to dance for him while singing in a voice so strange and beautiful that he felt he would go mad. He begged freedom from his bounds that he might embrace her. She smiled on him and continued her dance, revealing her flesh naked under the fur, pale as the smooth marble of the walls. While she danced and sang, her lover was tortured with knouts and spikes until, kneeling in a pool of his own blood, he fell unconscious and his limbs were hacked away. At the end, his head was cut off and given the enchantress, who threw down the fur and finished her naked dance with the bloody head in her embracing arms, her feet stained bright red by the blood in which she danced, her face shining with a look of ecstasy."

"An unpleasant woman," said Kathrin, who had just arrived.

The men stood, bowed and kissed her hand as Leo introduced them. She was stunning, Joseph felt. "And yet," he said, "it is easy to understand that a man may lose his head over a beautiful woman."

Kathrin laughed. He looked at her mouth: the sharp teeth, the hot tongue captured in the small cavern. Then the wet lips came together and she said, "For me, I prefer a man with a head on his shoulders." In their laughter, she let her eyes rest a moment on Friedl's face, and he grew warm, like the earth when the sun shines on it.

Leo wanted to be noticed. "But the story is also a para-ble."

"Of course," said Kathrin immediately, turning serious. To the others, she said, "Sacher-Masoch is a philosopher. The cruel woman is the earth, and he shows how it heartlessly treats the people."

"And Man—is he handsome and stupid?" asked Joseph.

She pondered a moment, appraising his black-pomaded wavy hair and the long lashes of his emerald eyes. "Men are stupid, yes," she said. "They will not see that the world is only what is there. They make for themselves big words like gold epaulettes and they walk stiffly, carrying high their 'Honor' or 'Duty' or 'Liberty' or whatever. They are stupid when they are 'believing' and not living."

"Those words are essential to life," said Joseph.

She cocked her head. "Men will always believe the best of themselves, even when they know it is a lie."

"And yet," Leo contradicted mildly, "ideals exist, faith exists, and love also—because men spend their lives in quest of these. Intelligent human life moves forward on the paths of its ideals."

"The moment exists," said Kathrin, "and in it is all the world." Again she looked over at Friedl, who nodded gravely. To look at her, slim and pale, burdened his heart, as though she were a treasure he'd lost a long time ago and now saw again in someone else's possession.

Hans stared at her while he served the wine and could only mumble when Leo presented him. Kathrin raised the glass by its stem and drank deeply, swallowing wine like water, the cool yellow-green liquid flowing into the red mouth. She drank in the way that she ate, or talked, or smoked, giving the present activity her full attention, but only for a moment. Kathrin couldn't sip wine or nibble food. She puffed cigarettes quickly to the end and stubbed them out. She spoke and moved quickly. Leo saw in her voracious-ness a wild magnificence, and a sensation in his groin as he watched her drinking reminded him that he wished to be devoured by her.

On their way home, he told her she was wonderful. He was nearly breathless in the effort of matching her brisk pace, and he stumbled frequently. Each time she smiled at him. "Ah," he said, "how you torment me!"

Her laughter was light and clear as a child's. "Do I?" she asked with pleasure, sweeping through the Palace Gate with him at her heels.

"You are fabulous. You could have any man you chose."

She didn't deny it, but took his arm to steady him. "Sweet Leo. It is so good to be alive and beautiful. I sometimes feel I have too much, too much of everything, and I want to give some away. Look there, to your left, that beautiful young man."

"Who? That one, the delivery boy?"

She laughed at his incredulity. "You see his mouth? It is a passionate one, and I feel I would like to kiss it. Yes," she said, disengaging herself from Leo. "Wait here."

She marched quickly toward the young man, who looked up questioningly as the elegant lady approached. When she was upon him, she reached out with both arms, took his face between her gloved hands and kissed him fiercely on the mouth. She turned and strode back to Leo, who, like the young man, was staring with lips agape. She took his arm again, and he applauded her by gripping it tightly to his side. He'd found his woman, he thought, free and fickle as nature, an incorruptible egoist with the innocence and danger of a tigress. "I am yours," he said. "You may do with me what you like."

"My good friend, you are dear to me. Slaves bore me. I am no Wanda. I like to give, you see. I give my body. When I see a man who is handsome and poor, I want to make him a present of myself so that he will be happy for a moment and rich. You understand, my dear. You too love the common people. You give your mind and your talent to them, in what you are writing. I do it in another way. We will be good friends. I do with myself what I like, but not with you. No slaves. To have slaves you must lose your freedom."

He didn't argue, but his hopes remained firm. When they reached the house, Wanda was already dressed for the theater in her pale lavender silk. Both kissed her, and she glowed with the praise. Then Leo turned abruptly to Kathrin. "Will you do something for me?"

"If it gives you pleasure," she answered graciously.

"Come." He led her by the hand to Wanda's wardrobe, where he selected the long ermine. "Will you wear this to-night? For me?" He watched her face, not daring to breathe.

She turned her back to him so he could help her into the fur. Then she went to the long mirror and admired herself slowly, striking different poses to study herself from different angles. After long scrutiny she announced, "Yes. I will give you that pleasure. And now"—she turned to him, shrugging off the cloak so it fell to the ground—"I will go and rest. Then I will dress and we will come late, so all the people look at our entrance."

When they arrived, the audience did as she'd predicted. Kathrin and Wanda entered the box with Leo behind them and arranged themselves opulently in their seats, throwing back the rich furs to reveal deep décolletés. Around Wanda's neck hung a collar of amethysts. Her shoulders were bare until held by the pale lavender, which deepened by contrast the chestnut of her hair. Next to her sat Kathrin, in a dress of deep forest green, nearly black, with black lace at breasts and wrists to bring out the paleness of her skin, her true blondness. She wore a thin chain of white gold with a diamond cross as pendant. Opera glasses and lorgnettes were raised to the magnificent pair, and women muttered to their husbands in disapproving tones that late arrivals should be made to wait until the first intermission, while the men nodded vaguely, plotting to get a message into the box. A spray of camellias was brought to Kathrin, white roses to Wanda, and Leo was delighted that neither woman expressed surprise or gratitude, but merely took his offering as their natural due. Then the messenger returned, with a sprig of speckled pale green orchids for Kathrin. She fastened it to the bodice of her dress, her torso haughty in awareness that all eyes were on her. The pale green rested against the deeper green like a mountain river against the moss. She read the card aloud: *In deep and unabiding admiration—Count A.* She half turned in her seat to address both Leo and Wanda. "Who could it be, this count?" She smiled and patted the corsage, beautiful as Titania, while women in the parterre smoothed their long gloves with sighs of exasperation.

267

"Perhaps it's written backwards and should read, '*A count,*'" whispered Leo, unable to resist.

Kathrin laughed and turned her eyes to the stage. But during the first act she and Wanda whispered to each other, annoying Leo by the disrespect they showed Nestroy, that great dramatist, as though his wit were nothing more than background atmosphere. During intermission, he chastised them. Wanda gave him a mournful look, but Kathrin was immediately contrite, apologized on grounds that she was too excited at being in an Austrian theater, and promised to come see the play again, when she would "hold every word in my ears like a beautiful shell."

Now a stream of men poured into their box: civil servants, army officers, bank directors and tired younger sons who whined effusiveness to Leo, twitching head or shoulder to show they wished an introduction. To Leo's astonishment, Kathrin received all with the charming smile or patter he'd thought she reserved for those of value. Every man left her feeling assured he had made an impression, and that she'd be waiting for him to call. When the box had emptied and the lights dimmed, Leo whispered, "You'll turn my house into a circus with all these clowns."

She placed a finger to her lips and indicated the rising curtain. He was helpless and annoyed.

At home, after Wanda had gone to bed, he questioned her. She told him she had taken an apartment of her own, where she was moving on the morrow. It was in a Renaissance Hapsburg building, color of egg yolk, on Beethoven Strasse, two streets from Wanda's birthplace. She hadn't mentioned it earlier because "I didn't want to offend your hospitality."

"But why did you tell all those men that they could find you here?"

"Maybe in one of them," she said with a naughty look, "you find a Greek for Wanda, no?"

"No." He was angry, and when she saw that she had overstepped, Kathrin reached out her hand, her face softened into innocence and she looked so vulnerable that he was forced to forgive her.

Next day he helped her move and in the evening called on her, at her invitation. She received him in a champagne-colored kimono, haloed by the smoke of a Turkish cigarette. She opened a bottle of Moët & Chandon for the two of them. "You are clever, Leo," she said. "Yesterday when the flowers came, you understood."

He looked at her blankly. "From the count? Did you discover who sent them?"

"What 'discover'? You hit with your pun. I sent them—Count A was of course A count, my account."

"*You?*" He gave a loud laugh.

"Why not? My first time in an Austrian theater. All must think I am much admired. All men want what they think other men want. If they think, This woman is desired by a count, they think, Ah, this is a woman for me. Men are very vain, Leo. They are little kings, and they want someone to go ahead of them, to taste to see it is not poisoned."

"You understand men so well?" he asked lovingly.

"Of course."

"Do you understand that I'm dying for love of you?" He went down on his knees and reached for her hand. With the other, she stubbed out her cigarette viciously. In dying, its aroma became stronger and sweeter. "Stop, Leo, or I shall not talk with you. You want what you cannot have. Sit beside me and I will tell you of my lovers. All men when they meet me are saying, 'I am not worthy to kiss your hand.' That is true, of course, but I do not say so. If I like the man, I will have him."

"What man is worthy of you, Kathrin?" asked Leo, who had no choice but to obey her, and was now next to her on the sofa watching her roll another cigarette.

"Whoever I desire. A woman takes a man and he becomes her ideal. He says before, 'I am not worthy,' and then, when he is in the arms of an intelligent woman, in only a few minutes he is convinced he deserves everything. She talks to him and strokes him, and he believes everything she tells him he is. Men are waiting to be invented by a woman, and they take as the truth what she says. They are vain, you see, my dear. In only a few minutes, a stupid man will believe that this woman understands him, and that no one else has understood him before. He thinks he really is what she has made up, and she—well"—her eyes were laughing—"she feeds him the words so he will perform as she likes."

"And afterward?"

"Maybe she will throw him away, if she is bored. Or maybe she will make up something else, so he will be leaving her and feeling sorrow."

"You speak of stupid men—" Leo realized that he had never before heard a woman speak as Kathrin did, had never before considered the possibility that a woman could think like a man, with the sexes reversed. Though the accent was different, and her speech was like music, Kathrin expressed sentiments similar to Karl's. Karl was still unmarried, still dedicated to a quixotic hedonism, having expanded his arena beyond the empire. Now he was in Paris. When he returned, would he recognize Kathrin as a sister, or would the battle between them be like two ferocious cats, for the kill? "Stupid men," he repeated, "but I don't believe you can love them. What of clever men?" Her danger was so exciting it caused confusion in his thoughts, and he was again like a very young man, hardly daring to speak to her.

"I have all my pleasure in the moment," she told him carefully, as though repeating a lesson for a dull child. "I am very happy and thanking the man who gives me his body and takes mine. You say 'love,' Leo—but what is it? You are speaking of something that lasts an instant, only when each one thinks he has the other, and when each is free to believe what he likes about the other."

"Kathrin," he begged. "I need what no other man needs. You recognize me more than any other woman—"

"Then why must I be making love with you?" She stood up and paced the room, exhaling smoke. "No. We are two poles. You belong to Werther and the soul. I am not like that. I am admiring you, for you are an important writer, and you say many things that no other writer says. You understand the peasants, the simple people. The stories you are writing about the Jews will be a great work. Your soul has much suffering. For you, love is pain, and I want to give you no pain."

"Kathrin," he moaned.

She stopped short and looked at him with curiosity. "It is so bad, then?"

He nodded.

"I cannot bed with you, but if you like, I will talk to you of my lovers, and I will let you watch me while I am making love. Are you happy with that?"

"The thought is agony. My beautiful queen, you have complete dominion over me. Use me as you will. I am grateful to be used in any way you like."

"You are not very beautiful, Leo," she said thoughtfully.

"I know," he said in embarrassment.

"You are quite ugly."

"Yes."

"And still, you can be exciting to many women. I know how it is—in your face is something many women can want. But Leo, I can never be making love with you. Still, you are a man I like better than any other. Give me your hand and you must go to Wanda. It is late."

He bowed his head over her hand, curiously grateful for the favor of her touch. He also felt alarm to realize her power over him, so different in kind from all other women, and infinitely more dangerous.

*　　*　　*

Hunters and huntresses, of whatever prey, share the thrill of the chase. Hunting levels people, and Crown Prince Rudolph went off at dawn with Gyula, a peasant's son, to enter the shy ways of wild creatures and outwit them through his own patience. Against nature, all men are defined by their species. Just as King Ludwig charged the night and found company with foresters, so his cousin Rudolph sought no loftier friend than Gyula. Hunting was his passion, to which he turned when affairs of state permitted him respite. His mother found her calm in speed, but he needed long hours of silence to restore himself. After leading soldiers, or battling with papers, the heir to the throne crouched in perfect stillness, his ears tuned to the slightest sound and his mind free.

Since his majority, it had been overtaxed. Rudolph was an intelligent man, and a frank one. He disagreed with his father and with Bismarck. They suspected him and tracked

271

him down through spies. Occasionally, when he went hunting at Gödöllö or elsewhere in the empire, Rudolph felt the desperate irony of being hunted. As statesman, he had to learn the tricks of deer and rabbits—either freezing in place to blend with the landscape or running so fast no one could keep up with him. He understood fear very well and had obtained a human skull for his desk. He felt terror whenever he looked into the eyes of a dying animal, and supplicated his own fate by dealing it to other creatures.

*   *   *

The advent of Kathrin brought a new contentment to the Sacher-Masochs' marriage. Her personality was a diversion necessary to their calm, and the net of marriage was quickly repaired to hold the glittering, thrashing fish. Wanda beat her husband with regularity and without complaint, wearing a *kazabaika*. He, assured of the lash that expiated him from cruelty, was hard at work on his *Jewish Stories,* a cycle of short stories about Jews in all countries, from England to Turkey, and in all situations, from wealthy Rothschilds to illiterate rural peasants. The stories were often gay, and all were chockful of anecdotes. Now he wrote about Adolph Tigerson, the *Possenreisser* (official buffoon) of the Jewish community in Lindenberg, northern Germany, who married a pretty, clever girl named Fischele.

Theirs was a happy, fun-loving household. . . . On one occasion Fischele prepared for the Friday evening supper a kugel (a Sabbath dish), which she had carried to the baker's to have roasted. Small was the modest kugel when she had taken it to the baker's, but when she returned, it was much larger and gave off a delicious aroma.

"Our kugel has been changed," said the husband as he drew up to the table.

"What difference does that make?" responded Fischele. "I met the cook of that rich Moritz Weintraub at the bakery. It won't hurt him to eat our little kugel for once."

"You are right," said the *Possenreisser* with a sigh.

At that moment there was a knock at the door. A *schnorrer* entered and asked for something to eat and drink. "Here, my friend," said Tigerson, "come, draw up a chair and eat with us." As he spoke, the hospitable host helped the astonished guest to the first piece of the kugel.

Scarcely had the beggar thanked them and taken his departure when Fischele said drily, "You have not asked for your deserved slap in the face today."

"For what, pray?"

"For having served the beggar before anyone else."

"Oh, that was done with premeditation. When Weintraub sees our little kugel on his well-spread table, there's no doubt he will get red in the face with anger and cry at the top of his lungs, 'May he who first tastes of my kugel choke on it.' So, my dear, that is the reason why I helped the *schnorrer* before you."

Fischele was satisfied with the explanation, and laughed as she put away the remains of the delicacy.

Next day, the merry philosopher of Lindenberg prepared a surprise for his wife. . . .

Leo put down his pen and looked at Wanda lovingly. A handsome woman she was, wonderful mother and devoted wife. She lacked nothing except danger; she was woman incarnate. But in that moment, before she was aware of his gaze and could meet it, Leo remembered an amazing conversation with Kathrin the evening before, when she had told him, "A woman is excited by mystery. Many times I am making love with a man who has not what you call intellect. Sometimes I am falling in love. If a man is not so clever as the woman, he should remain quiet and she can imagine him as she likes. She can make him clever and talented, if he says nothing to interrupt her. But if he is really stupid, he tells everything to the woman, and right away she sees he is a nothing. If a man is a fool, he should be wise and keep still, so his mistress can make of him a king." Then she'd smiled, her face opening like clouds to reveal her blond light, and added, "You, Leo, believe that no woman has a brain. It is all right so, for you. For me, it is all the same if a man has a brain or not. Rochefort had a big brain, the pig. It is no matter."

Remembering what that extraordinary woman had said, Leo let his eyes return to the paper. Perhaps she could tutor Wanda, initiate her into delights of the flesh and teach her desire for a man. Then Wanda, too, could become dangerous, with the power of infidelity, the bright cross on which he longed to hang himself, to feel pain racking his limbs and his heart torn.

She was coming today for the midday meal. Wanda showed restlessness, the slight fidgets of anticipation. He understood her concerns as hostess and freed her. "I have the next few paragraphs firmly in mind," he told her, "You may go and attend to your other duties."

She thanked him with a small smile and rose, going first to her own room to shed the fur, then to the nursery where Mitschi played alone (the others were in school), a sad little monkey, mournful with the bright beads of his abacus, incomprehension destroying his serenity. She took him in her arms and carried him to the kitchen, where she placed him in the laundry basket. In it, he rocked happily to distant lands, crooning, while she floured her hands and rolled out the dough for dumplings.

"Bah," said Kathrin, walking in the back entrance without a knock, flinging her hat on the table dangerously close to the dough. "Small minds give me a stomachache."

Holding her hands up before her, Wanda kissed her friend on both cheeks. "What is it, my angel?"

Kathrin saw Mitschi in the wicker basket and bent to kiss him. "*Servus*, little captain. Are you riding to America?"

The child beamed, and his hand reached out for the lump of sugar she'd brought. She straightened up and took a seat by the table. "They must all talk about me. Chatter-chatter, go the neighbors. I am a free spirit, am I not? Who is Frau Schinkenmaier or Fräulein Plotz or Herr Whatever-he's-called to talk about my affairs? The looks they give me! It is my apartment, I may entertain who I choose, no?"

"Of course, my darling," said Wanda soothingly. "What are they saying?"

"Bah. That I am a prostitute, a bad woman. I say back to them, *Merde*. Better to be a good prostitute than a cold fish."

"But you're not a prostitute!"

"Of course not, sweet one. Why would I take money? I have my own. You see, here." She pulled out her purse and began peeling off banknotes from a thick wad. She walked over to the window, opened it and, as Wanda gasped, flung out the notes. Kathrin laughed. "Money is nothing. But small minds, they think money is all things to everyone. Not so, not so. It is good to have and sometimes good not to have. Sometimes I starve myself for a few days—then I can take more joy in my meal."

"Kathrin, my life, what are you doing?" asked Leo in a shocked tone as he entered the kitchen, the Jewish endearment rising naturally to his lips.

"Getting thinner," she said, laughing. "My purse was too stuffed." Leo wondered if she was mad, but when she embraced him he was comforted. "I have never taken a man for money," she said. "That is stupid."

Now he understood. For a young and beautiful woman to live alone in Graz was highly suspect; if she was as unconventional as Kathrin, her situation alone would produce ugly rumors. And Kathrin added to her situation through action. Leo had heard of many escapades, most of them based on some germ of truth, which then bloomed and ripened into gaudy exaggeration. She was being wooed by a captain and one day admitted his messenger while she was taking a bath. He emerged from her apartment an hour later, clocked by the neighbors, and within a few days the sole messenger had become a regiment. So the men multiplied, through envy or malice, and finally, when the doctor was seen leaving her doorstep at two in the morning, the ladies of Graz closed their doors with finality to her. (The doctor, a good family man, had come in earnest to attend to sharp cramps in her legs and stomach.) Now Leo and Wanda could no longer take Kathrin along to invitations for tea or dinner, and their own guest list was cut short by husbands inquiring discreetly, before accepting, whether the "French miss" would be attending—in which case they would have to decline, as their wives could not be expected to present themselves in such company.

Conventional minds move along strange tracks, choosing as destination whatever they most disapprove of. So the virtuous wives made a study of Kathrin's promiscuity and assumed that her interests, like their own, were entirely prurient. But Kathrin explained to Wanda and Leo that "It's stupid to give such importance to something so simple and natural as love," and, in fact, expended little thought on the matter. Her appetite was quixotic and catholic; though her interest in politics had declined through living in a foreign country, her love of literature and of the whole broad study known as "human civilization" was strong as ever. Her appetite included a hunger for learning, and at present she was studying pre-Christian and specifically Egyptian art, a direction shown her by Rochefort.

At dinner, she brought out a letter she'd received that morning from one Sefer Pasha, a Polish count who had been the all-powerful minister of the Egyptian viceroy and now lived close to Graz in his castle of Bertholdstein, where, it was rumored, he kept a priceless collection of Egyptian art. Kathrin had written to him, mentioning her friendship with Rochefort and her present occupation in Graz as Sacher-Masoch's translator and expressing "overwhelming desire" to see his treasures.

The reply, which she held in her hand, had come by return mail. Sefer Pasha begged for "the honor" of a visit both from her and from Sacher-Masoch, "whom I have admired for many years as a great writer with deep understanding for Slavs, particularly Poles, such as myself."

"Will you accompany me?" asked Kathrin.

Leo was struck with inspiration. This Pasha was obviously a Greek, living among treasures in a castle. If Kathrin took Wanda with her, both women clothed in finery, then probably, this time at least, he could depend on debauch. Under Kathrin's tutelage, Wanda would ripen—and the Pasha, who had surely spent his life in voluptuousness, would find the deflowering of a virtuous wife more piquant than simple aquiescence to Kathrin's candor. And if not, if the man was a lion, then he would copulate with the lioness. Leo felt weak. "Yes," he said softly, "we'll all go. And Wanda must have a new dress made."

Kathrin's look pierced him, and then she laughed. "You

old schemer," she said. "I, too, will have a dress made." She clapped her hands. "It's settled, then. I will write that we will honor him in ten days' time. More dumplings, please. They are light as clouds and I am feeling much better."

15

SEFER PASHA, who had retired from public life at the age of forty a few years earlier, was proud of his fitness. His waist was taut, his muscles strong, and his teeth—which he liked to display—were sound and white. He rose every morning at six and galloped through his park before returning for breakfast. Now, on the morning of the day when he expected the writer and two women as his visitors, he watched the groom take the Isabella horses through their paces. They were magnificent animals, with delicate pink heads—a gift from the Empress Elisabeth in return for the Nubian he had sent her after she'd expressed her fancy for the black boy. He'd been a good Nubian, that one, much better than the one remaining in Pascha's possession. The other had whiter teeth and flashed them more dangerously when he danced. His legs were longer, he was faster and more graceful. A pity, to lose one like that. At sixteen, he still had many more years in him. But the horses were beautiful, and not every man possessed such a token from the Empress. He'd also received a photograph of her, mounted on an elegant white stallion, holding the reins in white gloves, her hat and habit dark. From the billowing skirt rose the famous waist, slim as a milkweed stem. Written by her own hand in the right corner was an expression of thanks and her signature. Another treasure.

Sefer had taken, loved and been feared by many women. But, except for an eleven-year-old girl from the Cairo marketplace, he'd never had a woman with such small hands, such birdlike bones as the Empress. He liked women who were slim, fair and virtuous, elegant as cats and pure of heart. Chastity delighted him and virginity was his greatest joy. Like most libertines, he felt noble, even pious, when he was able to bequeath himself to one who had never been shown pleasure before. His sacrifice was her ecstasy, and his generous nature contemplated nubile girls of good families like a philanthropist about to bestow a fortune on a beggar.

Seasoned women, too, could be delectable, though theirs was a reliable flavor. And great ladies, countesses or higher, were like exotic birds that gave greatest pleasure to their owner when they were caged. The ladies arriving today would be sparrows, he guessed, but perhaps their trainer, Sacher-Masoch, had taught them tricks.

*   *   *

When Elisabeth emerged from her bath of warm olive oil, she was brought a sprig of jasmine. Only one person could have sent it, and she ordered her maids to discover quickly where he could be found. Then she urged them to hurry while dressing her, and she sped out to meet him in Schönbrunn.

Her eagle had grown far too stout. He took hold of his cousin's slim hands and stepped back to admire again her wonderful face. "My white seagull," he said. "My restless bird."

"Ludwig," she whispered. With him, she felt at home, even in hated Vienna. Only he could bring her out of prison and soar with her. He lived in an aerie built on an icy crag and yet was safe. He ruled the night and wove his loneliness through Wagnerian strains into glorious edifices of crystal, porcelain, lapis lazuli, gold, silver—all of them reflected in mirrors, mirrored themselves in other mirrors like long halls of dreams.

The cousins remained together a few hours, speaking of shared memories and hopes, of the castles they were building or planning to build, of Rudolph, who—they both agreed—had wings of a Wittelsbach (though sadly pinioned), of Byzantium and Greece. They dipped into each other and were refreshed. Then he took his leave. "Adieu, Sissi. May the Lord keep you and love you and shine His light upon you."

*   *   *

Sasha stood waving until he couldn't see the carriage any more. Then he asked solemnly, "Where is our mama going?"

"To a beautiful castle," Leo told his son, one hand covering his swollen cheek, "where she will be treated like a queen. Come inside now, the breeze is too fresh."

After many hours of thought, Leo had decided it would be best to let the women travel alone. Sefer Pasha was unquestionably well-bred; he would therefore show discretion toward a woman accompanied by her husband. Since the married couple would be given a room, possibly a bed to share, intimacy between host and guest was precluded. Taking advantage of a slight pain, Leo had worked out a plan.

On the day before their departure, he complained of a toothache. A dentist was summoned, who examined the offending tooth and made out a prescription. Leo insisted medicine was not enough. He could feel that the tooth had eroded, he said, and demanded an extraction.

While the dentist—a meek man—prepared, Leo took Wanda aside and told her she must sit with them in her *kazabaika*, watching his suffering. She began to protest, but Leo grabbed her arm roughly and hissed, "Do it!"

In the chair, the patient's face was dead white and perspiration glazed the skin. The dentist secured the offending tooth and pulled. Blood gushed from Leo's mouth, the dentist mopped it with a towel, and Wanda's faint haughty smile remained on her lips. Natural color returned to Leo's face. He was trembling strongly. The dentist shook his head over the diabolical wife, who sat regally on a chair in furs, watching her husband's agony with disdain.

Afterward, a handkerchief covering the swollen cheek, Leo helped Wanda pack, selecting with great care the garments she was to appear in at different times of day. He took his time, designing complete ensembles from underclothes to jewelry, holding up this color against her face, then another, then laying it against skirt or bodice. He insisted she memorize the combinations and made her repeat the occasions when she was to wear which.

The costumes were charming, intended to bring out the full measure of Wanda's vulnerability. If Pasha was, as Kathrin imagined, an oriental type and despotic, then he would be most enticed by the picture of a chaste wife, a demure little woman with soft frills. To Leo himself, no woman was so exciting as Kathrin. But he knew also that other men might quickly discern her attitude to love, which she could sip nonchalantly like tea or down as quickly as *schnaps* and show no aftereffects. When she recounted her "affairs" to him she was a brilliant child, fantasy adorning or shaping the incidents, her humor enlivening them as she watched his face eagerly to see her effect. Lovely prattle, but Kathrin's conquests held no poetry and never placed her in danger.

Wanda, however, was terrified by love, and so the man who could make her unfaithful would be ravaging her spirit. The thought of Wanda lusting for a man excited and tormented him, her husband, for whom she'd never felt desire, he knew. Her coldness made her appear majestic and allowed him to perceive her as cruel; though he was aware that when she whipped him or lay beside him, she felt nothing beyond hollow duty. If some man filled that hollowness, if some man made her cry out for him, her cruelty could become self-serving and passionate.

On the morning of her departure, he supervised the loading of baggage, kissed Kathrin good-bye, asked her to convey his regrets to Sefer Pasha that his indisposition prevented the journey and embraced Wanda with the admonition to "be brave and beautiful." As the carriage rolled off, little Sasha ran out to wave. The smaller boy was in the nursery, weeping softly in the strong arms of the nursemaid because his mama had left him and he didn't know why.

Wanda and Kathrin rode through the valley of the Mur, then turned east up onto the mountain's ridge, reaching a peak at Ungerdorf, descending to Pöllau and Gnas. Fields bloomed in purple, blue, yellow, white; oxen stood harnessed to plows and peasant women walked with bowed backs, dark scarves printed with small flowers protecting their heads from the sun. Cows grazed among the poppies; hens and chicks scuttled back to the farmhouse when they passed, in alarm at the wheels and hoofbeats. Old men and women pumped wells in the farm courtyards, and small children who were making themselves important by chasing baby animals away from the flowers stopped in their work and waved. Small yellow serins swooped through the air, cutting in on the flight of dancing goldfinches, while hidden warblers trilled from inside bushes and shrubs. The early mist had risen and the valley below them was sharp and freshly scrubbed in morning light. It was warm already, with a forecast in the thickening air of summer heat. Wanda thought of her furs and sighed.

"You will not wear them," said Kathrin. "In the warm weather it is crazy."

"I gave Leo my promise," she said, and sighed again. "Maybe the evenings will be cool."

"You are not content with this journey we are making, little Wanda?" asked Kathrin, squeezing her friend's hands in reassurance.

Wanda looked at her with gratitude. "It's a wonderful adventure to be going off with you," she said. "I have never before traveled with a friend. But I think of the babies at home—they're so small; I hate to leave them."

Kathrin smiled warmly. "Such sweet things. Mitschi I love, so dark like a Bohemian, and terribly serious, but sweet like a little monkey."

"Leo calls him a monkey too. He thinks Mitschi is ugly and loves only Sasha."

"That must not be. One must love all one's babies. I would never have one—such a terrible mother I would be! Always forgetting I had the baby, or losing it somewhere. But you are a very wonderful mother, and Leo must love them all. Sasha is like a little god of the sun—he is a poem. And Mitschi, he is something else—like gypsy music, very sad and lovely."

Wanda's eyes filled as she looked out the window, seeing only a blur of pastel. Leo forgot he had children, most of the time. Then he would come home with presents and weave stories out of air, holding the little ones in a golden filigree of words. Sasha loved his father like a god, but how did Leo provide for them? Despite the presence of her beloved Kathrin beside her, Wanda was conscious of familiar bitterness, grown from a fear that her children might come to know the same poverty she had lived in. She could still remember clearly the dinners of potato peelings and fat; nights so cold she was kept awake by the chattering of her own teeth.

Now she had a servant, a title and a splendid wardrobe —and so Wanda's resentment of her husband turned inward, as it does with many women, making her ill at times and leading her toward a life of overscrupulousness. She was beginning to expect perfection in all things (delicious meals served on time, bright days with warm breezes, perfect order in the household, sweetened coffee, soft silks), the better to enable her to find fault. Like other wives who hide their unhappiness from themselves (because they have neither means nor imagination to change it), Wanda was developing the disease of expectations, a slow strangulation that deprives the victim of surprise and beauty first, then goes on to destroy even the simplest pleasures of the senses, making a crystal day in early spring *too* lovely, *too* bright—because the sufferer knows it must pass before she possesses it. Though Wanda was not yet in the terminal stages—and the appearance of Kathrin had slowed the disease and even reversed it at times —she was already gripped by the cancer of expectation and on her way to becoming one of those people whose measurement takes in only the distance between actuality and perfection.

They passed apple trees and cabbage fields and circles of sharp mountains sectioned like an orange, joined at the base by a village. At noon they arrived at the old castle of Bertholdstein, near Trautmannsdorf, whose partial ruins seemed an intentional effect to heighten romance. Willows swept the fallen stone and paths lined with cypress and sculptures radiated from the main entrance.

Sefer Pasha stood at the door to welcome them, his black eyes flickering like quick tongues over their bodies as they descended from the carriage. He was dressed in a dark oriental robe with white embroidery and wore a heavy chain around his neck, hung with a pendant of gold adders. He bent over the hand of each woman, his full lips hovering a millimeter above their white gloves, then straightened and shouted to the servants to bring out the luggage. He gave a quick nod, acknowledging Leo's regrets conveyed by Kathrin.

"The ladies will permit me to show them my modest castle," he said, his voice falling at the end to make the question a command. He turned abruptly to lead them. Kathrin and Wanda exchanged looks and shrugged. He acted more like a curator than host, Kathrin thought, and he himself was obviously his most valued exhibit. But they followed the tall man in his long robe, to treasures fabulous and astonishing as the surprise of a garden on Easter morning. Kathrin gasped and clapped her hands.

"Mademoiselle flatters me by her interest," said Pasha formally. Egyptian stone lions crouched before medieval Gobelins; Louis XV furniture stood on Persian carpets of brilliant and intricate design, laid over a black and white marble floor; Egyptian handmaidens with bare breasts brought fruit to their king above a lacquered Chinese cabinet, and a bust of Cleopatra stared out from its marble pedestal at a window frame held in place by Italian cherubs, their plump legs molded in relief.

He was pleased by her enthusiasm (the other woman was polite, but not stimulated and aroused like the blonde) and brought out his hidden collections, telling them the history of each artifact and how he had come to acquire it. One chest was reserved exclusively for gold—coins and jewelry used by ancient rulers to procure and placate mistresses, acquire slaves or purchase land. Most precious was a rare emerald pendant, the large stone set in heavy gold. Another collection was composed of boxes, in various sizes and shapes, of different materials, most of them showing an animal carved in relief on the lid. Some were decorated with jewels, a few were made entirely of jade. He opened them to display rings, brooches, earrings, scarabs. A makeup box still contained traces of kohl—a snake box which might have belonged to Cleopatra, said Pasha, and Kathrin saw before her the kohl-encircled eyes of the queen as she lay in the arms of Caesar.

When the tour was completed, he gave them a few minutes to refresh themselves. In their rooms, Wanda told Kathrin, "I'm afraid of him. There's something terrible in his eyes."

Kathrin, in her delight at what he offered, had not yet consulted her reactions to the man. In any case, she preferred not to contemplate the characters of rich men, and if a man was draped in glory or fable, she suspended judgment entirely. It was not money in itself but those personalities formed through wealth and power that fascinated her, rendering her helpless as a cobra's prey. "We will amuse ourselves," she said to Wanda. "It will be an adventure." But Wanda's spirit recoiled from his blank ebony eyes.

They took their apéritifs in a small dining room lined with porcelain, its round mahogony table set for three. Pasha poured cherry liquid from a crystal decanter braceleted by an English silver plate engraved with WHISKY. He handed each woman her glass and raised his own in tribute to "my beautiful guests." Kathrin took a sip and set it down.

"You would prefer something else?" asked her host with attentiveness.

She smiled charmingly, excusing herself. "It is too sweet. I like bitterness better."

He pulled on a golden rope beside the lacquered cabinet where the liqueur was kept. They could hear the tinkling in the distance, and an old man entered the room with bowed head, his gray hairs lowered deferentially before the master, his body tired but tensed for command.

"Whisky for the lady. Be quick."

The old man nodded and shuffled rapidly toward the door, barely raising his feet as he moved. He returned almost immediately with a bottle of honey-colored liquid, hugging it in his arms like an infant. Wanda felt pity for him.

"Here, you lout," said Pasha. "Or do you mean to keep it for yourself, eh?" The old man handed over the bottle, and Wanda saw that his hands shook violently. Pasha grunted, uncorked it and, finding no proper glass to pour into, shouted, "You old drunkard! You expect the lady to drink from the bottle, like you do? I should have done away with you years ago. Out, you piece of filth, and bring a glass." He kicked the old man, nearly causing him to fall, and turned to Kathrin with a sleek smile of apology. Wanda set down her own glass and a hard expression locked her face.

At dinner, a plate dropped from the old man's trembling

hands. Pasha roared his rage. "You cur! You worm! Better I had let you die in the gutter. But no, I save your life—and what gratitude do I get? You steal my liquor and break my dishes. Better your neck were broken. Here! On your knees, you vomit of a she-dog." He kicked his servant, whose trembling mouth attempted to kiss the boot. "I should have you flogged. I treat you too well. Out of my sight now—you sicken me."

The old man rose painfully and shuffled out, his face blind and impassive. Wanda looked down at her plate, her appetite replaced by sick anger.

Pasha turned to Kathrin. "I picked up the old tramp from a drunken gutter in Cairo. He's a thief, always was. I kept him out of prison and brought him here because I have a soft spot for old men. I saw my father murdered by young hoodlums when I was a boy. But this one! No gratitude. I should have left him to rot in his own breath. A thief always remains a thief."

Kathrin smiled politely and distantly, not listening. Something wonderful had entered the room, in the form of a beautiful coal-black young man, nearly naked except for a beaded deerskin, his muscles rippling under the shining skin of his long chest. Pasha noticed her gaze. "You like my Nubian? I had an even better one, but I gave him to the Empress. This one is sometimes lazy."

Kathrin's eyes never left the Negro, and her breathing quickened. His full lips were deeply curved like the silhouette of a gull, his high cheekbones glistened, his head was held proudly over a long neck. Her own fingers moved in a pantomime of caress. She saw their bodies together, white limbs on black, thrashing on sable. The naked blond goddess held out her hand to the black prince in ermine. Fair Venus lay with dusky Mars, her pale hair streaming over his exhausted flesh as he slept, his limbs gracefully spread, held in her open eyes where the black light softly ebbed.

Pasha watched her, aroused by her lust. She was a cat about to pounce, a hawk just before the drop. Bright color stood in her cheeks, her fever suffused the room. Contemplating her, Pasha shared Sacher-Masoch's desire for the predatory female, magnificent in her overwhelming, mindless need, in the command of her nature. Lions fell on gazelles and foxes broke the necks of chickens with no thought, no malice. This woman, now, was ready to devour the African—she was a fierce jewel, and Pasha decided he wanted it for his collection.

Next morning, Wanda's first blurred sight of day was a pale vision on her balcony, a slim bride. She closed her eyes, drifted on the veils, and opened them again to see Kathrin, in a long white peignoir, puffing a cigarette. Kathrin smiled, resembling a vestal priestess in romantic rendition, the billowing gown trailing laces and ribbons. But her hair was thick and uncombed, circling her head like a lion's mane, a savage head rising in clouds above the decorous civility of French elegance.

She came to the bed, sat down and slapped her palms quickly against each other, as though to finish off the remains of night. "That's that," she said happily.

"Pasha?"

"Mmm." She smiled like a sated cat.

"Oh, why?" Wanda's cry came from the heart. "He's a despot, a terrible man. He thinks he can buy any woman he chooses."

Kathrin shrugged. "It was amusing for me. After you came upstairs, we were talking. He was saying to me he is afraid of being assassinated. His many enemies, they are trying to kill him. No, he is not inventing. I feel it's true. He has secret doors built in his bedroom, part of the wall, you cannot see them. A door behind his bed opens to a little staircase, then to a passage, and is leading to a hidden door behind my bed. He told me of this and I said, 'Impossible. You must show me.' He smiled, but he looked like a dangerous snake, his eyes all small and sharp like cold fire cutting through the skin, and he said, 'Come.' "

"Weren't you afraid?" asked Wanda, shuddering.

"Of what afraid? Nobody is assassinating me. I would like him to give me a horse. He is a strange man, I have not had one like him before," She wrinkled her forehead, trying to find words to characterize him. "He is like a dagger, cold and sharp, but then he is hot." He had completely satisfied her, his strangeness, the total "otherness" of his egotistical manhood drawing out such a range of actions from her, such violence and single-minded absorption in the long night's game, that she now felt the freedom of one recovering from major illness, for whom the past siege is as unreal as life was when he lay unconscious.

"I'd like to leave," said Wanda. In seeming irrelevance she confided, "Leo will be very angry at me."

Kathrin understood. "We could tell him it was the other way," she offered. But Wanda shook her head. Her sense of honesty was quaint as some women's honor, and though she could live comfortably for years in falsehood, she was unable to tell Leo lies about a "Greek." Kathrin's quick understanding of her plight made Wanda suddenly want to confide everything in her. Of all the people who had known them, Kathrin, a woman and at the same time nearly a biographer of Leo's work, knew most about their lives.

"Forgive me," she said, "but have you ever . . . were you and Leo . . . I mean . . ."

"No," replied Kathrin, realizing this was at once a relief and disappointment to Wanda.

"What he asks is . . ." began Wanda again, but she had never before talked to anyone about that aspect of her marriage.

"Not customary," Kathrin finished for her, smiling. She took Wanda in her arms and allowed her to weep there, quietly, while she murmured to her. When she had finished weeping, Wanda took both Kathrin's hands and kissed them passionately. "You are wonderful," she said.

"Not so. You are unhappy in bed with your man. But I am thinking, Wanda, you would not be happy with any man. If you were married to a clerk or a peasant who would come one time in the week when all was dark and crawl into you a moment, you would also not be pleased."

"Men have desires and women must obey."

"Rubbish. There is no 'men' or 'women' in that. Some people want some things, others want something else. Some like to eat very much, others are filled up with a little bit. Some people will be drunk with a glass of Burgundy, but some drink all the night through and are clear as the dawn. My angel, you are taking all things too seriously. Every meal is not the Last Supper," she finished enigmatically.

"It's so difficult for me. . . ." She needed sympathy and Kathrin's embrace again. "The children, and the furs, and . . ." This intimacy was making her inarticulate.

"Your man is not the most beautiful," Kathrin told her, "but he is honest. That is a rare thing in men, I find. You can be proud."

"I suppose," she said listlessly. Then she burst out, "Oh, Kathrin, isn't there anything more? I sometimes feel life is just a nasty habit. And it takes so long! And it's terribly boring. If I didn't have my children, I don't know what I would do."

"You would go on."

"Maybe. Who can know? Did Leo ever tell you about Marika?" Kathrin nodded. "She waited until the children were big enough. Life becomes a habit you can't break. It's so tiresome, it just repeats itself."

"You must be falling in love, all the time."

"But how?" It was a genuine question.

"If you are expecting nothing, then each moment may perhaps be a feast. You don't plan it, but you are always prepared for it."

"I don't know," she said unhappily. Kathrin raised her up and kissed her softly on the mouth. To Wanda, the touch of her lips felt like the down of a young bird. It was the gentlest touch she'd ever felt, and she burst into tears.

"Come, now," said Kathrin motheringly. She raised Wanda's chin by the crook of her forefinger. "We will wash your face and put on your prettiest clothes and go downstairs and tell our host we must be leaving because your husband is ill."

"Thank you." Her voice was choked, but she looked at Kathrin with adoration.

To Wanda's astonishment, Kathrin and Pasha greeted each other diffidently, with not the faintest sign of intimacy.

She felt a child's sense of the adult world around her, which she would never know unless she was transformed into an adult herself—and if that happened, she would not know herself, she would be someone else. They all dined together, and then the carriage was sent for. Pasha gave Wanda a small bronze lion as a gift to her husband, a token of his admiration. He kissed the hands of both ladies and escorted them to the carriage, begging them to give him the honor of accepting a few small trinkets he would send to Graz by messenger. Kathrin nodded disdainfully, then broke free of his arm as she caught sight of the Nubian. She walked up to the young man slowly, embraced him and kissed him. Wanda and Pasha watched, seeing the bright blondness of her hair in the sun and the man's naked skin, gleaming like malachite. Kathrin returned, offered her arm to her host that he might help her into the carriage and embarked like a queen, her pale green skirt softly ushered in by a breeze.

He saluted them as they drove off, regretting that he'd not tried the virtuous wife as well. But she had promised to come back soon in the company of her husband, and perhaps that would be even more piquant. Kathrin was like a force of nature, Northern Lights that swelled the sky and held you captive until they disappeared, taking with them the belief that they'd ever existed. She was something like himself, more than an adventuress. He recognized her pace; he too had once been forced to flee authorities. Her life would be abrupt, he foresaw; her quickness and her dazzle were the bright shimmer before death. Her speed was flight.

She waved to him from the carriage window and told Wanda, "That man knows me, but I do not mind. However, I shall not be seeing him again."

"I feel he's evil," said Wanda. "Such a man could be a murderer."

Kathrin smiled softly and said nothing, pressing her friend's hand in warmth at her simplicity.

16

ON A FLOAT of deep blue velvet Aphrodite lay, pulled slowly by white horses, as stilled waves of silver gauze lapped against her skin. Her blond hair was tangled with pearls, silk seaweed wrapped her limbs. She was caught in the moment after birth, assisted by lovely handmaidens on either side. The crowd gasped, and the Emperor and Empress applauded.

In the next tableau, moving slowly up the Ringstrasse toward the Hofburg, bejeweled Helen gazed out through the intricately wrought golden gates of Troy, her ringed fingers caught in the hair of Paris, who slumped at her side after love had defeated him. Behind them, a black-haired Orpheus dreamed beneath his tree, which bore, instead of fruit or leaves, the sculpted heads of Eurydice.

More Greeks followed, to the theme of love: the great swan spread thundering wings over a half-concealed Leda, and the bright egg was already laid which would bring forth Helen. Hermes sped down the Ringstrasse with the fleet Huntress at his heels. Then love ceded to power, as Pallas Athene in a long brown toga stood among the ruins of a temple, holding out the scales of justice in one hand, while under her other arm she clutched a heavy tome containing the wisdom of the world. Poseidon rose with sapphire trident to calm a sea boiling with monsters. Agamemnon lay dead at the feet of Clytemnestra, as Cassandra stood at her side. This float was linked to the next, where Orestes fled the hags of fate.

Next came the rule of Charlemagne. Stout Babenbergs,

in a frieze of virility, stood erect beneath their crest. The House of Hapsburg was born again nearly six hundred years earlier under a handsome Rudolph dressed in skins; and the Hungarian Corvinus, Matyas I, held out the motto of the Magyar conquerors: *Extra Hungarium non est vita, et si est vita, non est ita.* (Outside Hungary there is no life, and if it is life, it isn't this one.)

So rolled the gods and conquerors before Their watching Majesties on the occasion of their silver wedding anniversary. Never before had Vienna seen such a pageant, as ten thousand citizens rode or marched in the parade to commemorate this jubilee. The floats were sumptuous as Renaissance paintings; no detail had been overlooked in the tableaux, where history joined allegory, immortals and humans met in lavish settings, lovers embraced forever, and bright flags married again the blue-white of Bavaria to Austria's black-gold. Music swept the procession like a train.

Leading the magic display, on a white charger, rode the man who had designed it all, Vienna's most sensational party-giver, the painter who transformed his mistresses into orgiastic nude arabesques on canvas: Hans Makart. He was dressed in furs to resemble Rubens, and the Viennese who saw him and applauded remembered his voluptuous paintings, extravagances of flesh looped in allegorical settings, where secret lusts of Viennese society ladies bloomed in the respectable hothouse of art.

"Austria," said Karl to Leo. "It must exist. Nobody in their right minds could invent it."

Since his return from Paris, Karl observed his native land with that curious defensiveness of grown children who have discovered their parents are weaker than themselves. Hans Makart, the orgiast, received the imperial commission to design and organize the silver jubilee, in a country where most women were afraid of their bodies and didn't like making love.

Leo, whose erotic stories of female sultans appeared in Austria's most popular family magazine, said, "It's because they take nothing seriously. This is a country of bureaucrats, without enough imagination to conceive of the passions underneath. They see the details—the kind of cloth from which these costumes are made, the numbers of stitches that went into each. When they read my stories, they find nothing strange in the passions of the characters because the setting is exotic, and the inhabitants of it have picturesque tribal customs."

"Theater," said Karl. "All Austria is a stage and nothing that happens on it can be really shocking. If there is such a thing as life, it's out in the wings. But on the boards themselves anything can take place because you have the comforting knowledge that it's all made up. After the passions or deaths or love affairs, the actors change into new costumes and play their parts again. I am struck," he said, turning to his friend, "by unreality in the heart of Europe."

"And the French," asked Leo, "are they so admirable?"

Karl laughed bitterly. "Only in their inability to conceal flaws. If a Parisienne has a birthmark on her face, she won't try to cover it up—instead, she adds more rouge to it, or pencils around it, and imagines that she makes a virtue out of a vice. The French character is obvious, and often unpleasant. You meet the characters of Balzac in every drawing room. But they excuse themselves so well by their 'civility' and polish that the entire world mistakes their self-confidence for brilliance and allows them to say anything at all, however unpleasant, because they articulate so well."

Leo laughed. The game of national comparisons was a great balm to him. Kathrin had ravaged his mind, thrown him off the tracks of his work. Wanda's solicitous administrations had not been able to restore him; her disdain for Pasha and her hopeless "virtue" depressed his spirit, and he felt locked in the worst kind of bourgeois marriage, where man and wife inhabit different planes of existence, meeting only to talk of rent or the children. He'd been invited to Vienna for the Jubilee by a number of litterateurs, had viewed the invitation listlessly until Karl's telegram came, saying, PARIS VAUT UN ADIEU LES MOTS DOR ME PESENT JE VAIS A VIENNE POUR LARGENT VIENS MON VIEUX. So Leo decided to accept and take his first vacation from Wanda since their marriage. He'd tried, but without much hope, to have Kathrin accompany him. She'd answered, insultingly, that she never traveled with men who were not her lovers.

Now he was glad of her refusal. For years, he hadn't felt the easy pleasure of male company. In Vienna with his friend, his brother, Leo had a sense of hopefulness, as though he could look back on what he left behind and make a new pattern of it.

He'd told Karl about Kathrin, her extravagance and her beauty, her mockery of men, her cleverness, her selfishness, her complete lack of values. She was a creature of gestures, he said, and yet a *Lebenskünstlerin*—an artist of life.

"For whom there is no truth?" asked Karl.

"None. Life to her is a series of episodes. Not even series; nothing is joined."

"I'd like to meet her."

"You will."

"Yes. Tell me, old man, does she shock you? We've both reached '*il mezzo del camin di nostra vita*'—in fact, we're moving rapidly down the hill. You're a year younger, forty-three, yet old enough to be a grandfather. And you still think—don't you?—that the road ends in a magnificent temple, or a brillance of light."

"I have never been a believer," Leo defended himself.

"Of course not," said Karl impatiently. "Not the salon variety. You don't accept a God who goes to the best tailor, and you've naturally despised our parlor game of clericalism. But you believe—don't you, old man?—that belief is possible. You're still the old dreamer, with an old-country faith that faith exists. You keep banging yourself on the walls looking for that secret door."

Leo nodded mutely. Another band was coming up the street, men in white jackets with gold piping, playing the "Radetzky March." "Let's have a coffee," he suggested, taking Karl's arm.

They walked only a few steps, behind the opera, to the new hotel that had just come into vogue. There, at the Sacher, they ordered coffee and cake with *schlag*, like schoolboys lavishing a week's pocket money. With white flecks on the tip of his nose and on his chin, Leo smiled at Karl lovingly. "And you believe in nothing at all?" he asked.

"Belief, ah. To me it is the same as experience. The cake is good, it is chocolate, it is"—he waved the last forkful a moment under Leo's eyes before putting it in his mouth—"eaten."

"Did you love any woman in Paris?"

"Many."

"Do you ever want to marry?"

"What for?"

"Have children?"

"To perpetuate my seed?" He laughed. "Yes, I admit, I thought of that. I remembered talks that we had, you and I, about women. You believed that love nourishes a woman and brings her into glory. You said her destiny requires the love of a man and the love of children. That was in our Schopenhauer springtime. You told me the words dearest to a woman's soul are 'beloved' and 'mama.' " Leo was nodding as Karl spoke. "But," his friend went on, "that was young men's fancy. The only word a woman wants to hear is 'Bravo!' "

"You sound just like Kathrin," said Leo, feeling depressed. He wondered what they would do to each other, if either would be able to affect the other. Leo couldn't be sure, yet, how deeply Karl's "cynicism" went. Paris had hardened him, but perhaps the veneer would crack or melt before Kathrin's sun, that shined on all indifferently and could hide itself at will. He would be dazzled by her, Leo was sure, if only by the powerful young beauty she wore like a challenge. And Karl was still a wonderful-looking man. He seemed to have led the years to himself, not been overtaken by them. He was heavier than he'd been, and his hair had faded slightly. But age suited him as handsomely as youth, as though he'd come in from hard riding and was now perfectly attired for tea—simply moving from one part of the day to another, always in exquisite taste. His manners still had the careless ease of the aristocrat; a slight twitch of the eyebrow brought waiters running. Doors were held open for him and women paused a moment on entering a room, to allow him scrutiny of themselves.

Karl placed a hand on Leo's arm to reassure him. Leo was thinner and paler than formerly, and still worlds away from elegance. His slenderness did not prevent clothes from bunching up—he was still the old ragamuffin, encumbered by too many body parts, shuffling through life like a hobo or tramp. But words spilled from him still like sparkling streams, he was still magic's son when he wrote or told stories. "My old dear," said Karl affectionately. There was no man he'd ever liked so much—and yet, he had to admit Leo was growing old. Physically, there seemed to be less of him, as though the hunger that always gnawed about his face had managed to devour some parts of his flesh. But the most disturbing sign of age was in repeating patterns, the repetition that turns an artist into a hack when he begins to imitate his own work, or that makes a man appear a fool to his intimates because they can predict the following sentence from the first. A small scene with Wanda in Bruck, years ago . . . Karl smothered the memory. Perhaps this would pass; Leo was sequestered within himself like a prisoner.

"I have an invitation," Karl said. "To a ball, a small one, but elegant. Will you be my companion?"

"With pleasure, *monsieur,* " Leo answered, making a small bow over the table, banging against it and upsetting the coffee cup. The brown liquid ran across the marble top and dripped over the sides.

"We'll rent the clothes," said Karl, offering a small supplication in advance to the patron of merrymakers that the white jacket would remain unsullied for at least an hour. "It's tomorrow."

Leo was as grateful for the invitation as if he were a young woman. A ball was a distraction, and he'd realized, by his spirit's plunge after they left the pageant, that he needed to be held up by occasions. Time for himself was heavy as air before a storm, held down by phrases of Kathrin that reappeared in his mind. He knew he was in love with her, knew he would give over his soul to her if she asked it, and prescience of the pain she would bring him already depressed his emotions. He had never yet watched her make love, but she had promised she would permit him to be an audience, and the agony of that would be far worse than any he had yet known. And if the man with her were Karl . . . ? With Anna, with Fanny, the pain was terrible, and yet those men were strangers. Kathrin could devastate him. He longed for it with fear like a condemned man who, at each postponement of the execution, learns to hate hope because it is a sign of life. He wanted to be rescued but not pardoned, so that his fate would always be awaiting him.

Karl paid for their refreshment and stood up like a prince as the waiter pulled back his chair. He walked out of the hotel, where he had never been before, on waves of "Your Excellency" and quick interest in women's eyes. Leo tried to batten down his envy with reminders that Karl, his brother, his love, was once again trying to restore him to health and was the paragon of friendship, who rescued him from prison by melting the bars.

*　　*　　*

Ida Ferenczy surveyed the ballroom below for a likely candidate. He must be lively and intelligent, not so young that he might blunder into presumption, and, of course, he had to be unaccompanied. She noticed an elegant blond man, extraordinarily good-looking, but his manner indicated he belonged to court circles. That disqualified him, of course— far too dangerous. There were so few to choose from! She wished she had never encouraged it; no matter what her final selection, the choice would be momentous and the situation unprecedented. Possible consequences darted at her with jeers; she longed for a fairy's wand to make everything disappear.

But it was too late. Arrayed in the gallery, mask to mask with her fabulous mistress, Ida had no choice but to continue the masquerade and offer assurances. Despite her experience of the all-seeing eye of police security, Elisabeth had resolved on this lark. The Jubilee had disturbed her deeply, Ida knew; her mistress had been shown twenty-five years of marriage and they passed in her thoughts like the parade on Ringstrasse, an ornamented stream moving down a prearranged path, propelled forward by the invisible specter at the end. She had studied Sissi for many years and knew the turnings of her mind. Twenty-five years had left little mark on her amazing beauty, but the Empress had not been protected from the ugly picture at the end, the slow walk and deep wrinkles, the hideous smile on the face that had devoured youth. She had seen something, Ida knew, and her hard need for adventure now was an attempt to find an offering that would placate the monster.

The Empress looked at her handsome friend in red domino, the intelligent face concealed behind a black mask, and thought that at least one of life's gifts, friendship, was in her possession. The friends were few, but she could rely on their love. This woman would risk everything, including her life, if she asked. Darling Mutzerl, her radiant child, was at the center, her sun securing her mother's world. And Ludwig, twin of her soul, who had been waiting for her after the pageant, who greeted her with, "My rare jewel, did you think I could leave you orphaned in Vienna on your silver anniversary?", he was the man who trod the same path, whose dreams were reflected in hers. They had talked into the night, and this morning Sissi had risen early, filled with energy that led her straight to her secretaire before being dressed. She was thirsty for work and her hand reached automatically for the pen. She drew her chair closer, recognizing the voluptuous sadness in herself as a sign of incipient creation.

Her literary work was private, usually kept from the Emperor, and a source of pride. Early in their marriage, she had tried applying her quick mind to politics. That time was exciting, with Andrássy, Deák, and the others—now held like student days, when intellectual ferment was compounded of insights and hopes. They'd worked toward the Compromise, and she knew how necessary her part had been. But she'd never received enough credit for her work, she felt; the Emperor still treated her like a child. After Hungary, nothing could again rouse her political dedication. Her husband regarded her mind as though it were simply another aspect of her charm, and felt flattered by it.

Speed and horses took her breath away, and though the mind had learned to live on small nourishment, it often called out for exercise. Franz Joseph ignored its products, her translations of Shakespeare, her poems, her insights about Heine. (But Rudolph had given her an original manuscript of Heine for Christmas last year.) Her husband was deaf to the beauty of language, she felt. He sounded a foreigner in every tongue, and only Viennese came naturally from his lips, a vulgar, nasal sound that mocked any elegance which might be lingering in the words. (Rudolph, however, shared her facility for languages, and he read the poets.)

She brought the pen to paper and allowed it a life of its own. Inspiration carried the lines and set them gently down. When the pattern was completed, the critical mind stepped forward and began rewriting, crossing out this word, that phrase, growing blank until it found the proper substitute. After forty-five minutes the sonnet was written, and Elisabeth called for her maids to dress her and bring to her a breakfast of milk. Then she copied out the poem again in her neat hand, designing elegant capitals at the beginning of each line:

> Oh, how the golden hours of my youth
> Revolve about me in my prison cell.
> They taunt these lips, that kiss the warder's hand—
> And slip away before the evening bell.
> How often have they brought me food and drink
> When I was hungry for the taste of home—
> Or when I thirsted for my childhood lake,
> And wished it had not been my fate to roam!
> Oh, golden hours—I will keep you bright!
> You shall not tarnish, neither shall you fade—
> But someday with an eagle you shall fly,
> And shine upon the world that lies in shade.
>   For where the eagle swoops, he builds his nest—
>   Then calls the seagull to her longed-for rest.

Shakespearean, she thought, as she carefully put it away. While they were still fresh, her poems had a nakedness about them that made her afraid to let anyone see. But perhaps, she thought, she'd make another copy for her eagle and send it by messenger to his grotto of Venus.

"Ida, my darling, I am feeling bored. Where is my adventure? I am waiting to be presented with a cavalier."

Ida left her mistress with a heavy heart, descending to the crowd on the floor below. She noticed a long-faced man, with a sensitive, melancholy expression. He seemed to be alone, and his posture revealed he was not connected with the court. A possibility. A short, cheerful man with clipped reddish mustache stood near her, entertaining a small crowd. His liveliness made you smile to see him; his stocky stance, his active face reminded her of Bay Middleton. Perhaps . . . but Sissi might not want to be reminded. The captain had married some years ago and had not been seen at Gödöllö since. The melancholy man sipped thoughtfully from his glass. Perhaps a scholar, maybe he spoke Greek.

As she came closer to him, Ida saw that his coat was not fresh. Too shabby for presentation. But his eyes were deep and soulful and his face resembled an early Saint Anthony she'd seen hanging in Budapest. He noticed her next to him, a majestic woman in red domino, and asked her softly if she was amusing herself. His voice was melodious. She smiled pleasantly, aware that time was passing while the Empress waited alone, and resolved to question him until she was satisfied.

"There once was a woman in Galicia," he said, his speech sounding like poetry, "a great Polish lady who went to a ball in Lemberg in a red domino. All the young men fell in love with her on sight, and when they had gained the favor of a dance with her, each was determined that she would be his mistress. . . ."

She let him weave the little tale around her, a saga of flattery, and when he'd finished, she questioned him in an offhand way, not to arouse suspicions. His answers reassured her that he didn't belong to the court and, in fact, didn't even live in Vienna. He seemed educated and erudite, and the more he talked, the less shabby did his coat appear. It was merely a trifle large for him, she decided. "Herr von Sacher," she said, having made up her mind, "it is a pleasure for me to listen to you. But upstairs in the gallery sits my beautiful mistress, who is feeling bored. Will you come and amuse her?"

"It will be a great honor," he answered, bowing. He'd last seen Karl with an auburn-tressed woman on his arms, a wonderful creature in green silks, and now both of them had disappeared. He had been wondering how long to wait and had begun to feel impatient. But this duenna was rescuing him into adventure.

Her mistress was an unusual woman—one sensed that immediately. Each gesture of hers was carefully placed, as though not to damage her, yet this was not the care taken by an invalid. When she moved, authority controlled her movement. An actress, maybe? No, the essential coquetry was lacking. A grand lady she was, certainly—not just the grande dame of a salon but a true aristocrat, at least a countess. She maintained a physical distance between them completely inappropriate to the informality of the situation, making it appear that she was granting him an audience. This impression carried through in the way she interrogated him. She was graceful and very slender. Her domino was a rich commanding white. Wisps of hair that had strayed from the cap were chestnut. She asked him about world events, his opinion on Bosnia-Herzegovina, his feelings about Andrássy, Bismarck, Czar Alexander II. He answered guardedly, as most Austrians had learned to do until they could know their interviewer. He replied that he'd come to Vienna for the Jubilee.

"What do you think of the Emperor?" the beautiful woman asked. Her gloved hands, fingers slim as twigs encased tightly in gleaming leather, played in front of her lips as though to shield them.

"A man of goodwill and commitment to duty. If his political vision were as long as his working hours, he would be Europe's greatest monarch."

Her laughter was high and spontaneous. He couldn't tell how old she was. "And the Empress? Do you admire her?"

"Of course," he said, as an utterly fantastic idea came to him. "Every man in Austria loves his wife only because he cannot have the Empress."

She grew thoughtful. "All the men in Austria are in love with her?"

"Of course."

"And in Hungary?"

"I'm sure they love her too, and more passionately."

"Ah." She breathed in as though sucking on an important piece of information. Then she changed the subject abruptly. "Do you speak many languages?"

"A few."

"Do you like to read?"

"Very much."

"Do you read poetry?"

"I do."

"Which poets do you most admire?"

"It's difficult; I don't know: Goethe, Mickiewicz, Byron, Shakespeare—"

"The great Shakespeare," she interrupted. "Yes. I too read him, especially the sonnets. I have been translating them."

"A difficult task."

"Perhaps," she said, in a tone implying she did not find it so. "I translate them into Greek also. Sometimes I write my own. And you," she asked peremptorily, "Do you ever write?"

"Sometimes," he admitted.

She clapped her hands together lightly, and her voice was happy. "Then we shall get on famously, you and I."

It was obvious she was not accustomed to strangers. She seemed unaccustomed even to conversation, which could never progress in the usual sense, never became more intimate, although she remained very friendly and curious about whatever he had to say. Yet she skipped from one topic to the next, bouncing along the surface, sometimes sealing the subject with a quick phrase that admitted no further discussion. She was quick-witted, he decided, with the easy brilliance of a child, the brightness and fascination of a dappled brook, too shallow for immersion, giving back the sunrays as it ran between two banks, oblivious to any existence beyond its own.

The conversation never deepened, never stayed on course, and yet it was not flirtatious in the manner of prattling charmers who know they may never take hold of an idea because it might explode on their pretty faces. She was baffling, this quicksilver woman who was both childlike and regal, overcultivated and free as a mountain stream, who resembled Marika not only in build, who fluttered like an imprisoned bird and tried out her notes. Intriguing and baffling, though all could be explained if his incredible idea proved true. Not possible, he told himself. After all, you just came along with Karl to be diverted for a few hours and at best return home with a pretty kitten. Your ideas are too fantastic, always were. Isn't it enough to be here with this Her, whoever she is? Why do you always permit your imagination to run off to the highest throne? This woman, calling herself Gabrielle—you're probably right to assume it's not her true name; why should she give it to you?—she's probably married. This woman certainly belongs in the high reaches of society, but can you honestly believe that the one you're thinking of would be attending a masked ball and appear there in the company of only a lady's maid?

And yet, as the artifact of their conversation began to take on high polish, the fantastic idea hardened and turned into suspicion. She was still flashing from philosophy to politics to literature, and still interviewing him. She asked direct questions about his life in a manner showing she customarily did this, demanding whatever she wished of a person without offering something similar in return. She was spoiled, but not in the usual way of pampered women whose whine can be heard even when they express their pleasure in a gift that, really, *shouldn't* have been made. She was spoiled in a grand way, as it were, never thinking to question her own absolute dominance. She was assured that whatever she had to say was extremely important (despite the nervous sentries of her hands), that her every gesture had an audience, and that her whim was an imperative. Extraordinary woman, in heavy white brocade like a lake frozen beneath a January moon.

"Do you have children?"

"Yes."

"A daughter?"

"Also."

She appeared satisfied. "I have a daughter," she told him, as though that information equaled a tome.

"Do you ever tell stories to your children?" she asked him.

"Yes."

303

"I always told stories to my daughter."

He had a scheme. If she were the One, what kind of stories did she tell her children? Of woodcutters and elves? Demons and spirits? Or of kings and queens? "May I hear one? It would be a great honor."

Her back stiffened; she was not used to the impertinence of requests. Even her maid sat up straighter. For a moment they remained in silence, and then the white lady's laughter released them. "Why not? It will amuse me. I have told no stories for a long time. Yes, I will tell you one now." She relaxed in her chair, drew a deep breath and began, in the manner of an accomplished storyteller:

"Once upon a time, there lived a young Queen. She was married to a king who ruled over two countries, and she was very unhappy. Every day she wandered alone through the woods until she came to a still lake. There she sat down and wept, because she had no children and the king paid no attention to her.

"One day, as she sat by the lake with tears running down her face, the lilies parted and a handsome man stepped out. She shrank back, but he came over to her saying he was her friend. His beauty amazed her; his eyes were black and deep. He said he was the Spirit of the Lake, and he had watched her every day as she came to the lakeside and wept. He gathered her tears. 'Your tears turned into pearls,' he told her, 'and I have been keeping them in a golden casket at the bottom of the lake. Come there with me, to my castle in the water, and forget the world.'

"The young Queen looked at him and sighed. He was very beautiful, dressed in a coat made of the shimmering wings of dragonflies. In his black eyes she could read his deep love. But she remembered her husband and her duties as a Queen, and she told him, sadly, 'I cannot come.'

"Then a drowsiness overtook her limbs and moved up her body. The Spirit gathered her in his arms and carried her into the lake, down a crystal staircase spiraling to his home. When she awoke, she found herself in a magic country, with brilliantly colored fish and shells, white and red coral islands, also pink, and water flowers that shone like emeralds and rubies. At the center of each gleamed a pearl, black as the eyes of the Water King.

"He brought her ropes of pearls and draped them around her. She was astonished to see how many tears she had shed, for now they covered her completely. The Queen lived with the handsome Spirit in his crystal palace and reigned with him over the beautiful water nymphs. The two of them slept among the lilies in each other's arms and awoke in aquamarine gardens.

"But the Queen knew that she would have to go back to her husband in the land above the lake. One day she heard him calling her and told the Spirit that she must leave. With heavy heart, he brought her out of the lake and back to her own country.

"She returned to the King's palace. A short while later she knew herself to be heavy with child. As her time approached, she hoped for a son who would return to the palace in the lake and rule over the naiads when his father was no more. Then the child was born, and it was a little daughter, with black pearls for eyes, just like the Water Spirit."

Here she ended, her slender hands resting against her mouth, and she waited for response. Her maid asked, "Did the Queen ever see the kingdom under the lake again?"

"I think not," she said briskly. "In any case, the baby meant the end of the love affair."

Leo looked at her curiously. "A beautiful story," he said.

"Yes?" She had a strange way of smiling, without parting her lips.

"And magnificently told."

"Ah." Then softly, as though to herself, she mumbled, "Yes. I can tell stories if I wish." She turned to dismiss him, holding out her hand. He bowed low over it, straightened, and protested, "Madame, I must remind you that the laws of a ball such as this do not permit a lady to select a cavalier and then send him off without showing a single favor." She looked at him in cold surprise, but he persevered: "You might remove your gloves, madame, and let me kiss your hands before I take my leave."

Her eyes signaled alarm. Her maid placed herself between them. Then the lady trilled her high laughter and he thought that if his suspicions were true, his audacity had reassured her. She rose, accepted his arm and went downstairs with him to dance. Ida watched them and her lips moved in prayer, imploring the Lord to watchfulness.

Leo noticed that she shied in the crowd like a young horse. Even the possibility of physical contact made her cringe. When they danced, he learned to keep his hold on her very loose and slack; the merest tightening made her rigid. She moved regally, and her domino was the most splendid in the room, its high boss catching licks of light from the candles of the chandeliers. She had the smallest waist he'd ever felt, like a child's. Her movements had a nervous, high-bred grace like a Lipizzaner's. Over her shoulder, Leo saw Karl staring at him with amazement.

Then they were joined by the red domino, coming to tell her mistress they must leave. She seemed almost regretful as she disengaged herself.

Leo accompanied them out to their carriage, an unnumbered fiacre of the kind people rented when they didn't want to be recognized. She extended her gloved hand for him to kiss. "I enjoyed the evening," she said. "I will write to you. In the letter you will find an address for me. Now I can give you no address. I am always traveling, like a gypsy." She stopped to laugh, enjoying the joke. "But we will correspond, and you will give me your opinions on literature and philosophy. Perhaps we will send poems. We will exchange thoughts. We may never meet again." She looked at him thoughtfully. "It will be sad for you. You will remember this evening always, and you will try to find your Gabrielle again. You will peer in the faces of women you meet, hoping to find me. But you never will, you'll never find such a woman as I. Good-bye, Sacher." She entered the carriage, her maid followed and they drove off without a wave.

He stood watching the fiacre rumble down the street, and when it had disappeared he felt a hand on his shoulder. "Well done, old man," said Karl jovially, "you picked the most magnificent woman at the ball."

"That was the Empress," he whispered fervently. "She was in my arms!"

306

Karl patted him again with a laugh. "Right, my dear, and I spent the evening with Scheherazade!" Leo put his arm around Karl and, in the highest spirits imaginable, the two men danced and shuffled through the streets of Vienna until they found a drowsy innkeeper who served them wine, and Leo's jacket was soon drenched with it.

17

WHEN THEY ARRIVED back at the hotel in the early hours of morning, Leo found a note waiting for him. He recognized the handwriting, the bold, simple address: Sacher-Masoch. Kathrin had arrived in the evening and was willing to meet him the following day for lunch. She was in Vienna, she wrote, to "restore my spirits and wardrobe."

"Now," said Leo to Karl, his elation churned through conflicting feelings, "you will meet her. The most fascinating woman alive."

"If she's anything like your 'empress,' it will be an unspeakable pleasure."

"You know?" said Leo. "It really was She. The joke is, I've called many women 'empress,' but the true one I called 'madame.' "

"It would be justice indeed if you actually met the Empress of Austria," Karl agreed, "but you're not going to find her at masked balls, I'm afraid."

"She reminded me of Marika."

"Lovely Marika." They both paid her the tribute of silence as she rose, slim and fair in each man's mind. Karl asked, "Is Friedl well?"

"He's a strong man, but he'll never recover. His sadness accompanies him everywhere, like a shadow, and will not leave him until he dies."

"Poor man," said Karl with genuine sympathy. Friedl was one of life's rarities, a good person. "But now, master, we must to bed. The beautiful Kathrin awaits us on the morrow."

"Good night, my hero. And thank you for the Empress."

"It's nothing," said Karl.

*　　*　　*

On the following day, they went to a restaurant off the Graben, a fifteenth-century place with high ceilings, old farm implements displayed on the wall, saints sculpted of wood and painted, in the traditional way, on glass. They chose a table under a plump Saint Katherine draped in burgundy folds with a fat halo over her head. The living woman under it mocked saintliness by a far more exciting quality. She was hatless, her fair hair groomed in a French style, with a double chignon: from the thick knot at the base of her head a heavy golden rope proceeded up to her crown. Her dress was gray silk, with white ruffles at the neck and wrists. It had no bustle, was long-waisted, and the skirt ended in a small flounce. Her posture showed she was well aware that the demure attire was provocative. Her breasts strained against the gray silk and small pearls gleamed in her ears. The neutral color set off the peach of her skin, her honey hair and eyes darker than chocolate. She appeared fragile and her long hands were clasped modestly in her lap. Leo flushed with pride, complimenting her. She smiled, cocked her head slightly in Karl's direction to catch his praise. Instead, he admired the glass paintings. "Their charm is in simplicity. I like them better than the statues. Their primitivism is perfectly appropriate to Christianity."

Kathrin turned and studied her namesake. "Yes. She looks like a good Austrian housewife who can always stretch a dinner for unexpected guests." Karl watched the line of her neck, bearing the stately head. She was a pleasure to look at.

He watched her again while she studied the menu, her forehead wrinkling in the effort of choice. He offered to help her, suggesting asparagus as appetizer, followed by a beef roast, and was flattered that she accepted at least one of his proposals. Instead of the beef, however, she decided on veal, cooked in wine with mushrooms, because "it goes better with the white wine, and I do not like to change in the course of a meal."

He secretly agreed, but chose the beef anyway, remind-

309

ing the waiter to bring a quarter red with it. For now, he ordered them all a bottle of dry, fruity white from the Krems valley. He answered her questions about Paris. They chatted a few minutes in French. She told him she liked living in the Monarchy. "It is all a great theater, no? Here is more interesting than in France, because here live many different kinds of people, and each kind is living in a different epoch."

"Sometimes Austria-Hungary seems to me like a miniature continent," said Leo. "It goes by a different time from other countries. Or—wait. I have it: we're living in a great Imperial pie, baked very slowly, over centuries, retaining the flavor of each of the ingredients."

They laughed. Then Kathrin said, "We are all Austrians."

"Not me," said Leo. "I'm Ruthenian."

"Rubbish," said Kathrin. "All actors are Austrians. Here is where *les grands gestes* have their home."

"And life is gesture?" asked Karl.

She nodded.

"There is no continuum?"

She shook her head.

"Kathrin," Leo explained, "lives on islands of the present, hopping from one to the next so quickly she has no idea how she came to be there."

She looked at him gratefully. He blushed, feeling superfluous. All these words would be swept away, and he along with them, when the true encounter began. He wondered how they would talk to each other alone. Conversation would be a form of preparation—at a certain point it would end and they would have nothing more to say in the presence, the obstruction, of their bodies. Then the phrases would become less rational, sentences would shrink to ejaculations, until the inevitable moment when their gaze locked and could not be loosened. Their hands, in a mindless, purposeful dance, would come together, the muscles around their mouths would tense, their bodies would become erect, their breathing expectant as the space between them was appropriated and the lips met.

"You look pale," said Karl. "Is something the matter?"

"No. No, nothing at all."

"You are tired," he said understandingly. "The ball was exhausting."

"You were at a ball?" asked Kathrin.

"Last night. Leo danced with the . . ." But the look on Leo's face stopped him, though he didn't understand. The game was an amusing one; why couldn't he tease his friend about the Empress? Too serious, too deadly serious, he was—but then Karl realized his poor friend was in love with Kathrin.

"It's a pity," said Karl, "that you didn't come to Vienna earlier. You missed the Jubilee, a splendid pageant. We're returning to Graz tonight."

She looked at Leo disapprovingly. "You won't stay a few days and escort me?"

Feeling miserable, he couldn't answer. "We've already been here a few days," said Karl. "Time to go back to work."

Her eyes blazed at him. "The work can't wait?"

"No more than you," he replied, and she felt a flash of hatred at his insolence. He seemed not to notice. "We'll meet again in Graz, I'm sure," he said, as though to comfort her, and she wanted to strike him. He added fuel to her mute anger. "I've been in Paris so long, diverting myself with charming women, that I must now return to real life—which, as you know, is in the provinces."

Leo wanted to say something, to tell Kathrin he would stay with her, he would lead her through Vienna or wherever else she wanted to be, but her anger included them both; she ate her veal with such ferocity that he was silent, and the moment passed.

She ate rudely, noisily, until her dish was devoured. Then, her anger apparently satiated with her appetite, she said sweetly, "It is good to be doing something. Eating, working, traveling. One must always be moving. But soon I will be translating your *Jewish Stories*, and then I will be doing nothing else."

"I hear you are a fine translator," said Karl. "Perhaps you will let me read some of your translations?"

She shrugged.

He was determined to make her feel the misery she was causing poor Leo. "It's fine when a man has such a pretty translator—or when a woman can find her occupation through a man's work."

He succeeded. She was in a magnificent rage. Her cheeks took on a charming hue; her eyes were fierce and naughty. "What do you mean? A woman can always find occupation, and she needs no man. A woman can occupy herself, though a man cannot. A man is nobody—he needs a woman to invent him for himself. She shows him who he is, though she can invent herself alone. That's why men are always looking for women and can never be true to only one. A man is always hoping that he is more than he appears to be, and so he is looking for the woman who says he is." The looseness of her language signaled to Leo that Kathrin was upset. She could speak nearly perfect German now, but in moments of intensity precision abandoned her.

Karl was charmed by her attack. A real little tigress, a kitten with dangerous claws. It would be amusing to battle with such an adversary, and this woman was more intelligent than most—though as vain as any. For Leo's sake, he should teach her that man was her master. He should tame her for his friend and give her to him in harness. A delightful woman, an original being; surprising as a water sprite whose fires, now playing on her face, caused him a curious sensation near the stomach. He was appraising her like a connoisseur, but just as a gourmet in a strange country may confuse the ingredients and cry out at the unexpected sharpness, or feed, unknowing, on a dish prepared with opium, so Karl was as yet unprepared for the sensations and possible addiction she might bring. She had already decided to enslave him.

She found Leo's importunings cumbersome, and Karl infuriated her. His blond handsomeness affected her body temperature and rate of breathing, but she was determined, at least at the beginning, to reveal none of it and to treat him with the contempt he deserved. However, she was not able to practice her policy. After her return from Vienna, she rarely saw him. He didn't call on her, and though he frequently visited Leo and Wanda, circumstance or arrangement dictated that her visits almost never coincided with his.

To her alarm, she realized that the thought of him was often in her mind. Though she had nothing against love, it was despicable if not free. His lack of obeisance chained her, and this was intolerable. She began to acquire the stealth of lovers or beggars whose movements are controlled by the actions of those they seek to importune. She made a study of his habits as well as she could, and one Sunday was successful in meeting him at the coffeehouse as though by accident. She knew the others would be coming soon and, like an actress on the Greek stage, wasted no time in diverting dialog, but went directly to the central action: "You have been avoiding me."

"Have I? Forgive me. It is my loss." She was stunning in her light summer clothes, the thin voile stirring restlessly around her body. "Will you do me the honor of permitting me to call on you?"

"Yes."

The day was warm and soothing. Even inside, he could smell the fragrance of the air, mingling with Kathrin's deeper scent. The sun would continue to shine for many hours. It was a day that stroked away whatever years had accumulated since twenty-five, and the woman was young, beautiful, ripe. He touched her arm lightly. "If you have no objection . . ." She nodded briskly. He paid and followed her out.

They spoke little on the walk of twenty minutes to the house where she lived, matching their steps, breathing the same air, each constrained from words by expectation. In her sitting room, on a chair of gold velvet, he accepted wine in the same color. They toasted each other and small words were released, phrases as thoughtless as their sips. She waited, in a womanly way, for his physical initiative. Light gilded him, and she was too warm in her clothes. He leaned forward and kissed her, so gently it was almost painful for her not to increase the pressure. She trembled, and he kissed her again, his lips exploring her face with a blind man's delicacy, over her cheeks, eyelids, lashes. Again he moved down to her lips and her hands caught his face, held it firmly, her mouth pressed against his, opened the lips. She kept him a long time, released him by moving her hands along his shoulders. The small table stood between them, and her hands dropped away from him a second so she could rise. He rose too, and she came into his arms, pressing him against her, her arms encircling his large body, filling with him. She raised her lips—and his hands on her shoulders gently pushed her away. "Not yet," he said in a low tone.

"What do you mean?" She broke free, stepped back.

He grinned. "You are too accustomed to conquests. You make them and soon forget them. But I want to keep you awhile. And so, my lovely, I will make it a little difficult. We will come together in time, but not now." He felt the rightness of his action, though he hadn't planned it. She would make love wonderfully, when they did, but she needed time to fill up with him, to think about him and desire him so strongly that even fulfillment would not diminish it.

"Please leave." She was shaking.

He took his hat and went to the door, blowing kisses. When his footsteps faded, she amazed herself by a short burst of tears, a summer shower that left her refreshed afterward, moist and waiting and nearly happy.

This mood lasted only a few minutes. Then she reclaimed herself, a determined woman who was accustomed to holding all the reins and resolved that none should slip. She was no toy and would not be treated like one. He would see that he had no effect on her. She would show him, and lovesick Leo too, that her only path was triumphal. She'd entered their midst and would explode upon it. By next week Friedl would be ready to die for her and their happy little male congresses would be over. (She dismissed Joseph as too easy and therefore undramatic.) Karl would relive this afternoon again and again, cursing himself for his loss.

But Friedl was not as tractable as she'd imagined. He was obviously flattered by her attentions, but so unaccustomed to seduction that he merely smiled stupidly and didn't respond. They walked along the streets together with her arm through his. She prepared light delicacies for him and served them in her apartment. He smiled and repeated his gratitude, swearing she was the kindest and most beautiful woman in existence, the cleverest also, and he spoke to her in a voice of mourning about his beloved Marika—"an angel"—and his darling children, at home with their grandmother in Galicia.

Though he made her impatient, she found herself liking him. With him she felt as safe as though walking behind a guide in the mountains. He was not strictly good-looking, though his strength showed in his face, his movements attracting people by his manliness.

On an evening when she was invited to his house for supper, Kathrin stayed behind after the others had left. She was extremely tired, she said, and dreaded the long way home. Naturally, her host offered her a bed for the night. She chose his, and undressed when he did, quickly, in the dark of his room. He took her in his arms and pulled her down. He was powerful and heavy. Neither spoke, but she cried out softly with pleasure in the near-pain of his quick, deep movements, his groin striking hers at each thrust.

She woke in the first dawn and looked over at him, who slept with lips parted like a little boy. He felt her eyes on him through his sleep and moved slowly toward her. She pushed him away and he, not understanding, moved toward her again. She sat up. "You have a bad smell," she said.

He opened his eyes, amazed. "How is that possible? I always smell like this."

She laughed warmly, in affection at his bewilderment. Men never realized that they smelled, and yet each had his distinctive odor. Most powerful were working men and peasants, and their pungency seemed to increase through the night. By early morning they were distasteful as rotting meat. The upper classes were more subtle, or perfumed, like Pasha. Sometimes a man's odor rising from her own body had carried her on a new wave of desire, even after he'd gone. She'd often breathed in this aphrodisiac, sniffing the sheets, her hands, her cupped breasts, feeling her abandonment and yearning for him to come back.

But not with Friedl. The whole room smelled of him; the cloying aroma made her want to wash. He was looking at her with perplexity, still caught by sleep. She rose, shivering in dawn chill, wrapped herself in a blanket and went to heat water. Friedl scratched the hairless top of his head and tried to go back to sleep.

When she returned, he was fully awake. He smiled at her, she returned the smile and he sprang up to greet her. He removed the blanket roughly and pulled her to him, grinding against her. She struggled, but he was strong and held her fast. She protested and he covered her mouth with his own, one hand holding both of hers tightly behind her back. His other hand helped him work his way into her. Luckily, she was tall and it was soon accomplished. He released her when it was over. She looked at him with disapproval.

"No," he told her, "you can't play with a man. Either you come to him or not. You shouldn't be a whore, Kathrin. You're a beautiful woman, with a beautiful body. But you are too restless, you must try everything. In the end, you have nothing, no love, only your freedom. And then your freedom is nothing, because it brings you only loneliness."

She was curiously touched and felt a moment's sadness, in regret at not being simply a good woman who cared for her man. She listened to Friedl as though he brought her wisdom. But then she rallied. "What you call 'restlessness' is life. No one is living properly who is not free. You cannot live your life for love. It comes and goes."

"A woman must be loved," he said. "She needs the love of a man to be a true woman."

She laughed bitterly. "You sound like Leo." Except that Leo elaborated on the theme. "She can ignore the love," he'd said. "She can trample it, mutilate it, try to murder it—but she feeds off it, she needs it to become herself." The wild romanticism of a nineteenth-century author, she thought, deriving from the world he was born into, heavy with the sighs of Werther, and returning into it, to feed the simple folk who don't read books but take their beliefs from the genera-tion of their father's masters. The time was past, she thought. She herself was in the advance, but even the hefty bourgeoisie was beginning to recoil from the suffocation of love and death they had inherited from German Romantics. The twentieth century was only two decades off, and she predicted it would pay more attention to the inventions of Bell and Edison, regarding man through his machines, than it would to the great credos of literature and Christianity. One was always able to think more clearly after fornication, she reminded herself.

"No. Leo sees Woman as magnificent and cruel. I like his happy stories best, where the women are clever and pretty. But you are not the woman for any man. You are not womanly."

They were still naked, their bodies two facts of existence, drained of eroticism after the act. They sat on the edge of the bed in the slowly lightening room, where shadows shrank as the day brought its benediction of color. In the corner hung the crucifix, a bouquet of dried Alpine flowers at its base. The walls were white. The large wardrobe was painted in traditional peasant style, trimmed with wildflowers. She stroked his face and kissed him gently. Her hair was thick, tangled by the night, frizzed around her head in a blond aureole. Almost sadly, he removed her hand. "No," he said. "If I am to have a woman, she must belong to me. You are beautiful. You can excite any man. But I would rather be left alone and have my peace. Come now," he said, smiling in his old open way, "I'll make us breakfast."

She recognized that she could go no further. With men in the arts and politics, with civil servants and army officers, she could slacken the rope and then pull it in any time she pleased. Men who lived for sensation, who held their illusions in front of them, believing real life lay in suffering for a goal —they were easy prey and belonged to her for as long as she cared to intoxicate them. But a man who sought peace and lived by goodness eluded her net. She would have liked to make him pay for his insult, but was astute enough to see she lacked the means. She felt an unfamiliar sadness, a longing devoid of eroticism, something like homesickness. He had belittled her; he didn't want her, and yet she was not angry.

They drank milk and ate bread, the thick honey dripping onto her fingers. He rolled a cigarette for each of them afterward. They smoked peaceably, like two old friends. She wondered what would happen to her next, and thought of Karl.

*   *   *

At Gödöllö, the Empress opened her morning mail. The letter from Sacher had been forwarded through secret channels from Milan. It was longer than usual—she had been receiving at least one a week from him since sending him "her" address—in a hand not as good as it could be, each line sloping downward with angular strokes.

My Dear Gabrielle—

Most beauteous woman, peerless lady: Great humility comes over me as I read again your latest letter, and though my heart fills with compassion for you in your sad and lonely hours, it is also light in the knowledge that you see fit to confide in me. Your confidence is the dearest treasure I possess. I deeply believe that honesty is the highest form of friendship, though rarely achieved between a man and a woman. I hope to prove myself worthy of your trust, and to convince you of my good faith by returning your candor with full measure of my own.

Do you remember, most beautiful of women, that enchanted evening when we met, and you honored this poor supplicant by recounting a fairy story of your invention? It was a marvelous story, wonderfully told, and I would like to return that rare favor with a little fairy tale I made up for you:

Once upon a time, there lived a duke and duchess in a beautiful blue and white country of high mountains capped with snow against a sky blue as cornflowers. Lakes glistened in the sun and gleamed in moonlight, finches sang out against the dawn, and horses galloped with their fair riders across unbroken fields.

The duke was much loved by the people for his merriness and good cheer. The duchess was admired for her good looks and sensible manner. They had one daughter, and hoped for another.

On the day their second daughter was born, the duke decided to throw a great feast in her honor. She was the most beautiful child he had ever seen, she ruled his heart, and in her soft features he read signs of future greatness. He knew she would transcend both himself and his wife in power, wealth, beauty and fame.

Now, in this enchanting blue and white country dwelled many spirits of the woods, lakes and mountains. All the spirits took forms of women and all were beautiful, though not all of them were good. The duke issued a proclamation inviting everyone, even the spirits, to the feast honoring his daughter's christening. A boar was roasted and hundreds of sweet tarts were baked. Frothy meringues and cream puffs rose on mirrored trays in frames of lapis lazuli, these miniature mountains peaked with whipped cream reflected as in a lake.

The guests were as merry as their host. Acrobats and jugglers, clowns and magicians all came to the feast, performing their tricks, astonishing and delighting all guests. And the spirit women came down from the mountains, up from the lakes, to bring their blessings to the tiny girl.

One gave her wealth, another beauty. The third bestowed power, the fourth, intelligence. From the fifth spirit she received the ability to love; the sixth promised she would be adored. The seventh gave her health, the eighth, talent. The remaining four bestowed on her the gift of tongues, a life of ease, a good husband and healthy children, and the admiration of all the world.

The duke was very pleased with these gifts, and he presented golden coins and necklaces of pearls to the spirits. As they were about to leave with their treasures, another spirit entered, more beautiful than all the others, so radiant in her beauty that the christening guests could not look on her. Her voice was like music, her movements were graceful as fountains. She came over to where the baby lay and smiled down on her, a hideous smile. "She will have all those things," said the thirteenth spirit, "but I give her the inability to enjoy any of them." The people gasped and clutched their hearts, but when they looked up, the terrible and beautiful form had disappeared.

The child grew to charming girlhood and magnificent womanhood. The prophecies of all the spirits came true, including that of the thirteenth.

Thus ends the tale. A sad story, my dearest Gabrielle, but life is cruel. Behind all beauty stands vengeance, and the glories that Nature presents to us often mask danger, brutality and death. I shall not elaborate this theme, which is too sadly familiar to me, and too unhappy for your precious eyes.

Your divine voice still echoes in my ears, and the joy of your wonderful letters fills my heart. Your slender form haunts my mind, and I grieve that I must once again take leave of you.

But one word more, angelic creature. May I suggest that the name of Gabrielle, though exquisite in sound, does not express your extraordinary nature? I would prefer another for you, one that rings with your incomparable loveliness and true majesty. I mean the name Elisabeth.

Your devoted and adoring servant,
Leopold von Sacher

She read the letter with growing horror to the end, then tore it in half, tore that half in half again, and so on until each piece was no larger than a snowflake. She tossed the flecks in the air and threw herself on the bed. Her eyes were wide open, no tears came, and she resolved never again to write him and never to permit another communication from him to reach her sight.

18

THE TWO FOURS of his age seemed ominous: a sign of repetition. His life was growing flat, stale and unprofitable; inspiration seemed to be spent as quickly as the money it brought. He'd written *Harmless Stories from the Stage World* and *Silhouettes* and *Fake Ermine—Part II*, setting down the words almost compulsively, contributing only to the support of his family, not to the great search, which was life enlarged through literature. His *Legacy of Cain* wandered aimlessly through his mind, taking no hold. He wished he could stop writing, and that he could write more brilliantly and with more depth than he ever had; that he could immerse himself completely and drown in work, to be resurrected as a new man, or artist. But the stream was drying up—and yet he was compelled to write. At forty-four, Leo had a sense that his whole life was a compulsion toward uncertain ends. He'd reached the point where nothing is new, where everything has been tried or tasted, all books read, all women loved; and the future held nothing but a promise of staleness as he picked over his past life, trying to find morsels to nourish him.

His best work of recent years was, he knew, the *Jewish Stories*. Each story was built around a central ritual or celebration—marriage, death, the Day of Atonement, Tabernacles—and each was set in a different country, each contained its particular cast of characters. In the stories, ritual was animated through human actions, and so presented a double view of humanity. Individual acts gained significance by reflecting millions of similar ones throughout history. Ritual was made personal as the symbolic act was shown to reflect individual psychology. Perhaps he could write a sequel; the book was still receiving acclaim from many parts of the empire.

Jewish scholars in Budapest had invited him to come and speak. When the invitation was reinforced by another, from Hungarian writers, asking that he help establish a bilingual literary journal, he sensed a message. The prospect of a new country, new material (in the ghetto of Budapest) and travel appeared to him as part of whatever design had been planned for his life. He would be honored and paid, hopefully refreshed in spirit, and could experience life in the Dual Monarchy from the other side.

Two months after Leo's birthday, the family went to Budapest, living in rooms rented for them in a fifteenth-century pink house on the cobbled hill of Buda. Downstairs, the Gothic benches were nearly always occupied by visitors who'd come to honor the Austrian writer. On these stone seats, hewn out of the wall they lined, sat artists and aristocrats, journalists and bearded rabbinical figures from across the Danube, waiting for the porter to take up their cards or messages and return with word that the Author was receiving, or that he was engaged at present.

The Jews from Pest greeted Sacher-Masoch effusively, embracing and kissing him as they welcomed their "brother." Despite Leo's pride that his pen had proved sincere enough to enroll him in this fraternity, he was aware of belonging to Ruthenian nobility, and that his heritage sprang from the crown of thorns and the stained ground of Calvary. His book had grown from deep study, not experience, but his visitors from Pest assumed that his Gentile blood contained a large admixture of their own.

Christian admirers of his work suspected the same but were tactful enough not to mention it. In any case, it wasn't relevant in this country, where writers were taken to be the most important men in life's gallery, more important than generals or politicians. A writer of distinction was addressed as "Poet," and a poet in Budapest was treated like a fair-skinned blond child in Naples.

He enjoyed the praise and, later, the work on the journal. His colleagues here were lively and humorous. The food, spiced with paprika, rolled in pancakes, made every meal an occasion of pleasure. His wife and children were treated with great kindness—a well-known dramatist took the children to play hide-and-seek in ruins of the old cloister on Margaret Island—and, at the beginning, he felt expectancy, a new path opening.

But editorial affairs and constant visitors kept him from his proper work. The longer he was separated from it, the more his imagination howled toward the steppes, where she-devils feasted on wolves and blistering winds swept fresh carcasses. He needed an escape into writing, and gratefully accepted the invitation of a family named Reis to live with them in the small village of Écsed, twenty kilometers north of Hatván.

In May, they took the train and from Hatván (meaning sixty: its distance in kilometers from Budapest) continued by carriage over muddy roads, pulled by plow horses harnessed with old ropes and driven by barefoot boys in cloth trousers. They arrived late afternoon at the Reis house in the high part of the village, hens flying up to scold the horses, the garden wild as a jungle. "Our entrance to Jerusalem," he whispered to Wanda, who nodded wearily with the weight of sleeping Mitschi against her chest.

Frau Reis came running out, children scampering around her, and, blushing with pleasure, she embraced the visitors. Her stone house overlooked the valley where the sun was sinking toward a border of hills at the far end of the fields. Behind the house rose low mountains, the cemetery spread peacefully on a northern slope above the cupola'd church. The houses of the village were still lit by the sun, rust red cottages prefaced by gardens. In the courtyards, animals were taking their evening feed. The high poles above the wells cut diagonals against the sky. He could see the main square, dark under the flowering trees, and the small stream beside it. Everything was right; he had been brought here as to a village of his childhood, that he might renew himself at the source of his inspiration.

The household delighted him, in its Jewishness and generosity. Itinerants and *schnorrers* were given alms and bed. A young rabbi, looking greasy and unkempt, appeared at the Reises' in two long black caftans, one worn on top of the other, his pockets stuffed with melons, and was treated with veneration. Almost every evening the gypsies came by and frenzied the air with their violins as everyone, even the young children, danced the czardas until they were breathless. The air was heavily perfumed with the aroma of Spanish fly, a soft-bellied beetle, dulling the senses like an opiate.

It was a wonderful place, but Leo could not fight off the effects of his years, his life, his nature. He worked each morning in the room he shared with Wanda (the children, Sacher-Masochs and Reises, all shared a large communal room), and, as before, he needed her in furs. She sat in sable on days when village children played in the stream and the heat made her faint. She beat him midmorning and again before dinner. Though the Reises found the Herr Doctor "wonderfully kind" to their children and servants, Leo importuned their hefty Geza to wrestle with him and whip him. He played "Bandits" every evening, letting the children chase him up the mountainside until they could capture him and tie him up. The older girls wore fur jackets at his request and were encouraged to treat their prisoner roughy. The younger children found particular delight in the game at first, but after having played nightly for weeks, they tired of it and the "dear doctor" was forced to beg and plead with them to play.

He was working on a new cycle of Jewish stories, but at times the sense of déjà vu oppressed him so greatly that he was forced to stop. Everything had been done, and yet he still longed to be whipped into creativity, to suffer his unworthiness and through that suffering be granted the love necessary to creation. Even with his wife in the room, doing everything he asked of her, even under the whip of proud Geza, Leo still thought of the One who would be his cruel mistress, the true Wanda, imperious as Nature herself, before whom he could lay his painful humanity. He still imagined Kathrin, sometimes in the midst of work, other times in his dreams. She commanded him ruthlessly, and he obeyed—though then the dream faded and he knew he would never have her.

Out of lassitude came kindness. When the need to be exorcised was not on him, Leo told stories, danced with the village girls, picked flowers for his hostess and spoke to everyone in the house with a gentleness and interest that earned him their love. No servant was too low for Leo to stop and inquire how he was and to show concern about the man's life. If anything that he wore or carried was admired, Leo presented it immediately as a gift. He walked in the fields and learned from the laborers, sometimes offering his manual help or giving a suggestion for doing the job more effectively. He helped the younger children with their reading and figures and listened with happiness as the eldest daughter played piano.

At this stage in his life, Leo had learned nothing so well as compromise. He gave of himself over and over again to those around him, understanding that to each person the small details of daily life were a definition of himself. He knew that the ingredients of a stew or the number of stitches in a piece of needlework were the facts and symbols of a person's self-esteem, and those he spoke to felt he understood them and shared their lives. At the same time, Leo was shrinking further and further into private madness, separated from all creatures of the universe. His imagination filled his mind with monsters and demons; he longed for only one thing, which was punishment, and all else was subservient to it. He kept the torment to himself as well as he could, though he sometimes screamed at night, occasionally ranted when alone with Wanda and once in a while felt an inexplicable horror of the outdoors.

Wanda was concerned, but, seeing that he was able to conduct himself publicly and earn the admiration or devotion of those around him, her concern turned to indifference and then resentment. With others, he could be pleasant; with her, he was demanding, self-pitying and violent. She now completely loathed him physically and regarded him as an incarnation of evil, destroyer of health. She kept the children from him as much as she could, and saw what she called his "dark nature" imprinted on his face.

But her heart was singing in late June, when Karl and Kathrin arrived for a visit. Her darling Kathrin, who brought the sun with her, and dear Karl, the kind friend who paid her compliments. Just the sight of them, beautiful as saints, made her happy. Held tightly in Kathrin's arms, Wanda felt the hardness in her melt. She remembered her first sight of Kathrin, in the Graz railway station. Now she was even more magnificent, more vital, as the sun played over her hair and her eyes blazed.

Kathrin turned to Leo, kissing him firmly on the mouth while Karl stood to the side smiling. "I have come to see you," she said, "and the children—where are they?—because I will be taking a long trip. Austria is running out on me."

"And Karl is running off with you?" asked Leo.

She looked over at her lover with pride. "He is accompanying me."

"And what will *I* do without you?"

"Oh, that," she answered, shrugging. "Come now, greet Karl and take me in to meet your Jewish friends."

The two men embraced, Karl hugged Wanda, and they all went inside, to be met with joyful explosions from Sasha and Mitschi, a wide, flushed smile from Lina and a curtsy from Frau Reis, who appeared as happy to see the friends of dear doctor as if they were her own. Leo smiled lovingly at the good woman. Within ten minutes, he knew, she would have beds and fresh linen for them, and she had already set plates for them in her mind.

It was remarkably unpainful for Leo to see the two of them together. He told himself the lack of pain came through inevitability—they were so perfect as a couple it seemed they'd been paired at birth. This man and this woman deserved each other like Mars and Venus; they were here together simply because it had to be. They looked at each other proudly, but not flirtatiously. Each was known to the other; each had taken the other and given him back to himself. Leo felt no envy. He would never be worthy of such love, and his pride was that he had helped give them to each other.

In the evening, after supper when the gypsies played and the sky was pale apricot, Kathrin came over to Leo. "Will you walk with me?" she asked, offering him her arm. He rose, bowed to the others and went off with her, shuffling quickly to keep up with her pace. They walked down toward the main square. Kathrin, in a crisp white blouse and pearl-gray skirt patterned with tiny rosebuds, kept a determined step and said nothing. Leo felt something strange moving in her and now realized he'd had a sense of premonition when she arrived, and then again during the meal. She'd been gayer and louder than usual, the high polish of her brilliance isolating her from the others. Karl had been unusually subdued. Leo remembered her first words, "Austria is running out on me," and wanted to ask her about them. But she moved too quickly, and he needed all his breath and concentration to stop from dragging at her arm.

They crossed the tiny bridge over the stream and went into the inn. They ordered wine, and the villagers stared openly at this beautiful stranger, who smiled back loftily. When the music started, the bravest of the young men came forward, mumbled his request to Leo and turned to Kathrin. She nodded quickly, stood, and went into his arms.

For the next hour, or longer, she moved from one pair of arms to another, dancing gracefully with the young Hungarians. Leo watched her and sipped his wine. She was a phenomenon and he could think nothing about her, though an uneasiness in himself told him she was troubled. When she finally decided to stop, she marched rapidly to Leo and pulled him up. He had time only to throw down a few coins before she dragged him out of the room.

Outside, he displayed petulance. "How many conquests do you count?"

She laughed. "Poor Leo! Never mind, I still love you. Let's walk now. We'll go more slowly. I'm tired after all that dancing."

"Will you tell Karl?"

"Tell? What do you mean? I am amusing myself. He is a free person, is he not? And am I not a free person? And you —are you responsible to anyone but yourself?"

"I must be," he said almost angrily. Her words were childish. "I'm responsible to the state of which I'm a citizen, to my own family and to my fellow man."

"Rubbish. You are selfish. You live as you please. You

pay no attention to your wife or your children if they bore
you. In fact, the only child who interests you is Sasha. You
treat the others like a pig."

He stiffened. "Mitschi is morbid. The girl is not my fault,
her mother abandoned her."

"What difference does that make? Why are you judging
other people? Because you are selfish, of course. It doesn't
matter, the best ones are. You use people for your own purposes—never mind," she said suddenly, abandoning the subject. "It's all the same." She pulled him more closely to her
and he realized that, for the first time since he'd met her,
Kathrin was upset enough to be losing her powerful self-
control. "The Austrian police are hounding me."

"Why?"

"They are stupid, small-minded men."

He waited, feeling she must choose her own time. At the
crossroads she stopped before the small chapel, indicating he
should sit with her on the bench. They sat with their backs
to the Crucifixion, leaning against the iron grate, moonlight
illuminating Kathrin's face, though Leo's was held in the
shadow of a tree.

"I don't know if I'll tell you." She jerked her thumb in
the direction of the crucified Christ. "I hate a crown of thorns,
Leo. I hate the whole bloody business of Christianity. I hate
the wounds we're supposed to bathe in." She turned, and her
face flashed anger at him, as though he represented the object
of her hatred. "Blood and hypocrisy—that's what keeps our
society going." She was silent a long time. He could tell by
her breathing that she was calming herself. When she spoke
again, it was as though for the first time.

"My mother died soon after I was born. My father, they
tell me, had been a dissolute man. I'm not sure what was
meant by that, but in any case when his wife died, he became
pious, with all the vengeance and fury of converts. Instead of
stories, he recited sermons to me at bedtime. He never failed
to punish me for any naughty deed or thought, but I was
never rewarded for doing something well. It didn't matter to
me," she said, with a toss of her head. "I was clever and
learned while I was still very young how to get the better of

him. My marks at school were always first class—in the beginning, just because it came naturally to me; later, because I had gypsy eyes and blond hair. I knew how to use them very well. I entered puberty early and came out of it knowing that my face and body were instruments that I could play on whenever I wanted something. Oh, I couldn't do that at home, of course. My father thundered his God through the house and pinched his pennies. He married a rich, disagreeable woman who, happily, gave him back some of the misery he tried to drive into my life. I ignored her completely, and this confirmed her in my father's opinion that an evil spirit lived in me. She kept out of my way. He, on the other hand, was always trying to exorcise me." She laughed. "It was very funny, really, though quite painful at the time. He thought that by pulling out my tongue he'd catch the tail of the demon."

Enthralled, Leo forgot that she was talking about her actual childhood. A happy expression played over her face as she warmed up to her story. "When I was nineteen, I inherited my mother's money. Not without difficulty, of course, but by that age I had many friends and protectors who saw to it that I received what was legally mine. I took it and left home. I never saw my father or stepmother again. He lined his slippers with newspapers to save money, and when the soles had completely worn through, he attached the newspapers to the tops and walked on them. He used berry juice for ink because it cost nothing, but his letters were so pale that no one could read them." She laughed so long that Leo joined in. When she finished, sputtering, she said, *"Ce n'est rien, rien du tout.* It's nothing." She cleansed herself with laughter, like a cat.

She stood up, moonlight coating her skin and clothes, making all appear to be the same color, and waited for Leo to join her. They walked slowly, into the darkness of trees. "So where am I now? Oh, yes, I am telling you the story of my life and you are being wise and saying nothing. It is best. You think I am beautiful and clever, yes? Yes, and many men have thought the same. They have adored me and told me I am like no other woman. But in the moment I speak truthfully to them, their opinion changes. Take that Buloz, for example—he was completely in love with me. He would look at no other woman, he sent presents all the time, he said he would die if he couldn't have me. So he proposed, and I said, 'I cannot marry you.' The silly man asks why, and I say, 'because you are an imbecile.' It is completely true, but he stares at me as if I am not right in the head. His face turns a funny color and he races from the room. But he misses the door, runs straight into the wall and falls on the floor. After that Buloz never spoke to me again. I don't mind, it's all the same. But I was right that he's an imbecile."

Leo was laughing with her. In the soft darkness he couldn't see her face. Her voice was light and musical, but he suddenly remembered the rough voice of Anna. She'd told men what she thought of them and thereby preserved her honor. She'd been very strong until she fell in love with him. He'd never thought of her before in connection with Kathrin, but now it seemed that Kathrin had always reminded him of her, his Anna, the first—only?—true mistress he'd had.

"Ah, Leo, you are my dear good friend."

"Yes, my angel. And if there is anything that I can help you with . . ."

"Of course. Men always want to protect women—it makes them forget they're weaker. It is late. My story is long. Perhaps I will tell it to you, but now you are tired and you have work in the morning. We will meet when your work is over, and then maybe you will learn my 'secret.' " She said the word melodramatically, mocking it.

"Tomorrow is market day in Hort. They will all be going to it."

"Then I shall not. Maybe I shall stay behind and read your new stories, and afterward we will talk. Would you like that?"

"Very much," he answered fervently.

At the house she gave him her hand to kiss, then playfully slapped his face with it. "Good night, dear. Give Wanda a little kiss from me."

Next morning, bandits came down from the hills—three young men on horses, dressed in coarse shirts and trousers, carrying guns. Leo watched from inside the house as Frau Reis walked up to them, listened to their requests, nodded and went into the house. While she was gone, the young men patrolled fiercely, touching nothing that was not theirs, pacing the ground and grinning at each other (for reassurance? wondered Leo) until the lady of the house came out again, her arms full. She gave each a large bottle filled with clear *schnaps* and a piece of cloth, either wool or linen, in a neutral color. Now her hands were free, and she thrust them deeply in her apron pockets to bring out bright coins, which she counted first, before distributing evenly among the three. The men saluted her, mounted their horses and rode off with the speed of Cossacks.

"Goodness," she said when she saw Leo's pale face, "what's come over you?"

"Those men, with their guns—weren't you afraid?"

"The bandits? I'm used to them. They're mountainfolk, and they come into the valleys whenever they're hungry. They go to all the landowners and ask for 'contributions.' They're clever fellows, you know, though rough-looking. Not a thing goes on in the valley they don't know about. Even before they've come down, they know exactly what to ask from each."

"And from you it was *schnaps*, cloth and money?"

She smiled. "A small price. They're all Robin Hoods, you know. They make their demands in proportion to the landowner's wealth, or at least their assessment of it. Sometimes they make a mistake"—her smile was broad—"or they fall behind the times. Neighbors of ours had to give so much to the bandits that they had almost nothing left for themselves. Honest people, not poor, but they have only a small patch of land. However, their name is Ferenczy, an aristocratic name as you know, and the bandits confused them with the Ferenczys who live fifty hectares farther south and are extremely rich. Those Ferenczys"—her smile turned rueful—"were asked for only a bit of linen and a few heads of cabbage."

"And if the poorer Ferenczys had refused?" asked Leo.

She clapped her hands and opened her eyes wide. "Oh, my dear doctor! Nobody must refuse—unless he wants to find the red cock on his roof the same night, or have his supper interrupted by a bullet whizzing through the window. The bandits' bullets never miss their mark."

"I see." He shuddered. The distraction would probably prevent further work this morning. What if he had been here alone when they came? What if the others had already left for Hort, as they planned to do in a few hours? What then? Would they have murdered him? Though the danger was over, fear grew in Leo until he recognized panic. His palms were lined with cold sweat, his eyeballs ached, his heart was in his throat. He returned to his room with Wanda, who had accompanied him out, and went to bed.

"There," said Wanda, "were some chaps who really know your game. I'm sure they would have been happy to play 'Bandits' with you."

His panic was too strong still to admit feelings of hatred. Amazing, how life could imitate art. Between reality and illusion was a line so thin—if any line existed at all—that man could never know truth, even the truth of his senses. Life is metaphor, he remembered. Yet facts sometimes intruded. Or were these "facts" merely the manifestation of metaphor? Were they simply examples of the symbolic made active? The bandits were as "real" as Gabrielle, yet encountering the actual Empress brought no deeper knowledge of the imperial power of Woman. The Empress symbolized that majesty, as Christ symbolized humanity in its suffering and love, as Cain symbolized man's curse and his painful pilgrimage. This confusion eventually put Leo to sleep, and he was not woken by the others when they left.

He rose in the afternoon, feeling very hungry. In the kitchen he found Geza, kneading dough with her strong brown arms, but was too sick at heart to ask her for anything beyond food. She didn't look up from her work, but told him curtly she would serve him outside. He thanked her and went out to wait at the foot of an old plum tree, a few feet from where the children had made a secret cave.

He took his meal of cheese, bread and sausage at the table,

drinking only a single glass of Tokay to accompany it. As far as he could tell, no one was around. Kathrin and Karl had probably joined the others on their excursion and wouldn't return until night. His time was his own, but he couldn't put it to use. He tried work, and the blank paper spread blankness to his mind. He tried to read, but the letters made no sense, the words held no meaning. A sentence was simply a pattern, a progression of physical shapes indicating nothing beyond itself. He took a walk, then, behind the house, up the northern slope through the cemetery. After a time he was comforted by his body's movements, the breezes against his face, the calm of the countryside.

In the evening he found Kathrin, who had not gone to Hort, but had spent the day by herself, walking through the hills and reading his stories. She said they were fine, as good as those of the first volume, and her praise made him understand how much he had needed it, how his work had stopped and stood waiting until it could receive its reward.

They sat together in the hammock. The sun was still warm, the distant hills golden. A stork flew slowly and awkwardly above them toward its nest. "Sometimes, Kathrin," he said, feeling a desire to unburden himself in the soft evening, to offer her a small gift of himself, "I think of talent as an underground well. We can't know when it dries up. In some men, this talent gushes forth like a cataract, spilling over everything in its path, harming only whatever is too weak to take root. This great force, this creativity, purges and makes new—it renews even itself. I think of Goethe, and Shakespeare, and Dante."

He spoke to her profile. She listened quietly, without expression. "Others," he continued, "have felt that tremendous force within themselves, carving out its own path. When the talent dries up, these men don't know it, because the bed it made is still deep. So they go on—writing, painting, composing—but their energy is a dust storm.

"Energy is all the artist has left; the blood of creation has stopped pulsing; the veins are dry. Such a man should die early, or else he will know death in life and go mad." She turned and looked at him questioningly. He touched her hand and said in a voice so soft she had to read his lips to hear, "Such a one seeks punishment for destroying the promise given him, for having betrayed the godliness he was granted."

The golden ridge of hills on the horizon formed a frame for the pink fields. Kathrin was very beautiful in the dusk. Her skin gave back the color of the evening, and her brown eyes were endless. Their Tokay waited for them. They rocked gently for a long time, both silent.

"What is this perfume I smell, Leo?"

"It comes from a soft-bellied beetle. The smell of love."

"Too strong."

Again they were silent. His hand lay over hers in gratitude for his confession. She understood that he had given her something intense and private and, though she could make no use of the gift, she thanked him by reciprocating. "All right, I will tell you a story."

He removed his hand and watched her face, the brown eyes dancing. She addressed her words straight in front of her. "Some years ago, before I met you and when I was living with Rochefort from time to time, I went to a ball at the lake of Montreux—do you know Montreux? No, never mind. The people were beautiful or rich, which means their clothes were beautiful. I wore pearls in my hair and my ears and around my wrists. My dress was mother-of-pearl, a changing taffeta, with a very deep décolleté. I put a white rose between my breasts—men like to have their noses there.

"I looked very beautiful. I came to the ball to dance and be merry and also to win a bet I'd made with Rochefort. I will tell you about the bet:

"There was a young Russian prince in town, extremely handsome and tall, who had recently married a little cousin of his. Everyone talked about the bride and groom, saying they were so beautiful, so much in love, how wonderful to see such love—you know the kind of thing. Even Rochefort, who knew the prince well, said to me that he was completely in love with his wife. 'Rubbish,' I said to Rochefort. 'No one is completely in love.'

" 'You are wrong,' Rochefort told me. 'The prince is

totally in love with his delightful wife. No other woman exists for him.'

" 'Foolishness and foolishness,' I said. It annoyed me to hear such things. 'And you are a foolish man to believe it. So much love can not be.'

" 'Don't you believe in love, then?' he asked me, and I could tell he was a little nervous.

" 'It exists,' I answered him, 'but not for long.' You know, Leo, that it's a rainbow, and in the moment it appears it already begins to fade. So I said to Rochefort, 'You are a silly man to have such illusions. Fidelity is stupid, and only stupid people give it value. You must not have illusions about women—I have none about men.'

" 'Not even with me?' he asked.

" 'No,' I said, 'and I am right.'

"He looked at the floor when I told him that. You see, he had been sleeping with a young duchess the night before, though he didn't know I knew about it. I always know such things. They amuse me—what's the difference? 'Rochefort,' I said, 'your faithful prince is no different from you or any other man. If a pretty woman takes his fancy, he will sleep with her, even on his wedding night.'

" 'No!' Rochefort insisted. He was shouting. 'Not everyone is like you, Kathrin. There are men who have ideals and live by them. The prince is such a man. He is pure and chaste. His heart is simple and loving. He has given it to his young bride and will give it to no other woman.'

" 'You are making me annoyed,' I said to him. 'So you will now make a bet with me. I say the prince is like other men, and all men can be seduced. I say I will prove it to you.'

" 'Agreed!' said Rochefort, who was eager to prove me wrong; I could see. 'You will have your opportunity in five days' time, at a ball in Montreux. I'm so sure of winning the wager that I don't mind supplying the information that the prince will be alone. His bride has taken ill and is recovering in the sanatorium. He will go to the ball by himself at her request, because the hostess is a relative.'

"I had not much time, not enough to order a new dress. But the dressmaker remodeled one that I had, making the

335

sleeves tighter and the neckline lower, threading a silver ribbon under it.

"At the ball I danced with the prince, naturally. Later, as though by accident, I was in the same canoe with him on the lake. The moon's silver light always suits me well. My eyes look darker, and I'd made my lashes black. By the time we returned to shore, it had been arranged between us that I was to meet him next morning at his hotel, near the sanatorium. He stayed there alone and visited his wife, or received her visits, every day.

"To prove to Rochefort that I had won honestly, I left behind a silver comb he had once given me, with his initials and mine engraved on the handle. I hid it carefully, after the prince had left the bed, where I knew the chambermaid would find it.

"I was right. In the evening, the princess came to join her husband in his rooms. The chambermaid brought my comb, thinking it was hers. The princess saw it and understood, of course. The initials identified it.

"Without saying anything to her husband, she flew down the stairs and took a carriage to Rochefort's house. She pushed aside the servant who opened the door and ran into Rochefort's study. She held out the comb to him and tried to speak, but no words came. She just stood there, throwing her arms around wildly, her face moving in terrible grimaces. She opened her mouth wide and blood gushed out from it. She toppled and fell forward, hitting her head against the iron legs of a table. She was dead immediately.

"Later that evening, the prince shot himself." Kathrin cocked her head and looked at Leo sideways. "I won the bet."

He shivered. Beside him sat Judith. His lips moved, trying to form words, while she observed him with mocking eyes. Finally, he brought out, "The Austrian police—what have they to do with it?"

She tossed back her mane. "Nothing." She gave a small laugh. "At the time some stupids didn't believe it was suicide. What else? And Rochefort said he would get even with me. He was quite humorless sometimes." She chuckled softly, a sound like purring. "It bores me. I was bored in Switzerland.

I come to Austria and all the people with tiny minds peer at me as if I am something odd. They want to ask me about visas and how I earn money and why I came, and something else. They put chains on my spirit. They are mannikins, not people. I have used up Austria, I won't return."

"You used to say you were happy there."

"Perhaps." She tossed off former feelings like an old newspaper. "I want a place where people are generous."

"England? France?" he offered.

"Of course not. All Europe is the same. Old, used up, crammed with bureaucrats. I want people of a wild, generous spirit—across the seas."

"America?"

"Why not?" She left him swinging when she got up. She walked a few steps, turned and, with eyes twinkling, said, "I take souvenirs." She held out her hand, showing him a small Egyptian snake box and a gold pendant with an emerald large as a grape. She displayed them only an instant, gathered her hand into a fist and went inside. He rocked gently in the pale salmon evening, his eyes closed, his mind stunned and the untouched Tokay waiting on the table for their communion.

He was still in the hammock when the household returned, adults chattering, children sleepy, from market day. The sweet Tokay was now half drunk, and in the darkness no one could see its red stains on Leo's shirt. Frau Reis begged him to come indoors, worried that his lungs would be affected by the night air. He assured her he was fine, said he was hoping to have a few words with Karl and bade the rest of them good night. Surprised and relieved to be going to bed alone, Wanda admonished her husband, with wifely sweetness, not to stay up too late.

"Well, old man," said Leo softly when they were alone, "I haven't had a word with you yet."

"The beautiful Kathrin controls her subjects. She commands and we obey." His tone was gently ironic, as though he spoke of the world's inevitable ways.

"Do you love her?" asked Leo eagerly.

Karl's face was impassive in the light of the candle that

Frau Reis had brought them. "Old one, how shall I put it? She has a claim on me."

"You've heard her story?"

He nodded. "I knew she would tell you."

"And you're going with her? Even to America?"

Again he nodded.

"You'll leave your home, your rooms, your books and follow her? Even though you don't know if you love her?"

"Leo." He sighed. "How can I explain it to you? I'm forty-five. All my life I've had position and wealth. Women found me to their liking. I never had to earn money or take a wife—I had enough servants to care for me. I've been a dandy and a dilettante, and I've always played with life as though it were a rich man's toy—"

"But you have written!" Leo interrupted. "You've thought, you've painted—you've produced many things."

"I was also given a good mind," he admitted. "Another of fate's little gifts. I inherited everything and gave back nothing. You have dedication to your work. And you have a wife and children. The family forces you to make money, and an even greater force drives you to creation. You are a wonderful writer. You are Austria's pride. But look at me, old friend. What have I accomplished? And what lies ahead for me to do? A few more essays on so-called 'learned subjects' that only a handful will ever read? More conquests in the drawing rooms? More fittings at the tailor and conversations in the coffeehouse? You see, my dear, I'm quite a useless fellow."

"And Kathrin?"

"Is in flight. She's an astonishingly strong person, but now she needs someone." He decided not to reveal her confidences about Friedl to Leo. Friedl had humbled proud Kathrin, and when Karl returned to her he found her softened, more vulnerable, and grateful.

"And you're paying your debt to society through her?"

Karl smiled. "My mouth is dry. Let's finish the wine." He poured the glasses full and gulped his as though it were water. "Perhaps. *'L'âme a ses raisons.'*"

"*L'âme?* Not *le coeur?*"

"Perhaps also. Who knows?"

"You are expiating yourself through her?"

"It may be."

"And yet, in the end she may no longer need you."

"I know, but it's possible she will teach me something necessary. At any rate," he said brusquely, embarrassed by the transparency of words, "there are times when it's necessary to follow, and not ask too many questions."

Leo pondered a moment. "I shall miss you—both. Terribly."

"Let me embrace you." Leo stood up and knocked over his glass. Karl grinned, put his arms around his friend and kissed him on both cheeks. "Frau Reis is right. We'll get lung infections if we stay out much longer. The candle will show us the way. Follow me." They went into the house and to their rests. Leo's heart was pounding strongly. When he lay down beside Wanda he knew the night would be long and sleepless. Different sensations were playing around his heart; he mistook them for love, but he was very cold.

*   *   *

The castle at Gödöllö, on the route to Hatván, was particularly beautiful in summer, when the rich green and the bright profusion of flowers and blooming trees set off the egg-yolk building with festivity. Elisabeth had added two wings to the castle: the left one contained her stables and the right held a long greenhouse of palms and orchids, bougainvillea, frangipani, banana and cacao trees, brilliant little hummingbirds, scolding parrots—a Brazil in the heart of Hungary.

The grounds and building were empty now, except for the servants who maintained them. A few months earlier, Her Majesty had ridden here, when the Archduke Rudolph came to announce his wedding plans. He was formally betrothed to Stephanie of Belgium, a plump girl but a Catholic, platitudinous and premenstrual. This last fact had been discovered only after the proposal, and the marriage had to wait upon menarche. From Gödöllö, Rudolph had gone to visit his cousin Ludwig at Linderhof, a baroque jewel set in the Bavarian mountains. Rudolph had assured his cousin that "you are my dearest and most valued friend. . . . You have a noble spirit and lofty nature." And Ludwig had replied, "You are a true prince. In you resides the spirit of Maria Theresia and Joseph II. It is my fondest hope that after my death you receive Bavaria."

But the heir of Austria was more concerned with the future of his own peoples. He felt that his efforts were bearing fruit when the Emperor declared Czech to be an "official second language." The Czechs could take over the role of Hungarians when—if—Hungary was instated as a separate kingdom. Since the resignation of Andrássy and the appointment of terrible Taafe as prime minister, Rudolph knew that the Cause—of Hungary, of minorities—would be set back. He was being watched more carefully than ever. In Prague, where he was now, he felt a measure of relief.

None of the royal family saw Gödöllö in its bloom. In a little copse, a toga'd stone warrior poured sandstone water from his jug into a real pool. A niche in the stable walls held Saint George capturing a lion, in the shadow of blooming chestnut trees. The peasants amused themselves by debating whether the lion's head more closely resembled the Emperor or the Crown Prince. They missed the excitement and activity that Their Majesties' visits brought.

All was still at Gödöllö. Inside, the polished mirrors reflected porcelain chandeliers, the spiral stairs, the marble table where Deák had signed the manifesto of '48. History and art were long here. Former occupants still held sway in furniture, paintings, other objects of their choice and taste. But the emptiness of the castle was oppressive to the servants as air before a storm, and they perceived its vacancy as somehow ridiculous.

19

$\widehat{A}$T DINNER NEXT DAY, Leo said little, but his eyes would become brilliant with intensity, then go suddenly blank as though the mind that animated them were absent. He devoured a few mouthfuls hungrily, then forgot his food and played absentmindedly with his fork. His strangeness was remarked, but he assured his dining companions that he was fine, he was only suffering from the stuffiness of his room and the many cigarettes he'd smoked. After the meal, he said, he would air himself out in a long walk. Wanda waited for his invitation or command to accompany him, but when none came, she smiled happily at the prospect of joining the children this afternoon, gathering flowers in competition to see who had the most varied bouquet at the end.

On his walk, Leo became dizzy. He knew this was the earliest symptom of many illnesses. His pulse was too high. He felt weak. Spasms of heat and cold passed over him. He returned slowly, taking great care not to exert himself. He knew he must rest, and that a doctor should be sent for.

In front of his room, he had a premonition. The door was closed, but the latch hadn't caught. He pushed it open very gently, soundlessly, and at first had only the sense of something being wrong. Then he made it out: two figures on the bed, their fair heads together, torsos complicated into a single body. He stood transfixed, with a certainty that he was about to die. The scene blurred, then came into focus, and the images were projected to his mind in staccato progression, with the jerkiness of "moving" pictures—a sheaf of papers shuffled rapidly to give the illusion of animation. He was a young boy, a small child, lacking words that might come to his aid. He stared, while his body froze and burned. He couldn't ask for help, couldn't move, was rooted to the spot as that man and that woman took each other on his bed, and life was at its beginning, earlier than childhood, before mother and father, the blind sperm seeking the engulfing egg.

They didn't see him, they saw nothing in their lovemaking beyond patterns of flesh, hair, ceiling, bed. When they were consumed, they lay side by side in each other's arms, their bodies drying as they fell into light slumber on the hot afternoon. When they stirred again, he was gone and the door closed.

In the early evening, they came to call him for supper and found him in his room stretched naked on the floor at Wanda's feet. She wore a long *kazabaika* lined with sable, her hand wielding a knout with spikes. His back was already bleeding from small cuts and he was begging, piteously, in a high voice, "More, my savior, my mistress. Cruel vengeance, have your way. Take off my skin. Flay me alive. More, I must have it. Go on, go on." He continued his croon, in strange falsetto, prone on the floor.

Wanda turned her face to them and they could read in her eyes the mute appeal of a bound calf. "Stop it!" commanded Karl, but Leo didn't hear him, was aware of nothing but the form standing over him and of his need.

Karl went to Wanda, put his hands on her shoulders and drew her away. He took a blanket from the bed and threw it down over Leo, who still chanted for the lash. "You must stop," said Karl. "You are mad."

Slowly, the whimperings and beggings subsided. He lay unmoving, prostrate, silent. "Get up," said Karl angrily. "We have to wash those cuts."

Leo rose, pulling the blanket around his nakedness. He looked much thinner without his clothes; his skin, Kathrin thought, barely covered him. He saw her. "Kathrin," he said. "You must wear a *kazabaika*. You are made for it. You must be my cruel mistress."

"You are mad," repeated Karl.

"I am not!" he cried. "I am a great author. I understand

the sufferings of man. I have compassion for all. Jesus Christ hung from the cross of humanity. Why do you come in here? Why do you come in my room?" His face was wild—he seemed to lose the thread of his own words. Then he collected himself and shouted, "You see how cruelly my wife treats me! You see that for her I am a worthless slave! She beats me and whips me until my skin is broken."

"Disgusting," said Karl.

"Oh. Oh. You are hurting me. Disgusting? And what of all the critics who hail my work? What of all those around the world who are my admirers? What of the French? the English? Who are you to me? What are you doing here? Why are you in my room?" Leo pulled himself up stiffly and said in a cold voice, "I am the author of *Venus in Furs*. I have created the greatest women in German literature!"

"Ridiculous," said Karl. "Your women are ridiculous. You are ridiculous!" He started moving away, signaling Kathrin to leave with him. She shook her head.

Wanda put her hand shyly in Karl's, and he led her out of the room. She walked away from her husband with bowed head, like a child who has been discovered misbehaving and therefore cannot lie.

Kathrin sat on the edge of the bed and looked at him, deeply angry. This was the great writer whose works she had nearly memorized in hours, days, weeks of reading each line, struggling to bring the words to new life in another language. This was the friend, the author, who had been one of the most important men in her life. He had betrayed her. She felt no pity for him now, with his bleeding back. There was nothing further to say. Karl had said it already—his life, his work, himself were all ridiculous. To write of violence and cruelty in terms of sexual relations was an act of intellect, of will. To grovel at his wife's feet, terrifying Wanda to stupefaction, was abdication of will. Karl would eventually forgive him, she thought—Karl's anger burst from his chivalry, his aristocracy. He had despised his friend for being undignified, losing control, becoming a creature of blind desire. But the storm would end, and Leo would return to Karl's graces when he was restored to civility.

Kathrin's disappointment went deeper, to the tiny sliver

of faith she carried, the hidden splinter of belief that honor existed, that men could be relied upon. Her father had taught her contempt, but with Leo she had almost begun to accept that a friend could be like a father, worthy of respect, carrying authority. Leo and his books had given her work. She didn't despise his—or any man's—sexual predilections, so long as they didn't divest one of humanity. The beast on the floor who parodied a victim while making a slave was not Leo, not Sacher-Masoch. A strange beast, who showed her that any faith at all—even the slimmest token—was ridiculous. She stood and began to walk out, her feet bare under her light summer skirt.

"Stop!" he shouted with such force that she nearly lost her balance. She tripped forward and cried out as a thick nail, used to hold down the carpet, pierced her foot. She sat down in Wanda's chair and examined her injury. The nail was driven in so deeply that only a little blood surrounded it. She held her foot and looked up at Leo. Then she smiled.

"Take it out!" he cried.

His face was yellow. She looked steadily at him, keeping her smile. "Why? This is a charming sensation, Leo."

"Take it out!"

"The nail is deep in my flesh, Leo. I will keep it there, and whenever I decide to remove it, there will be new pain."

"No! No!"

"Calm yourself, my dear. This is highly interesting. Perhaps I shall rip it out and tear the flesh around it."

"No." He buried his face in his hands.

"Look at me, Leo."

"No." He began to sob quietly.

She sat a long time, her foot in her hands, while he sobbed drily. When he looked up, timorously, she took hold of the nail's head and yanked it out, tearing the flesh with viciousness, releasing a stream of blood from the deep hole in her foot. She made no sound. Their eyes met. She got up and walked out of the room, leaving a trail of blood behind her.

Karl and Kathrin, her foot bandaged, rode down to Hatván in the early morning, by wagon, and then took the train to Budapest. They would collect their few pieces of luggage and proceed to Trieste, where they would await the ship to America.

It was a hot morning, and the air was heavy. The sky darkened, the temperature rose, and storm was inevitable. At the Reises', shutters were drawn and the animals brought into the barn or coop. By noon, candles were lit against the darkness and the wind began to stir.

The wind churned the air, cooling it. Dust, leaves and small twigs whirled with bright petals and chicken feathers. No rain fell, but the wind became more violent. Wanda, standing in the kitchen with Geza, heard the loud cracks as branches were sliced and trees split. Saplings bent with the wind, stripped of their leaves, their suppleness ensuring their lives. Then came a violent sound as the sky opened and waters rushed out. In minutes, it seemed, streams turned to rivers and spilled down the mountains behind the house. Water poured through the gates of the lower courtyard, turning up feathers and fur, feed and excrement.

On the northern slope, left of the kitchen, waters claimed the cemetery, carrying off wreaths and flowers first. Roaring strength, the flood opened graves, splintered biers, ripped off crosses and bore down bones, skulls, earth and lime to the wall of the church, where it deposited its hideous cargo in great mounds.

Geza prayed loudly, her body rocking with incantation. Wanda mumbled the creed of her childhood: " 'I believe in God, the Father Almighty, Maker of Heaven and Earth . . .' " but was not comforted. And still the waters threw half-putrified cadavers and fresh corpses on the heaps.

* * *

Farther west, at Gödöllö, lightning struck the stables. The horses whinnied and rose up in terror. Panic struck them. They lashed out, reared and burst their stalls. They stampeded in their attempt to escape, and in their wild desire to be free, they trampled each other to death.

345

PART VI

Mayerling (DEATH)

And Cain said unto the Lord, My punishment is greater than I can bear.

—Genesis 4:13

20

HIS WIFE was cold, but there were many charmers in Vienna to warm him. In Prague, too—though Rudolph still felt the pain of that Jewish beauty whose eyes were like a dying doe's. He'd seen her when he made an official visit to the old ghetto of Prague and that face stared out at him, ancient in its beauty and yet completely new, unlike any face he'd ever seen. Their eyes met and locked. They had a few hours together after the official business, and he was as if hypnotized. If he could only learn to read her face, he felt, he would understand everything.

Her parents, seeing her in the company of the Crown Prince, sent her away from Prague to preserve her for a future husband. The taint of Imperial favor, they knew, would spoil her chances. But then she escaped from the country exile, returning to the city to seek her beloved (she loved him on sight; she had never seen a man so beautiful). She didn't find him and fell ill. A few days later she died. Her parents were able to get word through to His Highness that their daughter, age nineteen, was dead. He visited her grave in the old Jewish cemetery.

Whenever he was in Prague he went there, and her face haunted him often, as young as it had been, so Jewish and filled with pain. He thought of her on nights when he stayed awake, thinking and writing, and on early mornings when he crouched silently, waiting for game.

He loved hunting. It was an escape from affairs of state and the domestic rule of Stephanie. The hunting lodge at

Mayerling lay not far from Vienna—just beyond the Vienna Woods in the valley of Helenenthal—and he came out as often as he could. Fall was a marvelous time, for the landscape as well as the hunt, when trees were yellow and green and the pale henna squirrels competed busily with the long-eared gray ones for possession of the tree holes, to store their winter's rations. From his window, he could look across the fields of thistle and clover, above the hollow of evergreens, to the strong rock face rising in sharp gray peaks against a milky sky. His little room was bright with whitewashed walls. A wooden crucifix was mounted in the high corner and a glass painting of the Virgin hung over his bed. In the window boxes phlox and geranium burned, and the fence beneath his bedroom was wrapped with roses.

On the October Saturday, Rudolph rode out to Mayerling in advance of his father's party. He arrived at three in the afternoon, in time for a few quiet hours of hunting with Gyula, the gamekeeper. Gyula had already laid out the clothes on his bed, in the order that Rudolph would put them on. Gyula understood his master's ritual. The garments were old and loved, and gave him warmth. In the old clothes, he felt a new man, far from the Hofburg and his cold wife. He put his binoculars around his neck and carried his own rifle and pistol. Gyula brought the blankets and a small flask of *schnaps.*

They walked out to a blind and sat motionless, the blankets wrapped around their legs. Wind moved the leaves and swallows dived and soared between the slowly flapping crows. Rudolph and Gyula spoke to each other only with their eyes. As hunters, they were part of nature, their hearing tuned to forest and fields, competing with the wolf and fox as predators. A good hunter, like a wolf, never disturbed the natural balance; he picked off the old, sick or too-delicate young, the individuals nature had prepared for slaughter.

Rudolph hoped for boar. The deer would be hunted in tomorrow's party; pheasants, partridges and capercaillies were rare, as was the woodcock with its marvelous flesh. A sound. His gun was cocked, held under his left arm while his right hand raised the binoculars. He could see only the dark moving smudges far away, and knew they were deer. Gyula's eyes said Wait, they will come closer, they will circle around. Rudolph nodded, put down the glasses and accepted the flask, taking a swig of plum *schnaps*. He passed it, open, to Gyula.

This waiting was most difficult, and with impatience came the words and images Rudolph tried to keep out. Now they ran along his mind like deer on the horizon—Taafe, Bismarck, Austria, Hungary, Czechs, Stephanie. Take care not to kill the healthy ones. Waiting. Waiting so long already while the earth turns and makes you helpless.

Coming from the left now—Gyula was right—the swift herd, small and gray to the naked eye, was coming up browner in the sights; his finger on the trigger—and then it pulled.

Gyula looked at him with disbelief. "What of it?" said Rudolph.

"We must kill her now. Quickly."

The doe was kicking when they came up, lying on her back and struggling her broken legs. The bullet had passed just below the belly through both forelegs. She was two years old and healthy, except for the blood and the life running out of her eyes. Gyula waited for his master to shoot.

But Rudolph paused, looking down at the animal. "Does it know it will die? Do you think it is feeling pain? We should learn to read the signs of death, Gyula. Does it know anything at all, this animal? I think it knows fear. It senses that it will never run again, and running is its whole life. Does it fear death?"

He felt Gyula's quick breathing and said, "I'm sorry. It was a bad shot. Perhaps I was tired of waiting. Or perhaps it happened only because the gun was ready." He took a deep breath. "I'm sorry I hurt her. She didn't mean to come into my sights. Now I can't let her live." He took his pistol, stretched out his arm and shot cleanly between the eyes. They dragged the carcass to softer ground and buried it.

Next day the Emperor and his guests went out to hunt in the woods west of the lodge. Rudolph's stand was next to his father's. A herd of deer was driven past. Rudolph shot, missed and, when the deer had passed his father's stand and were speeding toward the horizon, he stepped out and shot again. Such an act was criminal according to the rules of hunting. His bullet missed the Emperor's head by a few centimeters and lodged in his gunbearer's arm. The incident was naturally kept secret, but the Emperor banished his son from his sight.

*   *   *

Leo and Wanda had been married nearly ten years and had attained the unpleasant and often inflammable truce of many couples, when a joint life is carefully divided into hemispheres, each inaccessible to the other. So Wanda cared for the house and children and finances; Leo wrote and arranged for his necessary rituals to be performed by servants or by his new, obliging translator. Wanda had progressed from resentment through disgust to indifference, and from her sphere everything "brutish" had been swept away. It suited her not to be touched, and though her husband was ridiculous, she stayed with him for the sake of the children and money. The last person she had loved, except for the little ones, was Kathrin, but what remained of Kathrin lay at the bottom of the Atlantic. She had died mysteriously on board ship and was buried at sea.

They'd learned of the death in a short letter from Karl, who had continued the journey alone and planned to remain indefinitely in America. A few months later, they had received another note from him, briefly describing the literary life of New York, the salons of a woman called Wharton, the dandified clothes and gastronomy, summing up with, "Kathrin would have been amused."

Kathrin still appeared in Wanda's dreams, and sometimes the image of her, slim and blond, would rise in the midst of household tasks or while marketing. But Kathrin was dead, Wanda had nothing beside the children, and her resolve to protect them against hunger became her only goal.

Leo's new translator was the dowdy Hülde Meister, a woman as sturdily Germanic in temperament as in body. Leo found her work excellent and was grateful for her understanding of him as artist and as man. She took his Slav peculiarities and his personal excesses in the manner of a German hausfrau who daily polishes even the most fussy and impractical objects. She did what he asked of her with humorless efficiency, showing such enthusiasm for work that she appeared almost ardent. When Leo thought of Kathrin, her memory was rendered "poetic": the beautiful, imperious woman he had loved, the extraterrestial spirit inhabiting the earth as the loveliest of its creatures, the magnificent demon, the soul-snatcher to whom he had bequeathed his soul. Rarely did he remember his last sight of her, and when he did, spasms racked his body until the recollection was driven out.

Hülde Meister was stolid and unpoetic. Wanda's immediate antipathy to her never faded, but she was forced to entrust the children to her care when she traveled to Leipzig to see editors who owed them money. They had been slow in payments, and when she wrote terse, insistent letters they'd responded by sending only half the amount due.

She planned a short trip and was able to accomplish her business a day early. She didn't telegraph ahead, intending to surprise the children, who would be home from school already when she arrived. From the carriage she saw her two sons on the street huddled against each other. She ran out to them, throwing the driver twice his charge. Mitschi was weeping loudly; Sasha accompanied his brother's sobs with frightened, impotent yelps. Blood covered Mitschi's leg, from short pants to his shoes, so much blood she couldn't see where the cut was. Then Sasha, shaking, pointed to the broken glass on the side, and Wanda saw the deep gash at the top of Mitschi's leg. She took him in her arms and carried him toward the house while Sasha, holding onto her skirt with a tight fist, stammered that they were locked out, the woman had told them to stay outside, he'd banged on the door as loudly as he could when Mitschi got hurt, but no one answered.

Cold with fury, but composed, Wanda shifted Mitschi's weight on her arm, reached for the key in her pocket and gave it to Sasha. He took a long time fitting it into the keyhole because of his shaking, but Wanda waited silently, and Mitschi was becoming more calm. Inside, she cleaned and bandaged his wound, while murmuring to both children in soothing tones until they were quiet and comforted. She kissed them and gave them chocolate, then brought out the chessboard and helped them set up the men. She left them together, playing, and went to look for her husband and the woman.

She found them both in the bedroom, naked in bed. Hülde screamed when she saw her, jumped out and pulled the sheet with her. Wanda's eyes were narrow, her lips set in a thin white line. She grabbed the whip near the bed and brought it down on Hülde. The woman cried out and dropped the sheet. Wanda whipped her again, with full force, then again and again, screaming as she lashed her, making sounds barely human, keening her rage, sounds terrifying as the murdering howls of a she-wolf. Hülde whimpered, running back and forth, calling on Leo to save her. But he was huddled in bed, blanket up to his face, his mouth open as he watched this savage scene in fascination, with Wanda more magnificent than she'd ever appeared: a predator.

"Hag! Witch! I'll kill you!" Wanda's anger turned human, female, as she chased the naked woman around the room, cutting her skin with the whip. Suddenly she dropped it, picked up a chair and ran at Hülde. "Murderess!" she screamed as she lunged, but Hülde found the door handle, pressed it and escaped, yelping, her heavy naked flesh shuddering as she ran. Wanda caught her balance, threw down the chair and coldly, in a low voice, said to Leo, "Insect. You are not my husband any more." She left the room to join her children.

Hülde departed as soon as she was dressed. Next day Leo followed her, with books and papers, his collection of photographs, his clothes, Sasha's clothes and Sasha. Hülde welcomed the man and his son, showing great attention to the boy, who was, she knew, his father's angel and, though unaware, possessed the power to drive Leo back to Wanda. She cooked him his favorite foods and read with him, but after a few weeks Sasha became ill. He was feverish and raved for his mother. The illness terrified Leo, unearthed in him deliriums buried by time, and he wrapped his son in blankets and took him home to Wanda.

She nursed him to health, rarely leaving his bedside. His thin smile broadened through her love, and a month after the onset of the fever, Sasha was able to return to school. He and Mitschi walked hand in hand, their books and lunches carried

354

on their backs. The other child had disappeared. A few days after her father left the house, Lina had run off. Wanda ordered a search, at first. A week went by with no sign, no hint of the girl. She was thirteen years old, of an age to look after herself, and members of the search party convinced Wanda that the girl could be anywhere by this time, perhaps beyond the borders of Austria. The search was abandoned.

On the first of January, Leo was honored at a celebration given for him in Paris, a silver jubilee commemorating his twenty-five years as author. He was embraced by the great lions of French literature—Dumas, Victor Hugo, François Coppée—and Zola called him "maître." At a dinner party given for him by Alphonse Daudet, Sacher-Masoch was asked by the editor of *Le Figaro* to accept the position left empty by the recent death of Turgenev, as International Author. He said he would think about it.

He returned to Hülde wearing the Légion d'Honneur, and for weeks carried the elation and pride bestowed on him by his French triumph. He worked; Hülde was good to him; she meted out his punishment and still served him with obeisance. But a sense of emptiness intruded. After having been a father for so many years, Leo felt the absence of children. He missed Sasha, his radiant little prince, the child who held the sun in his face. Hülde understood Leo's need, as she always did, and helped him plan a way of getting back the boy.

Together they traveled to Graz, took him out of his school—Wanda would say they kidnapped him—and brought him back with them. This time illness settled on the boy almost immediately, an illness more severe than the time before, rendering him limp and bloodless, so weak he couldn't be moved. He whispered prayerfully, then cried out for his darling mama. Leo telegraphed to Wanda, who arrived next day.

The child's face was white as the linen on which he lay. He strove for a smile when he saw her and reached for her hand, straining with the effort. She gave it to him, tears in her eyes, and he pressed it to his hot lips. "Little mama," he whispered, his eyes closing, "how good that you came."

She stayed with him through the night and allowed no

one else near him. The severity of Sasha's illness forced them to obey. He slept fitfully, his thin body recoiling from pain every few minutes, and he often hallucinated. Then came moments of stillness and clarity: "Little mama, you will be tired if you do not sleep." She shuddered and kissed him. Then again: "Don't worry about me, my angel mama, the dear Lord will care for me well." She sobbed, despite her tremendous strength, despite her resolve not to let him see her grieve. He was pale as death; his teeth chattered; he suddenly burned. When he opened his eyes, they were the color of his hair. He gave a small cry and was dead. His mother went away in the morning, leaving the small corpse to his father.

21

ELISABETH SPENT the year visiting shrines of past civilizations—in Greece, Egypt and the Troys Schliemann had excavated. She moved swiftly, riding her legs as she used to ride her horses, setting a pace not even bodyguards could match, though she was a woman of fifty and grandmothered by both her eldest daughter and her son. The ancient world remained beautiful and various—"O golden hours, I will keep you bright"—and her travels through civilization's youth brought her a longing to return to her "childhood lake."

In June, she was home in Bavaria. The glittering Starnberg was patched with sunlight. Here with an eagle she longed to fly. She felt that the years shot by too quickly; years passed like bright coins, spending youth and beauty. Her mother still lived there, disapproving of her daughter's ways with more explicitness than she'd shown when Max was alive. To sensible Ludovica, the Wittelsbachs were all mad; no wonder her poor dead sister Sophie had had such a difficult task with Sissi.

She kept away from her mother and spent her time with darling Mutzerl, now eighteen and sparkling. Sissi always rose early, to greet the day, but Whitsunday was gray and surprisingly cold for June. Brooding clouds watched over the mist and would not disperse it. At nine in the morning, Sissi's youngest brother arrived on horseback. The way he dismounted revealed that his news were somber: Ludwig had been taken prisoner at Berg.

"No!" cried Sissi. "They can't put him in a cage!"

"He is driving the country bankrupt with his extravagance. People believe he is growing mad, but he will not come to Munich and show himself."

"Yes, he will go mad if he is caged. It's illegal! He is the King!" She ran off, to be alone, and for the rest of the day she walked along the lakeside, despite the cold and the intermittent showers, looking out across the gray waters to where he was being held. In the late afternoon she returned and dispatched telegrams to Franz Joseph and Rudolph, begging them to protest the illegality of the king's incarceration. His wings must not be broken.

He knew what they were planning, but he was sure they'd never take him alive. Yet when he heard the scrapings and rustles as they closed in on Neuschwanstein, the champagne and arrack he had drunk made him too tired to flee, to soar over the mountains across the border to Tyrol. He called for another bottle and told his valet, "The worst is not that they want to steal my throne, they want to bury me alive."

Weber, the valet, knelt at his lord's feet. "I will dress you warmly, Your Majesty, and you shall escape."

Ludwig waved away the suggestion. "I am a king. A king cannot be afraid." He rose heavily and went to his desk. "Here, Weber, this is all I have left," he said, giving the young man 1,200 gold marks. "You were the most faithful of all. I shall not need it where I'm going." Weber buried his face in his master's robe and wept.

Shortly after midnight on June 13, 1886, guards rushed in and seized the King, bringing him to his bedroom, where the doctor was waiting. "Your Majesty! This is the saddest duty I have ever had to perform. Your Majesty's mental condition has been observed and diagnosed by four medical experts. They are unanimous in their opinion. Prince Luitpold has taken over the government as regent. I have orders to conduct Your Majesty to the castle of Berg this very night."

The King heard his valet sobbing quietly. To the doctor he said, "How did you manage to declare me insane? You have not even examined me."

"That was not necessary, Your Majesty. We received enough evidence from your staff."

"Ah. For how long do you plan to incarcerate me?"

"Your Majesty's cure should take about a year."

Ludwig smiled sadly. "No, not so long. It is a little thing to take a life. Come, Weber, we must be dressed."

At four in the morning, accompanied by a small personal staff, the doctors and their guards, Ludwig II of Bavaria, sometimes known as the Moon King, made his last journey through the night.

Before dinner on Whitsunday, the King took a promenade with Dr. von Gudden. Then he dined alone. In the late afternoon, around six o'clock, he expressed the wish to take another stroll. The doctor, pleased by his reasonableness and docility, agreed to the exercise. They wore overcoats against the unseasonable cold and carried umbrellas in the slight drizzle.

At seven in the evening, the doctors observed that the weather had become decidedly unpleasant, and that His Majesty's corpulence usually prevented him from undertaking long walks.

At eight, they were surprised, even concerned. They were not alarmed, however: the heavy downpour would have forced the men to seek refuge until it was over. Only a few guards were sent out to seek them.

An hour later, every man at Berg was scouring the area, particularly the path leading to the lake, where they had begun their promenade. On the water, not far from shore, floated a black object. It was the King's overcoat.

Both bodies were recovered near the bank, in shallow water. The King's watch had stopped at 6:54; von Gudden's neck and shoulders revealed bruises.

The Empress was informed by her daughter, wife of Prince Luitpold's son. She retired to her room and lay prostrate on the floor. After some time, she began to pray. She called upon Jehovah, God of Vengeance, God of Love, God of Wisdom. Her prayers turned to raving, and she could not be calmed until Rudolph came into the room and gathered her up in his arms. She sobbed against him while he stroked her. "Rudi," she said, "our great eagle has been murdered!"

"I loved him too," said her son quietly. "The Dream King is dead. His dream was to bring back the past; mine is to bring about the future. But Europe is overrun with drabness. The bureaucrats hound us. Through our dreams we die." He kissed her cheeks. "Be brave, Mother."

*   *   *

In the morning mail came a letter from Paris with Verlaine's poem on the death of Ludwig II, *"le seul vrai roi de ce siècle."* Leo, a blanket wrapped around his legs and the yellow cat on his lap, read the poem, approved and handed it to Hülde. She was expecting their second child, an event he ignored. Since Sasha's death three years earlier, Leo had lost his paternity. A child was merely an accident of fate. A person could have only one true child of his heart, and that one had been torn from Leo.

He stroked the pussy slowly, in accompaniment to its purring, and handed the bills to Hülde without opening them. He unwrapped the package that had arrived. In it was a large tome entitled *Psychopathia Sexualis,* written by Professor Krafft-Ebing, a man Leo was acquainted with. (Krafft-Ebing was hailed as brilliant by his peers, including his good friend Dr. von Gudden.) Leo had heard about this book, which he felt to be an atrocity, a monstrous text in which his own name was used to describe a form of sexual "illness." He looked at the index, found the page and read:

> By masochism I understand a peculiar perversion of the psychical *vita sexualis.* The individual affected is controlled by the idea of being completely and unconditionally subject to the will of a person of the opposite sex, of being treated by this person as by a master, humiliated and abused. This idea is colored by lustful feeling. The masochist lives in fantasies, creating situations which he often attempts to realize. Through this perversion his sexual instinct becomes more or less insensible to the normal charms of the opposite sex— incapable of a normal *vita sexualis*—psychically impotent. . . .

360

"Hülde! This ignoramus, this ass—ah, I feel ill. 'Psychically impotent'! Oh, that is very clever!" He threw the cat off his lap. It remained at his ankles, looking up with bewilderment, uncertain whether to rub against its master or go away. "And what of my seventy books? Look, he dares to say this: 'I feel justified in calling this sexual anomaly "masochism" because the author Sacher-Masoch frequently makes this perversion the substratum of his writings . . . We have proof that Sacher-Masoch is not only the poet of masochism, but is himself afflicted with this anomaly.'

"Who is this idiot? Since when have clinicians been permitted to stick their noses in the lives of artists? He is a degenerate, that man." Leo kicked impatiently at the supplicating animal. "My only comfort is his idiocy. Who would read such trash? No one, of course. Of course. It will be unread and forgotten. This rat attempts to bury my name in his loathsome excrement. But he is dust already, and the name of Sacher-Masoch will burn brightly through the ages, wherever men read books."

He comforted himself, but could not be comforted. "These people," he told Hülde, "will kill us. These 'experts' will turn us into little pegs, unworthy of the name man. They'll destroy our dreams, our spirits and our talents until our nature will be like that of a chair or table, fashioned for use by its owners. A terrible thing, Hülde—the scourge of man is upon us, our days are numbered, and we will be made into ciphers."

He asked to be beaten savagely, and after he had been lacerated, after his wounds had been cleaned and dressed, he asked for more. "I must return!" he shouted, "I must enter into the Great Woman who is eternal and gives death. Build her!" She attempted to calm him by her lashings, but still he raved. "You must take off my head, you must decapitate me! Crucify me until I am dead. No, I can see you haven't the heart. Build her, then! Order an iron maiden, have her constructed, that I may be crucified within her! Yes! Yes!"

He ran off shrieking and stumbled on the yellow cat. In fury, he pulled it up by its tail and rushed to the kitchen. The cat struggled hopelessly. Its natural weapons—teeth and claws—could attack only air. In impotence, it hissed and thrashed, but Leo held it firmly with one hand, while the other, having found a knife, slashed at the yellow fur, making wounds at every strike until the belly was wide open and entrails dropped on the kitchen floor. Then he continued his butchery, carving out the eyes, chopping off its tail. He plunged his hands into the bleeding carcass and removed the inner organs. It was dead and hideous. Leo took a seat at the kitchen table and methodically, with his small knife, sliced off its skin and fur.

Hülde came in while he was at his work and watched him silently, his hands dripping blood on the table and floor. He was unaware of her. She, who knew the world as an office where each event could be filed according to category, realized she could no longer keep him in the house.

He turned abruptly, his eyes burning, and pleaded, "I need her. I must be impaled on her. She must pierce my flesh, my skin, my organs—she must nail me with a hundred wounds, holes gouged in my body, her spikes running through me, holding me, me, her crucified dead son forever!"

She made the necessary arrangements. He was taken off begging her for decapitation and impalement.

When he was gone, she straightened the rooms, putting everything where it belonged. She held the spine of the Krafft-Ebing book loosely in her hands, and it opened naturally to a place where two pieces of paper had been inserted, tightly covered with Leo's handwriting. She read:

> Whether princess or peasant girl, in ermine or in sheepskin, the Woman is always the same to me: dressed in furs, wielding a whip, she treats men as slaves and is at once my creation and the true Sarmatian woman.
>
> At the age of ten, I yearned for a distant relative of my father's—whom I will call Countess Xenobia—the most beautiful and promiscuous woman in the country. One Sunday she found me hiding in her closet. She seized me by the hair and threw me on the carpet. She placed her knee on my shoulder and began to whip me viciously. I clenched my teeth but couldn't stop my tears. And yet, while I writhed under my aunt's cruel blows, I felt a strong sense of pleasure.

362

This event became branded on my soul as with a red-hot iron. I both hated and loved the creature who, by her strength and diabolical beauty, seemed preordained to place her foot insolently on the neck of humanity.

Over the years other strange scenes impressed me, until this particular type of woman crystallized in my mind and took definite shape in the heroine of an early novel. Much later, I isolated the ambiguity that inspired *Venus in Furs*. I became aware of the mysterious affinity between cruelty and lust, and of the natural hatred between the sexes—overcome temporarily through love, reappearing later with striking force as one becomes a hammer and the other an anvil.

I believe that artistic creation always develops in the way that this woman took shape in my imagination: First, the author seeks a subject that has escaped other artists; then his own experience intervenes to show him the living being whose prototype already dwells in his imagination. This figure preoccupies him, seduces him, captivates him—because it corresponds to his innate tendencies, to his particular nature. He then transmutes it, giving it body and soul. Finally, in the work of art, he confronts the ambiguity that is the source of all further images.

This is what I have done, and it is the artistic way.

22

JANUARY 29, 1889, was a very cold Tuesday. The ground was frozen, the trees bare, as though winter had ravished Nature and left her naked, ashamed to show herself. In the middle of the day, Rudolph traveled to Mayerling with friends. A few hours later he was joined by Mary Vetsera, a seventeen-year-old baroness who resembled the girl in Prague, and with whom he'd been in love for three months. She wore the iron ring he'd given her, engraved with both their initials and the motto, "Love unto Death." Finding his passion returned by Mary, Rudolph had asked his father for permission to divorce Stephanie—a request the Emperor found unseemly and dismissed with the word, "Impossible."

Rudolph was thirty, and trapped. He had written books and articles, had worked for the twin causes of democracy and egalitarianism, and had spent the years since his majority waiting for power, escaping his hunters. He'd been aware of spies for years, constantly—the spies sent by Bismarck from abroad, the spies employed by his father and his father's minister.

He'd thought his vision, his energy, could transform the bureaucratic empire into a land of justice where men were free, spiritually and economically, and where each nation maintained the dignity of its own character, its self-determination. Instead, he was trapped in his own country, spied on by men he hoped to rule, deprived of action, driven further back with each advance. At thirty, he was used up; as Crown Prince, his life had been accelerated, his possibilities defined decades earlier than with other men.

As a boy, he'd given his mind to politics, and now he gave his heart to Mary, who gave hers. They understood they could not be united in this life. Rudolph longed for death, had come to love it, had offered it to other women and been refused. Mary, in her youth, unhappiness, avarice for fame, accepted his proposal and together they planned their journey.

On the morning of January 30, her naked body was found in his bed, one eye hanging out of its socket. Next to her lay Austria's heir, who had watched her in death for seven hours before raising the pistol again and taking off the top of his skull.

The world mourned; the demons were driven out of Austria and their place taken by dutiful men.

Epilog

FRANZ JOSEPH, the All-Highest, consulted every day with the Almighty. The Empress Elisabeth went into deep mourning for a year, sometimes visiting her son's crypt at night. She was never able afterward to shed her grief. In 1898, she was fatally stabbed by Luccheni, an anarchist, near Geneva.

Sacher-Masoch's death was announced in 1895. The obituaries mentioned that he had written approximately ninety books and had once been regarded as the heir to Goethe.

Wanda lived with Mitschi in Switzerland, trying to support them both through her pen. In 1901 she published *Confessions of My Life*, an account of her life with Sacher-Masoch.

Ludwig II had been the last Wittelsbach after seven hundred years of uninterrupted rule. Bavaria was fused into the nation of Germany.

Rudolph's place as heir to the throne was in time taken by his cousin Franz Ferdinand, who would later be assassinated at Sarajevo, leading to Austria's declaration of war against Serbia.

Franz Joseph died in 1916; Hapsburg rule ended in 1918, and not long afterward the nations of Austria were taken up in another empire.